A HISTORY OF BASEBALL IN 100 OBJECTS

A Tour through the Bats,

Balls, Uniforms, Awards, Documents,

and Other Artifacts that Tell the Story

of the National Pastime

◆ ◆ ◆ ◆

JOSH LEVENTHAL

BLACK DOG
& LEVENTHAL
PUBLISHERS

Published by
Black Dog & Leventhal Publishers, Inc.
151 West 19th Street
New York, NY 10011

Distributed by
Workman Publishing Company
225 Varick Street
New York, NY 10014

Manufactured in China

Cover and interior design by Elizabeth Driesbach

ISBN-13: 978-1-57912-991-0

h g f e d c b a

Library of Congress Cataloging-in-Publication Data available on request.

CONTENTS

PART III: THE DEAD-BALL ERA

PART IV: BABE RUTH AND THE BIRTH OF THE LIVELY BALL ERA

PART V: WAR AND INTEGRATION

PART VI: EXPANSION

PART VII: THE FREE-AGENT ERA

PART VIII: STRIKES AND STEROIDS

Introduction

Baseball has a long and storied history, its evolution affected by pioneering executives and managers, legendary players, milestone moments, and changes to the rules of this tradition-loving pastime. While many of the sport's basic tenets have held strong for more than 150 years, each new era has seen signature developments that have altered the very experience that is baseball.

This book traces that evolution by examining the objects that represent game-changing moments and individuals from the sport's history. While equipment and objects, from bats to balls to uniforms, are very much central to baseball and have been transformed in many ways through the years, this book is not a history of those objects. Rather it is an exploration of the game of baseball as told through the equipment, documents, and other artifacts that illustrate its key eras and events.

We encounter a wide range of objects—from the well-known to the obscure, from equipment used on the field of play to documents penned in corporate offices, from rewards of triumph to symbols of disgrace. Each has its own story to tell and each one takes us further along the chronological unfolding of the sport's history.

The journey begins, perhaps surprisingly, in medieval Europe, centuries before Abner Doubleday, Alexander Cartwright, Henry Chadwick, Albert Spalding, or any of the other so-called fathers of baseball walked the diamond. A document from early fourteenth-century Flanders shows us that bat-and-ball games, baseball's distant ancestors, have been part of childhood recreation since long before words like "runs batted in" or even "innings" entered the vocabulary.

Leaping ahead nearly half a millennium, to the very earliest years of nationhood for the United States, another document, this one from late-eighteenth-century Massachusetts, reveals the first known appearance of the term "baseball" on these shores. By this time, the game was commonplace enough as to elicit town bylaws to limit when and where it could be played.

The next object on the path through baseball's history represents the role that legend plays in the national pastime. A ball believed (dubiously) to have been used by one Abner Doubleday in Cooperstown, New York, in 1839, helped to fuel the mythology of Doubleday as the game's inventor. Although the story was widely disputed from the moment it was presented in the early twentieth century, Doubleday's place in the baseball pantheon was cemented with this rendition of baseball's origin story.

The codified rules compiled by the Knickerbocker Base Ball Club in 1845 provide a firm foundation from which the sport evolved over the next 170 years. While some of the principles laid out in this document have long since been dropped from the rule book, the basic procedures and guidelines will be very familiar to baseball fans of subsequent generations up through today.

From there we find key documents establishing organized leagues and further defining the rules of play. A game ball from the first contest played within an enclosed ballpark, where tickets could be sold, takes us on a first step on the inevitable path toward baseball as commercial business.

Professionalism in the game was first introduced by the Cincinnati Red Stockings, whose 1869 game ball represents the dawning of the new era. The flip side of that era is seen with a political cartoon from the 1880s depicting baseball players as chattel to be auctioned off to the highest bidder. The ongoing battle between owners and players finds its roots in the earliest days of the sport.

Baseball's maturation was not just about economics; it was also about developing new equipment, such as gloves for fielders and masks for catchers. The continuing expansion of organized league play brought a need to honor championship teams. The "World's Series" trophy of 1888 and the Temple Cup of 1897 tell the story of the precursors to our modern World Series.

With the turn of the twentieth century came new leagues, new dynasties, and new stars. Awards given to Cy Young and Ty Cobb show the dominance of those players during the Dead-Ball Era, while Joe Jackson's shoes take us back to one of baseball's more shameful moments. Off the diamond, we experience the birth of new traditions with the original lyrics to "Take Me Out to the Ball Game," a bucket used to sell hot dogs at the ballpark, and the first ball pitched by a U.S. president at a major league game. Honus Wagner's tobacco card of 1909—today worth millions of dollars—exemplifies the phenomenon of baseball-card collecting through the decades.

The agreement that sent Babe Ruth from the Boston Red Sox to the New York Yankees in 1919, and the mighty Ruth's home run crown of 1921, bring us to the birth of the lively ball era and the emergence of the long ball as baseball's ultimate thrill. Technological advances, from radio and television broadcasts to lights illuminating ballparks for night baseball, further hastened the explosion in baseball's popularity in the years between the two world wars.

Objects representing the remarkable 1941 seasons of Ted Williams and Joe DiMaggio introduce a new generation of stars, and a War Department identification card belonging to Hank Greenberg reminds us of the impact that World War II had on the American pastime, not to mention the nation as a whole. The postwar years, in turn, brought baseball's ultimate progressive action, when Jackie Robinson first donned a Brooklyn Dodgers uniform in 1947. Two of the most dramatic on-field moments are on display with a ticket stub to the 1951 Giants-Dodgers playoff game and the glove used by Willie Mays to make one of the most memorable catches of all time.

In the following decade, a historic home run ball hit by Roger Maris and a Cy Young Award belonging to Sandy Koufax join the continuous narrative of heroic achievements on the field. And, once again, decisions made in owners' and commissioner's offices—from teams relocating across the country and new franchises coming into existence, to changes in the physical appearance of the playing field and the creation of a new position—illustrate the continuing evolution of how, where, and by whom the game is played.

The bat that Roberto Clemente used to reach the 3,000-hit milestone is about more than the accomplishment of one individual. It is a symbol of the changing face of baseball and a new generation of stars emerging from foreign lands and thriving at the major league level. The floodgates to a new economic structure were opened, as well, when Catfish Hunter used a 39-cent ballpoint pen to ink a contract worth more than $3 million. Big stars would earn big bucks, and one—Reggie Jackson—would even get a candy bar named after him.

Two of baseball's all-time greats—Pete Rose and Roger Clemens—would use a bat and a ball, respectively, to establish new records in the 1980s, but both would later leave the game with a cloud of disgrace hanging over them. The ultimate disgrace came in 1994, when the failure of the owners and players to settle on a new collective bargaining agreement led to the cancellation of the entire postseason. It is the absence of an object that tells the story there.

Ever-resilient, baseball bounced back in the second half of the decade. Cal Ripken Jr.'s name was written into a lineup card for the 2,130th consecutive game, as fans everywhere followed his incredible chase of the "iron man" record. Derek Jeter put on a Yankee uniform with the number 2 on the back and helped resuscitate the franchise, propelling it back to dynasty status. Another record-setting home run ball, this one hit by Mark McGwire in 1998, represents both fans' renewed exhilaration for the game and, subsequently, their renewed exasperation with it, thanks to the tainted nature of that record-setting performance.

A new century brought new heroes and new dynasties. Ichiro Suzuki's Seattle Mariners jersey and the Boston Red Sox's World Series ring of 2004 define the brilliance and beauty of baseball of the past 15 years. Alex Rodriguez's Texas Rangers jersey and the "Bartman Ball" from the 2003 Chicago Cubs playoffs represent the darker times that continue to capture a share of the headlines.

Following additional objects from inspiring players and awesome feats, the book concludes with an object that illustrates how far the sport has come on a global scale over the course of two centuries. No longer just one country's national pastime, baseball has truly caught on as a worldwide phenomenon. Although the competition has not reached the status of soccer's World Cup, the battle for the World Baseball Classic championship trophy is being waged by players from every continent and truly exemplifies the sport's global identity in the twenty-first century.

PART I

THE ORIGINS OF BASEBALL

• • • •

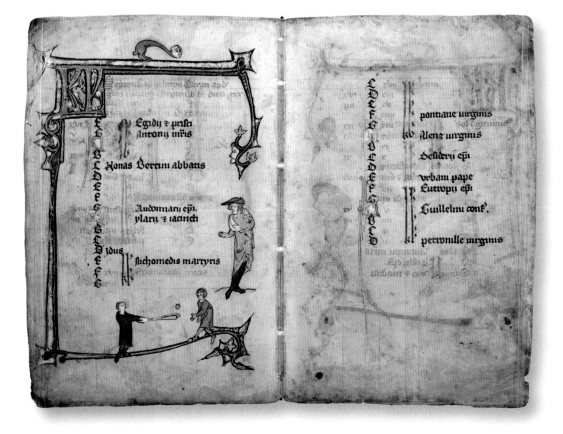

THE GHISTELLES CALENDAR, CIRCA 1301.

1

The Ghistelles Calendar, circa 1301

MEDIEVAL BASEBALL?

The question of who invented the game of baseball and when has fascinated genera-tions of experts and fans. Despite the propagation of the Abner-Doubleday-as-the-father-of-baseball story line for decades before it was fully debunked as engineered myth (see **Object #4**), the long search to pinpoint a moment, a place, and/or a person to credit with inventing the game has not produced a clear-cut moment of origin. Indeed, the sport has undergone a continuing evolution that makes it difficult to even define with certainty when baseball became baseball. What characteristics allow us to say *this* is baseball?

For centuries, millennia even, people have been engaged in games of throwing balls at other people who tried to knock said ball with an object of their own, such as a stick or a club. Bases of some kind entered the picture along the way, and the concepts of outs, runs, and innings followed various evolutionary paths as well. So while most experts agree that the fundamental tenets of the modern game took hold sometime around the middle of the nineteenth century, one can find glimpses of baseball-like sports long, long before that, and in some rather unexpected places.

References to ancient Egyptians playing stick-and-ball games can be traced to about 2400 BCE as part of religious rites and also simply for fun. Egyptologist Peter Piccione describes a scene depicted on a wall at the temple of Deir et-Bahari as an ancient precursor to baseball. The inscription, which dates to about 1460 BCE, shows pharaoh Thutmose III and priests playing *seker-hemat* ("batting the ball") as the goddess Hathor looks on. Other archeologists and anthropologists point to stick-and-ball games being played in ancient Mesoamerica as far back as 1500 BCE.

But without the basic structure of four bases and other rudimentary elements of the game that we have come to know and cherish, it is difficult to call these activities "baseball."

Nevertheless, most people today would look at this fourteenth-century Flemish illustration and say, "Hey, those kids are playing baseball!" The familiar swing of the bat, the fielder (or pitcher?) in position to field (or throw?) the ball—in many ways, this image represents the core of what we recognize as baseball.

The image dates to about 1301 and is the earliest known extant illustration of people playing a game that clearly evokes the modern game of baseball. It appears in the Ghistelles Hours or Calendar, a monthly calendar of saints' days that, according to the Walters Art Museum in Baltimore (which houses the piece), was produced for John III, Lord of Ghistelles and Ingelmunster, in a monastery in what is today northwest Belgium. This page represents the month of September.

Although the scene conjures up baseball, it is most likely an early form of a game known as "stoolball." Many variations of this folk game were played in England beginning around the eleventh century. The basic premise was for a pitcher to throw a ball at a target, such as a stool or a stump, while another player attempted to defend that target by striking the ball away with a bat or a stick. The earliest incarnations of the game simply required the batsman to prevent the ball from hitting the target, but later versions introduced bases. If the batsman succeeded in striking the ball, he or she—and it was traditionally a coed game—would run between the batter's stool and the pitcher's stool until the fielders got him or her out by throwing the ball at the batter's stool.

Stoolball was commonly played at Easter festivals, and some believe it originated among milkmaids, who used their milking stools for bases.

Other mentions and illustrations of stoolball can be found in documents from the eleventh to the sixteenth centuries. In his 1947 book *Ball, Bat and Bishop: The Origins of Ball Games*, Robert W. Henderson points to several such references, including one in the *Domesday Book*, a survey of life in England completed in 1086. Here the game is referred to as "bittle-battle," which is believed (though not confirmed) to be a primitive form of stoolball. Henderson also cites a fourteenth-century poem penned by a vicar in England advising parish priests against the playing of bat-and-ball games in churchyards.

In 1964, baseball writer and historian Harry Simmons cited an image of a bat-and-ball sport on a genealogical roll of the kings of England from the late thirteenth century. And A. F. Leach's *The Schools of Medieval England* (1915) includes a drawing from about 1310 that shows a student holding a large ball and a stick reminiscent of a bat.

References to stoolball became more commonplace by the sixteenth century, and the game continued to be played by a dedicated following in England well into the twentieth century. The National Stoolball Association was formed in 1979 and, renamed Stoolball England, is the official governing body of stoolball in that country.

Stoolball's development in England from the late Middle Ages into the Renaissance can be loosely traced through many documents and drawings of the period, and representations of different baseball precursors can be found in other European lands as well. The esteemed baseball scholar and official historian of Major League Baseball, John Thorn, wrote in 2006 about a small tableau in *Corn Harvest* (1565) by Flemish painter Pieter Bruegel the Elder that appears to show "a man with a bat, a fielder at a base, a runner, and spectators as well as participants in waiting." In addition, a fresco at the Casa Borromeo in Milan, Italy, depicts women from the nobility engaged in some sort of game consisting of a bat and a ball; it dates from about 1400. And German physician Guarinoni Hippolytus described, in 1600, a game being played in Prague that involved a ball, a club, and running back and forth between bases.

Because baseball has no clear or universally accepted origin story, direct connections between the modern sport and ancient stick-and-ball games are difficult to track. Stoolball appears to be a close ancestor of cricket, with the stools evolving into that sport's wickets. But the illustration from this early fourteenth-century Flemish *Book of Hours* undoubtedly brings our familiar baseball to mind and represents one step in the journey from the game's earliest precursors to America's national pastime. The evolution that took place over the next five and a half centuries underwent numerous twists and turns before the formalization of the "Knickerbocker Rules" in 1845 (see **Object #5**), codifying many of the fundamental rules of the modern game.

IMAGE DETAIL FROM
THE GHISTELLES CALENDAR.

BASE-BALL.

THE *Ball* once ftruck off,
 Away flies the *Boy*
To the next deftin'd Poft,
 And then Home with Joy.

MORAL.

Thus Seamen, for Lucre
 Fly over the Main,
But, with Pleafure tranfported
 Return back again.

2

A *Little Pretty Pocket-Book,* 1744

FIRST WRITTEN MENTION OF "BASEBALL"

A *Little Pretty Pocket-Book*, first published by John Newberry in England in 1744, was a collection of rhymes accompanying woodcut illustrations of children playing different outdoor activities. Bearing the rather wordy subtitle "Intended for the Instruction and Amusement of Little Master Tommy, and Pretty Miss Polly; with Two Letters from Jack the Giant-Killer; As Also a Ball and Pincushion; the Use of Which Will Infallibly Make Tommy a Good Boy, and Polly a Good Girl; To Which Is Added, a Little Song-Book, Being a New Attempt to Teach Children the Use of the English Alphabet, by Way of Diversion," A *Little Pretty Pocket-Book* is considered the first English-language children's book and—more notably for the purposes of this volume—contains the first known printed reference to the term "base-ball."

The book came packaged with a ball or a pincushion, depending on whether it was being purchased for a boy or a girl. No copies of the original 1744 publication survive, and the earliest extant Newberry edition dates to 1760. Pirated or imported editions of the book began appearing in the American colonies by the early 1760s, and the first major edition of A *Little Pretty Pocket-Book* for the American market was published by Isaiah Thomas in Worcester, Massachusetts, in 1787. This is the edition illustrated here.

With a letter of the alphabet topping each page, each activity featured in the book includes a woodcut illustration and accompanying verse describing the activity, followed by a "Moral" or a "Rule of Life." In addition to pages devoted to such bat-and-ball games as cricket, stoolball, trap-ball, and tip-cat, among the rhymes found in A *Little Pretty Pocket-Book* is the following:

BASE-BALL.

The *Ball* once struck off,
Away flies the *Boy*
To the next destin'd Post,
And then Home with Joy.

MORAL.

Thus Britons, for Lucre
Fly over the Main,
But, with Pleasure transported,
Return back again.

(For the American edition, "Britons" was changed to "Seamen" in the opening line of the Moral.)

The woodcut image for "Base-Ball" shows three boys stationed at different posts. One player is poised to pitch the ball to another, who stands ready to strike the ball. Evidently, it is the goal of the latter boy to hit the ball and run to the "next destin'd post" (posts commonly served the role of bases in ball-and-base games well into the nineteenth century). No bat is visible in the scene, however, so this form of "base-ball" may have been a version of handball with bases, as suggested by John Thorn.

Whereas this little children's book is significant because it represents the first time we see the term "base-ball" in print, it is not at all certain what game is being described as such, nor how the rules of this form of base-ball relate to our sport of today. As with many children's folk games of that time, activities involving a ball and base running developed in many different ways in different regions of England and America, and it's likely that the somewhat generic term "base-ball" was used to describe these diverse childhood pastimes. In some variations, a bat would have been involved, further connecting the game to the long journey toward modern baseball.

Discussions of a game or games called "base ball" continued to appear in booklets, or "chapbooks," about childhood games during the 1800s. William Clarke's *The Boy's Own Book: A Complete Encyclopedia of All the Diversions, Athletic, Scientific, and Recreative, of Boyhood and Youth*, published in London in 1828 and in Boston a year later, provides the earliest known printed account of the rules of the related English game of rounders. Robin Carver of Boston reprinted Clarke's rules in his 1834 publication *The Book of Sports* and featured it under the heading "Base, or Goal Ball," explaining, "This game is known under a variety of names. It is sometimes called 'round ball,' but I believe that 'base' or 'goal ball' are the names generally adopted in our country." Accompanying Carver's description was an engraving of boys "playing ball" on the grounds of Boston Common.

The following year, *The Boy's Book of Sports: A Description of the Exercises and Pastimes of Youth* made the leap from "Base, or Goal Ball" to, simply, "base ball" in describing the game that was on its way to becoming the national pastime. David Block, author of *Baseball Before We Knew It*, calls *The Boy's Book of Sports* "one of the two most historically important American baseball books to come forward in the first half of the nineteenth century" (along with Carver's earlier *Book of Sports*). Published by S. Babcock of New Haven, the 24-page chapbook featured "base ball" as the first game under the heading "Games at Ball," an indication of its popularity at the time. The book also reprinted the woodcut of boys playing ball on Boston Commons that had appeared in Carver's book, but this time it featured the caption "A Game of Base Ball."

The rules printed in the Babcock publication are similar to those in Carver's, but with a few key revisions. Whereas Carver (and Clarke before him) explained that the batter (or "striker") runs clockwise around the bases ("posts"), *The Boy's Book of*

BOYS PLAYING BALL ON BOSTON COMMON, CIRCA 1834.

Sports has the runners heading counterclockwise—as they do in the game as we now know it. This is also the first time we find the term "innings" used in the context of baseball, and the first use of "diamond" to describe the arrangement of the goals or bases. The three-strikes-and-you're-out concept is present here, whereas other rules, such as requiring that the batting team takes its turn until all its player are out, are vestiges of other bat-and-ball games that would soon fade from the game on its way to becoming baseball.

Although there is no neat and clear-cut evolutionary path from eighteenth-century childhood folk games to twenty-first-century baseball, A *Little Pretty Pocket-Book* provides a significant bridge in the journey: A game called "base-ball" was not only known in England in the mid-eighteenth century but was a popular and familiar enough pastime to be featured in this landmark children's book, one that was printed and reprinted on both sides of the Atlantic for decades. The game's use of multiple bases, the implicit stand-off between pitcher and batter, and perhaps most tellingly, the goal of reaching "Home with Joy," all ring true with our national pastime more than 270 years later.

3

Pittsfield Meeting House Bylaw, 1791

BALL GAMES BANNED IN EARLY AMERICA

On September 5, 1791, the following bylaw, proposed "for the Preservation of the Windows in the New Meeting House," was presented at an assembly of the inhabitants of the town of Pittsfield, Massachusetts:

> Be it ordained by the said Inhabitants that no Person, an Inhabitant of said Town, shall be permitted to play at any Game called Wicket, Cricket, Baseball, Batball, Football, Cat, Fives or any other Game or Games with Balls within the Distance of Eighty Yards from said Meeting House — And every such Person who shall play at any of the said Games or other Games with Balls within the Distance aforesaid, shall for any Instance thereof, forfeit the Sum of five shillings to be recovered by Action of Debt brought before any Justice of the Peace to the Use of the Person who shall sue and prosecute therefor.

This bylaw, uncovered at the Berkshire Athenaeum library as a result of research by John Thorn in 2004, represents the earliest written reference to *baseball* that originated in the United States. As with other early uses of the term, it is difficult to know exactly what form of the game is being referenced and whether it is the same sport we would recognize today. But this mention of baseball—distinguished here from the related games of cricket, wicket, batball, cat, and fives—shows that the playing of a game under this name was common enough in western Massachusetts of the late 1700s to be considered a threat to the town's meeting-house windows.

The Pittsfield ordinance also sheds light on the variety of bat-and-ball games that were prevalent during this time, in a relatively remote rural locale of Colonial Massachusetts. Most of the games mentioned have rich traditions in Colonial America and the early decades of the new nation.

At a legal Meeting of the Inhabitants of the Town of Pittsfield qualified to vote in Town Meetings, ~~or the Meeting~~ holden on Monday the fifth day of Sept. 1791 ~~Voted~~, The following Bye Law, for the Preservation of the Windows in the New Meeting House in said Town ——— viz,

Be it ordained by the said Inhabitants that no Person an Inhabitant of said Town, shall be permitted to play at any Game called Wicket, Cricket, Base ball, Bat ball, Foot ball, Cat, Fives or any other Game or Games with Balls, within the Distance of Eighty Yards from said Meeting House —— And every Person who shall play at any of the said Games or other Games with Balls within the Distance aforesaid, shall for every Instance thereof, forfeit the Sum of five Shillings to be recovered by Action of Debt brought before any Justice of the Peace to the Use of the Person who shall sue and prosecute therefor ——

And be it further ordained That in every Instance where any Minor shall be guilty of a Breach of this Law, his Parent, Master, Mistress or Guardian shall forfeit the like Sum to be recovered in Manner and to the Use aforesaid ——

PITTSFIELD MEETING HOUSE BYLAW, 1791.

Originating in England in the sixteenth century (possibly earlier), the game of cricket had established itself as the unofficial national game of that country by the time the residents of Pittsfield were seeking to limit its play near their meeting house. Cricket had been transported across the Atlantic by early British colonists by the beginning of the eighteenth century, and it was widely played here well into the next century. It was one of the first organized team sports in the American colonies, and leagues and newspaper coverage were especially prevalent during the Colonial Era. In 1754, Benjamin Franklin brought over from England a copy of the first official rules of cricket (published in England in 1744); Franklin's city of Philadelphia would prove to be one of the last holdouts of cricket in the United States, with matches attracting large crowds even into the 1900s. Cricket and baseball are often compared to each other, and the games do share some common lingo and rules, but the latter sport overtook its older British cousin in popularity on this side of the ocean by the time of the Civil War. In 1790s Pittsfield, however, cricket was likely the greater threat to the safety of the meeting-house windows, given its popularity at the time.

Wicket was akin to an informal variation of cricket, and references to that sport in the American colonies also date back to the early eighteenth century. Wicket even has connections to the father of the country: A May 1778 diary entry by Revolutionary War soldier George Ewing tells of "His Excellency," George Washington, playing wicket with the soldiers at Valley Forge. Other Revolutionary-Era mentions of wicket can be found in diaries and reports from both Colonial and British troops. Wicket was played through the first half of the nineteenth century, particularly in Connecticut but also elsewhere in the Northeast and as far west as Ohio. Though similar, wicket's rules had essential differences from those of the more established cricket. The wicket used in the game of that name was wider and lower to the ground than that

in cricket, and rather than being pitched through the air, the ball was rolled or skipped along the ground toward the batter's wicket. The batsman

WICKET MATCH AT
DARTMOUTH COLLEGE, 1793.

used a curved club, similar to a field hockey stick, to strike the ball. The game of wicket remained a popular pastime until about the 1850s, at which point it was completely overtaken by baseball in the American consciousness.

The game of "cat," referred to in the Pittsfield ordinance, was another widespread Colonial-Era childhood activity, and its origins and evolution (albeit murky) are closely tied to those of baseball. Early forms of "cat" developed in medieval England and typically were played with two pieces of wood (no ball), whereby one stick, the shorter "cat," was struck with a bat. Variations of the game commonly known as "tip-cat" involved pitching, bases, base running, and outs, but not until it was transported to the American colonies was a ball believed to be integral to the sport. In the basic version of the American game, called "one-old-cat" or "one-o'-cat," a striker or batter would attempt to hit the ball delivered by the pitcher and then run to a base and back before being struck with the ball, collecting points for each base touched. In "two-old-cat," two batsmen were positioned at opposite ends of the field and each would run to the other base when the ball was hit. "Three-old-cat" was the variation played with six or more players, three of them batsmen, on a triangular-shaped field. In many ways most similar to baseball was "four-old-cat," which had four bases arranged in a square and four pitchers/catchers taking turns throwing to four batters, one at each base. Four-old-cat could also be played with a single fielder serving as the pitcher, and this is the version most reminiscent of baseball. Both Albert Spalding and John Montgomery Ward, a Hall of Famer and pioneering player unionizer, cited four-old-cat as a direct predecessor of baseball. In truth, the games of baseball and old-cat evolved concurrently, and the earliest references to "one-old-cat" (as distinct from, simply, "cat") date only as far back as the 1830s.

It is not known for certain what "batball" in the Pittsfield rule refers to, but as it presumably involves a ball and a bat, one

Both Albert Spalding and John Montgomery Ward, a Hall of Famer and pioneering player unionizer, cited four-old-cat as a direct predecessor of baseball.

CRICKET MATCH IN PHILADELPHIA, 1879.

can imagine it bore some similarities to baseball and its relatives. The other games that the residents of this Massachusetts town insisted be played nowhere near their meeting house grounds are not bat-and-ball sports: the still-familiar football (before Americans started calling it "soccer") and the long-forgotten "fives," a form of hand-ball according to Thorn.

If all these near and not-so-near relations of baseball were being played at this particular time and place, what form of the game bearing that name was popular in late-eighteenth-century western Massachusetts? Again some speculation is required, but most likely it was a form of the sport that came to be known as the "Massachusetts game," also known as "round ball" or simply "base." The specific rules of the Massachusetts game, and its rivalry with the so-called New York game, are explored in later chapters (see **Object #8**).

The rediscovery of this Pittsfield bylaw in 2004 was in many ways a watershed moment in the search for baseball's origins. As the earliest known written reference to baseball in the United States, it provided documentary evidence that a game under that name was widely played in areas of this young nation even earlier than previously believed and that the game evolved alongside competing sports for many decades before asserting itself as our national pastime.

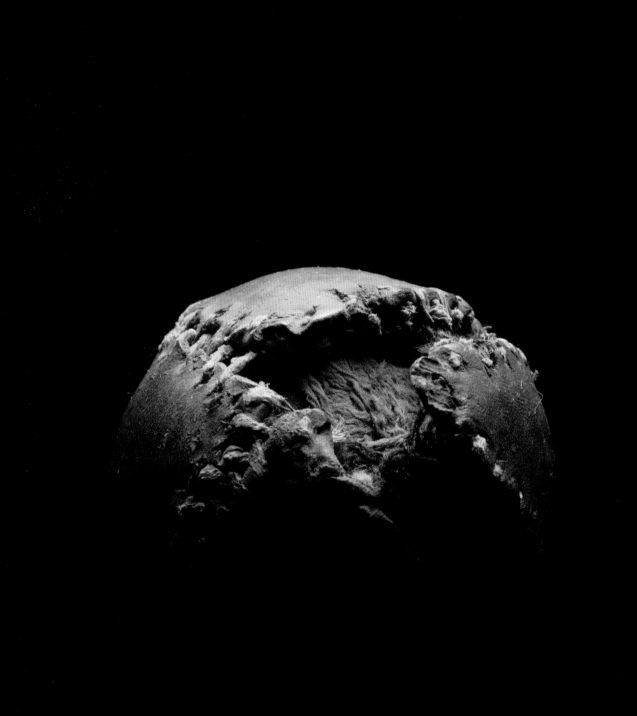

THE DOUBLEDAY BALL, 1839.

4

The Doubleday Ball, 1839

BASEBALL'S CREATION MYTH

For generations, it was a widely perpetuated story that the game of baseball was invented by Abner Doubleday in Cooperstown, New York, in 1839. It is the reason why the National Baseball Hall of Fame and Museum is located in that small town in upstate New York, and why the official opening of the Hall of Fame took place in 1939—the ostensible centennial of baseball's birth.

This ragged, handmade ball was the first object accessioned into the Hall of Fame's collection by its founder, Stephen C. Clark. It was found in a trunk allegedly belonging to Abner Graves, who in the early 1900s had been the source of the story that Doubleday first introduced the game of baseball to a group of Cooperstown schoolboys, including Graves, in 1839. The ball, thus, was linked to the so-called inventor of the game.

In fact, as we have seen, baseball, in some form, existed well before Doubleday, and indeed, there is considerable doubt as to whether Doubleday, a Union general during the Civil War, had any connection to baseball whatsoever. The Doubleday myth emerged from the Mills Commission, formed in 1905 with the purpose of determining the true origin of the sport. Headed by former National League president Abraham G. Mills, the committee included Morgan Bulkeley, the first NL president in 1876; Arthur Gorman, a one-time U.S. senator and former president of the Washington Nationals Base Ball Club; Alfred Reach, an ex-player and prominent sporting goods magnate; George Wright, one of baseball's biggest stars in the 1860s and '70s and also owner of a sporting goods company; Nick Young, NL president from 1885 to 1902; and James E. Sullivan, president of the Amateur Athletic Union.

Mills's report concluded that "the first scheme for playing [baseball], according to the best evidence available to date, was devised by Abner Doubleday at Cooperstown, N.Y., in 1839."

The impetus for the formation of the commission was the ongoing debate surrounding baseball's origins, most fervently undertaken by Albert Spalding and Henry Chadwick, two highly influential figures in the sport's growth. Chadwick, who was born in England in 1824, had been a leading promoter of baseball during its nascent years, and he was the prime advocate of the idea that the American pastime had originated from the English game of rounders. In the first edition of his *Beadle's Dime Base-Ball Player*, published in 1860 (see **Object #10**), Chadwick discusses "the English Game of Rounders, from which Base Ball is derived." In his 1867 article "The Ancient History of Base Ball," he wrote that, while rounders "was a mild and simple amusement compared with the American sport which has grown out of it . . . the English 'rounders' contained all the elements of our National game." He picked up his case again in the 1903 edition of the *Spalding Baseball Guide*, of which he was the editor.

Albert G. Spalding, the founder and publisher of that guide—as well as a star player in the 1870s before launching his A. G. Spalding Sporting Goods Company—took exception to Chadwick's claims, insisting that baseball was "purely of American origin." To put the matter to rest, Spalding assembled a committee to investigate and research baseball's origins.

Abraham Mills himself had long been an avid proponent of baseball as an American invention. At a banquet honoring the return of Spalding's "World Base Ball Tour" (see **Object #20**) in 1889, Mills gave a speech proclaiming that "patriotism and research alike vindicate the claim that [baseball] is American in its origins." His statement inspired a chant of "No rounders!" that reverberated through the hall.

In 1905, the Mills Commission sent out a call seeking information relating to the origins of baseball. Among the responses was a letter from Abner Graves, then a 71-year-old mining engineer living in Colorado. In it he claimed that Doubleday, a fellow student in Cooperstown, had modified the local game of town ball (not, crucially, rounders) and standardized it into a form that he called baseball.

The commission immediately embraced and embellished Graves's tale, ignoring considerable holes in the story—including, among other things, the fact that Doubleday himself, who had died in 1893, never mentioned baseball in any correspondence or in his personal diaries throughout his life, and that Doubleday was actually at West Point, not in Cooperstown, at the time Graves claimed he invented the game there. But tying baseball's invention to a Civil War hero in the pastoral farmland of small town U.S.A. was too juicy to pass up. Mills's report concluded that "the first scheme for playing [baseball], according to the best evidence available to date, was devised by Abner Doubleday at Cooperstown, N.Y., in 1839."

The Doubleday-as-inventor-of-baseball claim was received with skepticism almost immediately upon the release of the Mills Commission report in 1908, and histo-

rians continued to poke holes in the myth until it was effectively debunked. Still, the "Doubleday Ball" remains on prominent display, along with a portrait of General Abner Doubleday, in the Baseball Hall of Fame in Cooperstown as a symbol of the sport's long tradition in America, if not of its true origin.

MAJOR ABNER DOUBLEDAY,
CIRCA 1861.

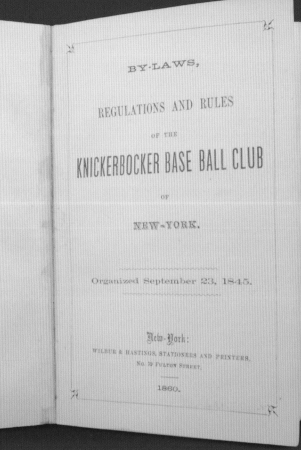

BY-LAWS,

REGULATIONS AND RULES

OF THE

KNICKERBOCKER BASE BALL CLUB

OF

NEW-YORK.

Organized September 23, 1845.

New-York:
WILBUR & HASTINGS, STATIONERS AND PRINTERS,
No. 39 Fulton Street.

1860.

5

By-laws and Rules of the Knickerbocker Base Ball Club, 1845

BASEBALL'S EARLIEST CODIFIED RULES

Despite the various chapbooks and booklets of childhood games, baseball in early America was not just for kids. Adult men's clubs were being organized for the myriad forms of bat-and-ball games of the early 1800s. The Olympic Ball Club was formed in Philadelphia in 1831 and published its own constitution in 1838. The surviving document focuses only on the operation and organization of the club—including extensive details on fines for absences, acts of negligence, and disorderly conduct—but offers

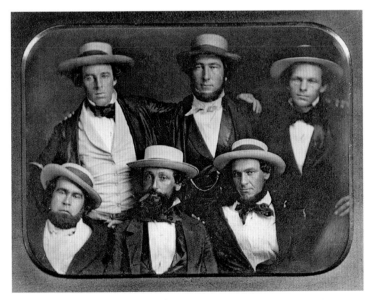

KNICKERBOCKER BASE BALL CLUB, CIRCA 1847.

little about how the game itself was to be played. Most likely, the Olympics played a regional variation known as town ball.

Clubs were also forming around New York City and Brooklyn beginning as early as the 1820s and 1830s. Members of such clubs often were "gentlemen" from the upper and middle classes, or skilled tradesmen, and they paid membership dues. The club games were as much about exercise and camaraderie as they were about winning and losing.

The Knickerbocker Base Ball Club was established on September 23, 1845, led by Alexander Joy Cartwright, for the purpose of "health and recreation." Prior to that, the members met for games at vacant lots in Manhattan, first at Madison Square and then Murray Hill. When urban growth overtook those spaces, the group formed the Knickerbocker Club and played its matches at Elysian Fields across the Hudson River in Hoboken, New Jersey.

The Knickerbockers were not the first organized baseball club, nor did Cartwright and company invent the rules of baseball. But the club's impact on the sport's history is significant in providing the oldest known codification of the rules of the game. Although a few of the practices outlined in the Knickerbocker Rules have evolved or been eliminated, the basic foundation of the rules of baseball today are evident.

1. Members must strictly observe the time agreed upon for exercise, and be punctual in their attendance.

2. When assembled for exercise, the President, or in his absence, the Vice-President, shall appoint an Umpire, who shall keep the game in a book provided for that purpose, and note all violations of the By-Laws and Rules during the time of exercise.

3. The presiding officer shall designate two members as Captains, who shall retire and make the match to be played, observing at the same time that the player's opposite to each other should be as nearly equal as possible, the choice of sides to be then tossed for, and the first in hand to be decided in like manner.

4. The bases shall be from "home" to second base, forty-two paces; from first to third base, forty-two paces, equidistant.

5. No stump match [truncated game] shall be played on a regular day of exercise.

6. If there should not be a sufficient number of members of the Club present at the time agreed upon to commence exercise, gentlemen not members may be chosen in to make up the match, which shall not be broken up to take in members that may afterwards appear; but in all cases, members shall have the preference, when present, at the making of the match.

7. If members appear after the game is commenced, they may be chosen in if mutually agreed upon.

8. The game to consist of twenty-one counts, or aces; but at the conclusion an equal number of hands must be played.

9. The ball must be pitched, not thrown, for the bat.

10. A ball knocked out of the field, or outside the range of the first and third base, is foul.

11. Three balls being struck at and missed and the last one caught, is a hand-out; if not caught is considered fair, and the striker bound to run.

12. If a ball be struck, or tipped, and caught, either flying or on the first bound, it is a hand-out.

13. A player running the bases shall be out, if the ball is in the hands of an adversary on the base, or the runner is touched with it before he makes his base; it being understood, however, that in no instance is a ball to be thrown at him.

14. A player running who shall prevent an adversary from catching or getting the ball before making his base, is a hand-out.

15. Three hands out, all out.

16. Players must take their strike in regular turn.

17. All disputes and differences relative to the game, to be decided by the Umpire, from which there is no appeal.

18. No ace or base can be made on a foul strike.

19. A runner cannot be put out in making one base, when a balk is made on the pitcher.

20. But one base allowed when a ball bounds out of the field when struck.

Most of the rules at the start of the list address the structure of the teams and how sides were chosen. Games played by the Knickerbockers tended to be intramural competitions among the members of the club; matches against competing clubs were less common at the time.

Many credit the Knickerbockers with establishing the 90-foot distance between bases, but in fact the club's regulations in that regard were not so specific. Rule 4 specifies the distances between home plate and second base and between first and third base as "forty-two paces, equidistant." If you assume a pace as equal to 3 feet, then, using Pythagorean geometry, you indeed get a distance just shy of 90 feet from base to base. But in *Baseball Before We Knew It*, David Block examines this question and concludes that, in the parlance of the time, a "pace" more likely was meant to indicate a distance of about 2 1/2 feet. With that assumption, the distance between bases, per the Knickerbocker Rules, would have been closer to 75 feet. That remained the commonly accepted distance until 1857, when it was officially changed to 90 feet in the rules of the National Association of Base Ball Players, the first governing body of baseball clubs.

A more striking difference in the Knickerbocker Rules, as compared to the way the game has been played for the last 150 years, can be found in rule 8, where the conclusion of the game is determined not by a preset number of innings ("hands") but rather by the number of runs ("counts" or "aces"). This meant that a game could last one inning or many innings, depending on the teams' ability to score. Incidentally, the term "runs" (like "innings" adopted from cricket) was known to be used in the context of baseball at the time, but it did not enter the official rule language until the following decade.

The directive to pitch, rather than throw, the ball in rule 9 meant that the ball had to be delivered underhand. In the days of "gentlemanly" baseball, the pitcher's role was to deliver the ball to the batter so that it could be put into play. Underhand delivery remained the standard until 1883, when sidearm delivery was permitted. Overhand delivery was finally allowed in major league baseball beginning in 1884.

Rule 10 defined the concept of foul territory, which, though not unique or original to the Knickerbockers, was not the norm in the 1840s. It was common practice in other forms of baseball, including the Massachusetts game and town ball, that any ball was considered in play, regardless of the direction in which it was hit. The regulations relating to foul balls are expanded in rule 18, which states that batters or runners could not advance on a foul ball. What is not entirely clear is whether a foul ball was counted as a strike under the Knickerbocker Rules. The use of the word "strike" in rule 18 leads some to believe that it was intended to count as a strike, whereas other historians contend that foul balls were not strikes during this period. The foul-ball-as-strike rule did not officially enter the rule books until after 1900.

The next three provisions, rules 11–13, are familiar definitions for how a batter can get out. The three-strikes-and-you're-out tradition, outlined in rule 11, was well established by the time of the Knickerbockers. Here they also included the proviso whereby a third strike dropped by the catcher meant fair game for the batter to attempt to reach base. There was no allowance for a "called strike," however; that did not become a rule for another decade. There is also no mention of "balls" or "walks," which did not come into practice until the 1870s.

The rule that a ball caught on the fly is an out also had a long tradition in baseball and its precursors, but rule 12's granting of an out for a ball caught on the first bounce is more of an anomaly. (Remember, back in those days, fielders played bare-handed, so catching a ball on the fly could sting quite a bit.) It was part of the official rules, but in practice whether or not to allow outs for balls caught on one bounce was generally left up to mutual agreement of the two team captains for a given match. It was removed from the baseball rule book in late 1864, and from that moment on, any fair ball had to be caught on the fly to be an out.

In one of the more significant advancements promoted by the Knickerbockers, rule 13 eliminated the practice of hitting runners with a thrown ball to get them out, also known as "soaking" or "plugging." This differentiated the New York game from other variations being played at the time.

The now-standard three-outs-per-side rule described in # 15 was not invented by the Knickerbockers, but it did solidify the evolution away from the "one out, all out" and "all out, all out" practices employed in other bat-and-ball games, including round ball and cricket.

Rule 13 eliminated the practice of hitting runners with a thrown ball to get them out, also known as "soaking" or "plugging." This differentiated the New York game from other variations being played at the time.

Rule 20 is an early variation of today's ground-rule double, only here it was scored a ground-rule single. This guideline was needed, given the lack of defined boundaries (i.e., no outfield wall) for the games being played on open fields in New York and New Jersey.

The regulations relating to interference, fixed batting orders, and the infallibility of the umpire, outlined in rules 14, 16, and 17, are also familiar to fans of today.

The Knickerbockers played their first intrasquad game under these rules in early October 1845. The first officially recorded contest between different clubs was held on June 19, 1846, when the New York Baseball Club defeated the Knickerbockers at Elysian Fields, 23–1, in four innings.

Many fundamental baseball practices are not addressed directly in the Knickerbocker Rules—such as number of players per side, the positions in the field, how runs were scored, the size and shape of the equipment, and so on—and the role of Cartwright and the Knickerbockers in *inventing* the rules of the sport may have been overstated over the years. Nevertheless, the Knickerbocker Rules provide a landmark object for tracing the evolution of baseball from its origins to today.

"GRAND MATCH FOR THE CHAMPIONSHIP, AT THE ELYSIAN FIELDS, HOBOKEN, N. J.," CURRIER & IVES LITHOGRAPH, 1866.

6

Constitution and By-Laws of the National Association of Base Ball Players, 1858

THE FIRST ORGANIZED LEAGUE

During the 1840s and 1850s, as growing numbers of men organized into clubs for the purpose of playing and competing in the game of baseball, the Knickerbocker Rules became the standard under which these disparate groups played, especially in and around New York City. Games between clubs were still largely informal, however, and no overarching body governed interclub matches or the rules of play.

This changed in 1857, when representatives of 14 baseball clubs, all from New York City or Brooklyn (at the time a separate city), convened at Smith's Hotel in Lower Manhattan to discuss the rules and competition among the clubs. Presiding over the convention as the senior organization, the Knickerbocker Club was joined by the fellow Manhattan-based Baltic, Eagle, Empire, Gotham, and Harlem clubs. Brooklyn was represented by the Atlantic, Bedford, Continental, Eckford, Excelsior, Harmony, Nassau, and Putnam clubs. Daniel "Doc" Adams of the Knickerbockers was elected president.

In March of the following year, with 22 clubs in attendance, a permanent organizing body was created: the National Association of Base Ball Players (NABBP). A league constitution and bylaws were drafted. Clubs wishing to join the association were required to submit an application; new clubs would be admitted with two-thirds approval of existing member clubs, to be voted at the annual conventions. The 1858 convention also established a Judiciary Committee to address rule violations and settle disputes between clubs. The NABBP regulated the actions of individual players as well.

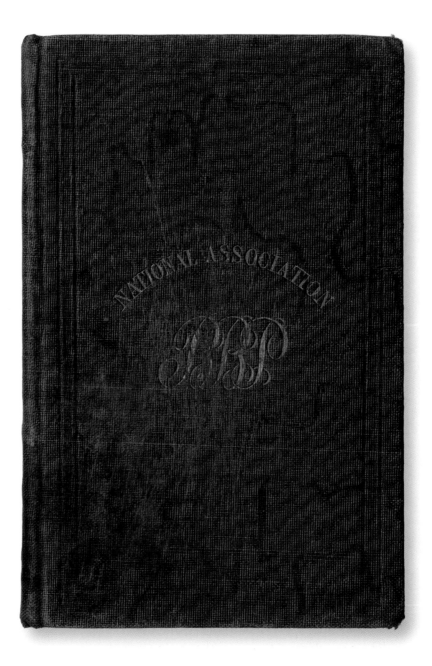

CONSTITUTION AND BY-LAWS OF THE NATIONAL ASSOCIATION
OF BASE BALL PLAYERS, 1859 EDITION.

Clearly not "national" in its initial membership, this pioneering association of baseball teams expanded over the next few years to encompass clubs from New Jersey, upstate New York (Albany, Rochester, Buffalo), New England (Boston and New Haven), and the Mid-Atlantic (Philadelphia, Baltimore, Washington, D.C.). By the end of the Civil War in 1865, teams from far-flung locations in the South, the Midwest, and the West had joined the association. At the 10th annual convention in 1866, the NABBP included more than 200 teams representing 17 states and the District of Columbia. The number of represented teams more than doubled at the 1867 convention. State and regional associations were organized to handle the rapid growth in the number of clubs and to serve as representatives at the annual national conventions.

In addition to regulating the member clubs and electing league officers, the annual conventions provided an opportunity to update and refine the rules of play. Doc Adams, who began playing baseball in New York in the 1830s and joined the Knickerbockers in the 1840s, headed the Rules and Regulations Committee at the 1858 convention. Adams had played a central role in writing the original Knickerbocker Rules of 1845, and he chaired that club's committee to revise the rules in 1848. (Adams is also credited with inventing the shortstop position, and he undertook the task of manufacturing the club's baseballs.)

At these first NABBP conventions, the distance between bases was formalized at 90 feet, and the distance from the pitcher's position to home plate was set at 45 feet. Nine innings was established as the length of a game. The called strike was introduced at the 1858 convention, and players were prohibited from using their hats to stop a batted ball.

Whereas discussions over the rules did spark disagreement among club representatives, the issue that came to dominate the debate in the latter years of the association was that of professionalism. The NABBP had been established as an amateur

Whereas discussions over the rules did spark disagreement among club representatives, the issue that came to dominate the debate in the latter years of the association was that of professionalism.

organization, but baseball's rapid growth, and the realization that there was money to be made, led owners to try to woo the top players with some form of financial compensation. This also led players to jump from team to team, or "revolve," in the course of a season, in search of bigger paychecks.

While the NABBP continued to officially ban professional players, many were paid under the table. By the end of the 1860s, the pull of professionalism grew too strong, however. The league established two distinct categories of players—amateurs and professionals—and teams were permitted to declare themselves professional. Ultimately, the NABBP collapsed, and the National Association of Professional Base Ball Players emerged in its place in 1871. The acceptance of paying players as part of the organization did not save the latter association either. It was not until 1876 and the formation of the National League that a central governing body would be founded on stable-enough principles, and by strong-willed-enough individuals, to sustain itself for decades.

7

Fashion Race Course Trophy Ball, 1858

PAID ADMISSIONS AND THE BIRTH OF THE BALLPARK

By the late 1850s, the rivalry between the baseball clubs of New York and Brooklyn was intensifying. Whereas the New York–based Knickerbockers had been a pioneer in establishing standards for the rule of play, clubs like the Eckfords and Atlantics from Brooklyn were making names for themselves on the playing field around the same time.

In an effort to settle the question of baseball supremacy between the two cities, and to celebrate the game's growing popularity, a best-of-three All-Star series was organized in 1858, to be played at the Fashion Race Course. Making up the New York nine were players from the Knickerbocker, Gotham, Eagle, Empire, Harlem, and Union clubs. Brooklyn, which was favored to win the series, was represented by an assemblage of Atlantics, Eckfords, Excelsiors, and Putnams.

The first game, played on July 20, drew an estimated 8,000 spectators, arriving by foot, horse, carriage, trolley, train, omnibus, and ferry. New York won the contest by a score of 22–18. The team was awarded the gilded ball shown here as a trophy. It is inscribed with the date of the game and the final score. In the words of the weekly *Spirit of the Times* newspaper, the match "will be long remembered with pleasure by all lovers of this noble and invigorating game."

Brooklyn evened the series in the second game, on August 17, with a 29–8 victory. In a highly detailed recap in the following day's paper, the *New York Times* reported that more than 6,000 attended, "over 500 of whom were ladies." The deciding game of the series was held on September 10, and the New Yorkers came away with the victory, 29–18.

FASHION RACE COURSE TROPHY BALL, 1858.

"GREAT BASE BALL MATCH" AT FASHION RACE COURSE,
ILLUSTRATION FROM THE NEW YORK CLIPPER, JULY 24, 1858.

Beyond symbolizing the sport's growth and marking the first baseball All-Star Game, the "Great Base Ball Match" of 1858 is especially significant for being the first time that a baseball game was played inside an enclosed park and the first time that admission was charged. The Fashion Race Course, located in what is now Flushing, Queens (not far from the current location of the New York Mets' Citi Field), was selected for its easy accessibility from both Manhattan and Brooklyn. The course already boasted a grandstand, but the track's infield had to be converted for baseball use. In order to earn back the funds spent on renting the track and converting the field, the teams decided to charge a 10-cent entry fee, with additional fees for horses and carriages. It was, as baseball historian Robert H. Schaefer described it, the first time that "baseball patrons would be charged a fee for the privilege of witnessing a match."

The decision to charge admission was not driven by a desire to raise money for the clubs or to pay the players, but rather simply to cover the costs of putting on the match. In fact, any surplus from the three games was donated to the widow and orphan funds of the New York and Brooklyn fire departments. But the three-game series was a revelation in showing that people were willing to pay money to watch a baseball game.

William Cammeyer was the first to fully seize upon this new development. In 1861, Cammeyer bought a property in the Williamsburg section of Brooklyn and opened the Union Skating Grounds, an enclosed skating rink. In an effort to generate year-round income, he converted the rink into a baseball field for the spring and summer months. He constructed a grandstand and bleachers, with "ample accommodation afforded to lady visitors, a grandstand having been erected especially for their use," according to the *Brooklyn Eagle*. Gamblers, meanwhile, were confined to their own segregated section. An eight-foot-high fence surrounded the playing field, and a clubhouse was built to accommodate three teams. Given the high quality of the Union Grounds in comparison to the other fields of the day, the Eckford, Putnam, and Constellation clubs all agreed to play their home games there.

Completed by the spring of 1862, the new baseball grounds hosted an opening exhibition game featuring players from all three resident teams on May 15. The contest featured the first known instance of the "Star-Spangled Banner" being played before a baseball game. Cammeyer did not charge admission for this inaugural match, hoping to attract fans to come and see his new ballpark. Thereafter, entry to the ballpark cost 10 cents; it was later increased to 25 cents.

Over the next decade, enclosed ballparks went up from Brooklyn to Philadelphia, Washington, D.C., to Cincinnati and St. Louis. The first to follow Union Grounds was the Capitoline Grounds, which opened just a few miles away in the Bedford neighborhood of Brooklyn in 1864. Named for one of the Seven Hills of Rome, the grounds featured bleacher seats, stables for patrons' horses, and clubhouses for the players. (Like the Union Grounds, it, too, served as a skating rink in the winter months.) The Brooklyn Atlantic club, winners of the National Association of Base Ball Players (NABBP) from 1859 to 1861, was the Capitoline Grounds' first tenant. The Atlantics defeated an All-Star team of other Brooklyn players, selected by sportswriter Henry Chadwick, in an exhibition for the ballpark's debut. The Atlantics went on to secure another championship that year. The Enterprise club shared the grounds with the Atlantics in 1864, and the Excelsiors called Capitoline home beginning in 1866.

Among the high-profile games played at Capitoline Grounds was a season-ending contest between the Atlantics and the Athletic Base Ball Club of Philadelphia in the fall of 1865. The *New York Tribune* reported that, with an estimated 15,000 to 18,000 in attendance, the game "created more excitement in the base-ball world than any previous contests this season." Brooklyn won by a thrilling 27–24 score. The following year, the same teams met at Athletics Park in Philadelphia for the league championship. The admittance fee was a hefty $1, but the game reportedly attracted nearly 20,000 spectators—many choosing to view the game from free perches outside the grounds.

In June 1870, Capitoline Grounds was the site of another epic battle, when the Atlantics hosted the Cincinnati Red Stockings. The Cincinnati club had been dominating teams throughout the country, mounting a winning streak that spanned more

BROOKLYN ATLANTICS
VS. CINCINNATI RED
STOCKINGS, AT
CAPITOLINE GROUNDS,
JUNE 1870.

than 80 games. Playing before a crowd of close to 15,000 at Capitoline, the Atlantics toppled the mighty Red Stockings in dramatic fashion, winning 8–7 in 11 innings.

While the *Brooklyn Eagle* called it the "greatest game ever played between the greatest clubs that ever played," the match highlights another revolution in baseball that had been sparked by the meeting of New York and Brooklyn All-Stars at Fashion Race Course 12 years earlier. Once fans had shown their willingness to pay money to watch a baseball game, the revenue generated could not only go to support new ballparks and the ballpark owners, but the income could be used to pay players. The Cincinnati Red Stockings were the first openly all-professional club (see **Object #12**), and they had clearly demonstrated what could be accomplished by attracting elite players with a paycheck. The Atlantic players, too, received a share of the gate receipts from the Red Stockings game in 1870. Club owners who were determined to keep baseball, at least on the surface, an amateur sport were rapidly losing out to those who saw the benefits of making baseball a professional endeavor.

Although the establishment of a professional league was more than a decade in the future, the All-Star baseball match at Fashion Race Course on July 20, 1858, was a landmark moment that would forever alter the place of baseball in American society. The advent of paid admission to games not only put the sport on the path to professionalism, but it also prompted the building of increasingly lavish ballparks, which would continue through the rest of the century. The relative comforts of these permanent wooden structures, combined with entry fees that served to keep out the "riffraff," made baseball games a more family-friendly event, exposing the game to more and more Americans.

THE BASE BALL PLAYER'S POCKET COMPANION, 1859.

8

The Base Ball Player's Pocket Companion, 1859

THE MASSACHUSETTS VERSUS NEW YORK GAMES

The writing of the Knickerbocker Rules in 1845 and the establishment of the National Association of Base Ball Players in 1857 under those rules show the growing maturity and popularity of what had come to be known as the "New York game." Meanwhile, the "Massachusetts game" was still going strong in New England. Through the first half of the nineteenth century, the rival Massachusetts and New York games followed their own evolutionary paths in their respective regions, along with another variation in Philadelphia, commonly known as "town ball."

The Base Ball Player's Pocket Companion of 1859, subtitled "containing rules and regulations for forming clubs, directions for playing the 'Massachusetts game,' and the 'New York game,' from official reports," marks the first time that the complete rules of the two games were presented in the same volume. The *Pocket Companion* was published by Mayhew and Baker of Boston, who not only presented the rules of their hometown version first, but were not shy about asserting that game's primacy: "The Game of Base Ball, as adopted by the 'Massachusetts Association of Base Ball Players,' May, 1858, which has ever been the favorite and principal game played throughout New England, . . . deservedly holds the first place in the estimation of all ball players and the public."

Also known as round ball, the Massachusetts game differed from the New York game in several fundamental respects. Each side consisted of 10 to 14 players; the additional players were needed because the Massachusetts game had no foul territory, and any struck ball, hit in any direction, was in play. The field was laid out in a square, with bases composed of upright stakes spaced 60 feet apart. The "striker" (batter) stood between first and fourth base (the equivalent of modern baseball's third base and home). The "thrower" stood 35 feet from the striker and could deliver the ball overhand. The game ended when one side recorded 100 tallies, or runs.

A side's turn at bat was over when one player was made out, and the methods for recording an out differed in several respects from the New York game. A struck ball was an out if caught on the fly; there was no allowance for catching the ball on the first bounce. The practice of "soaking" or "plugging" (hitting the runner with a thrown ball to get him out) was alive and well in the Massachusetts game long after the Knickerbockers had done away with it. Of course, the ball used in New England weighed half as much as that used in New York. Three strikes was an out in the Massachusetts game, but the umpire ("referee" in this version) could call a strike if a batter did not swing at "good balls thrown repeatedly at him, for the apparent purpose of delaying the game, or of giving advantage to players."

Whereas 19 pages of the *Pocket Companion* are devoted to the rules of the Massachusetts game and the officers, constitution, and bylaws of the Massachusetts Association of Base Ball Players, just 9 pages are given up to the New York game, which, Mayhew and Baker tell us, "is fast becoming, in this country, what Cricket is to England, a national game, combining, as it does, exciting sport and healthful exercise at a trifling expense."

The "Rules and Regulations of the Game of Base Ball Adopted by the National Association of Base Ball Players," presented in the 1859 *Pocket Companion*, reflect an updated version of the New York game compared to the Knickerbocker Rules of 14 years earlier. Further, with 32 items as compared to the Knickerbockers' 20, the 1859 edition goes deeper in laying out the basic rules, many of which remain in force to this day. It gives detailed specifications for the size and makeup of the ball ("not less than five and three-fourths nor more than six ounces avoirdupois. . . . not less than nine and three-fourths, nor more than ten inches in circumference. . . . composed of India rubber and yarn, and covered with leather"), the bat ("round, and must not exceed two and a half inches in diameter in the thickest part. It must be made of wood, and may be of any length to suit the striker"), and the bases ("must cover a space equal to one square foot of surface. The first, second and third bases shall be canvass bags painted white, and filled with sand or sawdust; the home base and pitcher's point to be each marked by a flat circular iron plate, pointed or enameled white").

Among other fundamental tenets represented in the 1859 rules were setting the length of the game at nine innings, with an allowance for extra innings in the event of a tie score, and five innings as the minimum length for a game to be official. The number of required players per side was also set at nine, provided they are "regular members of the club which they represent."

There is also a clause that specifically addresses gambling: "No person engaged in a match, either as umpire, scorer or player, shall be either directly or indirectly interested in any bet upon the game. . . . [T]he umpire may dismiss any transgressor."

While the Boston-published *Base Ball Player's Pocket Companion* presented the two games side by side, the rivalry and sniping between advocates of each side could be found in the press accounts of the day. An editorial in, of all places, the *New York Daily Tribune* on October 18, 1859, addressed the plans for New York and Brooklyn clubs to play a match with a visiting cricket team from England. The writer, whose provenance is not disclosed, scoffs at the idea that representatives of the "small potato" New York game would be worthy of such international competition:

> The so-called "Base Ball" played by the New York Clubs—what is falsely called the "National" game—is no more like the genuine game of baseball than single wicket is like a full field of cricket. The Clubs who have formed what they choose to call the "National Association," play a bastard game, worthy only of boys of ten years of age. The only genuine game is what is known as the "Massachusetts Game," and if the Englishmen . . . want to find foes worthy of their steel, let them challenge the "Excelsior" Club of Upton, Massachusetts, now the Champion Club of New England.

Suffice it to say, the days of the Excelsior Club of Upton, and those of most of the purveyors of the Massachusetts game, were numbered. By the end of the Civil War, the New York game would be synonymous with baseball throughout the country.

"The so-called 'Base Ball' played by the New York Clubs— what is falsely called the 'National' game— is no more like the genuine game of baseball than single wicket is like a full field of cricket."

KNICKERBOCKER CLUB OF NEW YORK AND EXCELSIOR CLUB OF BROOKLYN, 1859.

9

Knickerbocker Club of New York and Excelsior Club of Brooklyn, 1859

WHAT BASEBALL PLAYERS USED TO LOOK LIKE

On August 2, 1859, the Knickerbocker and Excelsior Base Ball Clubs met for a match at the Excelsiors' grounds near Court Street in Red Hook, Brooklyn. The home squad emerged victorious, 20–5, in front of an estimated 6,000 spectators. The *New York Clipper* reported that the game was "decidedly the most brilliant contest of the season." The *Brooklyn Daily Eagle*, meanwhile, hailed the orderly and respectful fans, "of both sexes," on hand to witness "this manly and noble exercise, and exciting and exhilarating game."

Neither the game itself nor the politeness of its spectators are of particular significance in the broader history of baseball, however. Rather, the two clubs agreeing to pose for a group photograph before the game gives us the oldest on-field baseball photograph, according to the National Baseball Hall of Fame. The man at center in the top hat and those to the right of him in the photo represent the Excelsior Base Ball Club of Brooklyn; the members of the Knickerbocker Base Ball Club stand to the left. Included among the Knickerbocker nine is future Hall of Famer Harry Wright (sixth from the left), who would later lead the formidable Cincinnati Red Stockings, baseball's first openly professional team.

A decade before this photo was taken, the Knickerbockers became the first club to adopt an official uniform. The wide belts, wool pants, and flannel shirts seen here might not seem the most comfortable attire for summer athletic activity, but it reflected the gentlemanly look that the clubs wanted to project. By 1859, the Knickerbockers had abandoned the straw hats that accompanied their first official uniforms and had switched to visored caps made of merino wool. The blue pants and white shirt remained the Knickerbocker uniform throughout the duration of the club.

The flat-topped, pillbox-style cap worn by the 1859 Knickerbockers remained one of the popular cap styles until the late 1800s, when it faded out of fashion. It was brought back into vogue by the Philadelphia Athletics of the early 1900s. Sixty years later, the Pittsburgh Pirates wore the "retro" style pillbox cap from 1976 to 1986, including their championship season of 1979.

First established in 1854, the Excelsior club, for its part, was known for introducing, in 1860, the so-called Brooklyn-style cap, featuring a rounded crown, a long visor, and a button on top—the precursor to the modern baseball cap.

Neither the Knickerbockers nor the Excelsiors of 1859 displayed any logo or insignia on their caps or jerseys (one member of the Excelsiors does appear to have an old-style "E" printed on his jersey shield). Later in the 1800s, teams began displaying the first letter of their city or nickname on their caps, a practice that did not become commonplace until after the turn of the twentieth century. In 1905, the Washington Nationals (later known as the Senators) became the first team to spell out the team nickname on their uniforms, printing the word "Nationals" in plain lettering on their home jerseys.

In 1860, however, the Excelsiors added the team nickname to their belts, embossed in Old English lettering; it is the first known instance of a nickname displayed on a baseball uniform. Belts served both practical and decorative roles on these early uniforms, although they became less ornate over time. By the early 1900s, most teams wore narrow, solid-color belts. The Pirates introduced the first beltless uniform in 1970, wearing pants with an elastic waistband. This style became nearly universal in the major leagues, lasting until the early 1990s, when the belt made its comeback.

The pants, or "pantaloons," of the earliest baseball uniforms

> Later in the 1800s, teams began displaying the first letter of their city or nickname on their caps, a practice that did not become commonplace until after the turn of the twentieth century.

were soon adapted to give a tighter, tapered fit at the cuffs. This then gave way to the knickers style, first worn by the Cincinnati Red Stockings in 1868. As the Baseball Hall of Fame points out in its "Dressed to the Nines" online exhibit of baseball uniforms, the knee-high knickers not only eliminated the problem of loose leg openings, but it also allowed the Red Stockings to display their red stockings. Cincinnati and other clubs of the day wore their knickers to come just below the knee, revealing socks of solid colors, stripes of varying widths, or other patterns. Over time, however, the length of the pant leg has traveled up and down as fashions change. Many players today wear their pant legs down to the tops of their shoes, completely covering the socks—although not quite in the style of the Excelsiors and Knickerbockers of 1859.

The collared shirts donned by these clubs remained the style through the first decades of the twentieth century, and the collars took various shapes and sizes. Some teams in the nineteenth century even wore ties with their collared shirts, either bow ties or short ties tucked into the jersey. Completely collarless jerseys became the norm by the late 1920s and 1930s. Teams also experimented with different styles of buttons, laces, and pullovers; zippers were not used on baseball uniforms until the 1930s.

Flannel uniforms of wool or cotton-wool blends remained the standard for more than a century after the Excelsiors and Knickerbockers took the field in August 1859. Lighter-weight wool blends were employed around the middle of the twentieth century, but it wasn't until the introduction of lighter and more durable synthetic double knits in the 1970s, first worn by the Pittsburgh Pirates, that flannel uniforms were hung in the closet for good. The Pirates of the 1970s looked quite a bit different from these clubs of the 1850s.

BASEBALL UNIFORMS
DEPICTED IN "NEW YORK
FASHIONS FOR MARCH
1870" LITHOGRAPH.

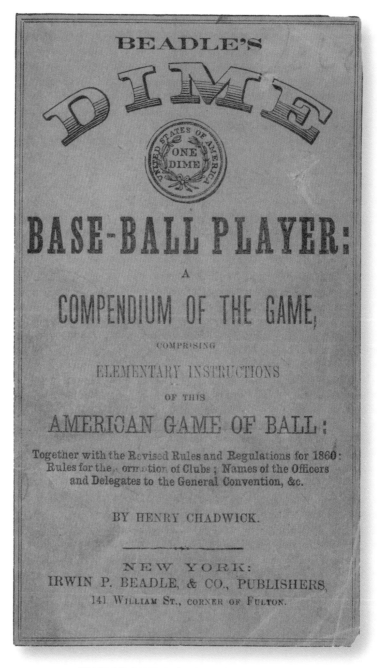

BEADLE'S DIME BASE-BALL PLAYER, 1860.

10

Beadle's Dime Base-Ball Player, 1860

THE EMERGENCE OF THE ANNUAL
BASEBALL GUIDE

In 1860, Irwin P. Beadle & Company of New York, originator of the so-called "dime novel" paperback, published *Beadle's Dime Base-Ball Player: A Compendium of the Game, Comprising Elementary Instructions of the American Game of Ball*. Written by Henry Chadwick, the booklet marks the first edition of the first annual guide to baseball. As Chadwick states in his introduction:

> In presenting this work to our readers, we claim for it the merit of being the first publication of its kind yet issued, as all previous works on Base Ball—and there are but very few published—have been confined to the history of the game as contained in the proceedings of the National Convention of Base-Ball Players, together with the rules and regulations of the game adopted by the National Association. We, therefore, introduce this book to our readers, feeling confident that it will be interesting to all, and beneficial to many, especially to those who have but a limited practical knowledge of the game.

Published every year from 1860 to 1881, the guide spawned a wave of baseball annuals that continues to this day.

The first edition of *Beadle's Dime Base-Ball Player* opens with a brief history of baseball to that point and lists the Knickerbocker Rules of 1845. Chadwick discusses the establishment of the National Association of Base Ball Players and includes a

UNION PRISONERS AT SALISBURY, N.C., 1863.

soldiers and officers, from all classes, would participate in side by side. As a soldier from the 10th Massachusetts Regiment wrote to his family, "Officer and men forget, for a time, the differences in rank and indulge in the invigorating sport with a schoolboy's ardor."

Beyond the physical and mental benefits to the players, baseball games among the troops and between regiments served to broaden the game's exposure to those who might not have been familiar with it. Even though by 1861 more than 60 different clubs belonged to the National Association of Base Ball Players, only a handful were located outside of the New York–New Jersey area. Matches between regiments from different states introduced the game to more far-flung regions on the East Coast and in the Midwest. And through the prison camps on both sides of the Mason-Dixon Line, the game's exposure was broadened in the South. There are even (unconfirmed) reports of games between Union and Confederate teams.

In the early days of the war, regiment teams would sometimes play organized "civilian" clubs. In June 1861 the Washington Nationals Base Ball Club played an assemblage from the 71st New York Regiment on a ball field behind the White House. The New Yorkers defeated the Washington club handily, 42–13. The 71st returned to Washington a year later, but with its ranks decimated by the First Battle of Bull Run, the depleted New York team lost the rematch.

A slightly more precarious game was described by George Putnam, who was encamped with his Union regiment in Texas: "We were playing baseball near the front lines after a break in our skirmish. Suddenly there came a scattering of fire of which three outfielders caught the brunt; the center field was hit and was captured, the left and right field managed to get back into our lines. The attack . . . was repelled without serious difficulty, but we had lost not only our center field, but . . . the only baseball in Alexandria, Texas."

> Wartime baseball also helped to break down the social divide that had characterized the sport in previous decades.

As much as it was a welcome diversion for soldiers on both sides of the "War between the States," the games declined dramatically as the war progressed and the casualties mounted. The sport not only faded among the troops, but many civilian clubs had to disband for lack of healthy bodies and as spectatorship dropped.

After the long and bloody war finally came to an end, however, baseball thrived. The game served as a way to forget the sorrow and devastation caused by the war. People in more and more cities and towns throughout the reunified nation had been exposed to the sport. The competing Massachusetts game and cricket lost steam as the New York game gained prominence. And after membership in the NABBP had declined from 62 clubs in 1861 to about 35 in 1863, a whopping 202 clubs were represented at the national convention in December 1866, including teams from former Confederate states Tennessee and Virginia and teams from as far away as Kansas and Oregon. Baseball was securing its place as a truly *national* pastime.

PART II

BASEBALL GOES PRO

◆ ◆ ◆ ◆

CINCINNATI RED STOCKINGS TROPHY BALL, 1869.

12

Cincinnati Red Stockings Game Ball, 1869

THE BIRTH OF PROFESSIONAL BASEBALL

A somewhat-ironic consequence of baseball's meteoric growth in the 1860s was the inevitable path toward one thing that the sport's earliest proponents advocated against: paid professional players. It was a game for gentlemen, men who played for pride and the physical benefits. But as the potential for revenue from ticket sales became evident, and as the democratization of the game among the lower and working classes was hastened during the Civil War, the momentum toward paying players for their work was virtually unstoppable. In 1869, the Cincinnati Red Stockings became the first openly all-professional team.

When the National Association of Base Ball Players was formed in 1857, the constitution and rules included no clauses preserving the amateur status of the member clubs; that was simply understood. In 1859 the association added an explicit ban on professionalism in its regulations: "No person who shall . . . at any time receive compensation for his services as player, shall be competent to play in any match."

Despite these restrictions, by the late 1860s most clubs were paying at least some of their players. As Henry Chadwick noted in his *Game of Baseball*, published in 1868, "The rules prohibit players from receiving compensation for their services in a match, but there is scarcely a club of note that has not infringed the rule, or that does not nullify it now in some form or other."

Following the 1868 season, the NABBP adopted a rule acknowledging two categories of players—professionals and amateurs. Clubs were permitted to declare themselves professional. Harry Wright and his Red Stockings jumped at the opportunity.

"FIRST NINE OF THE CINCINNATI
(RED STOCKINGS) BASE BALL CLUB," 1869.

The Cincinnati Base Ball Club was established in 1866 and joined the NABBP the following year, during which season it dominated the local competition. After the touring Washington Nationals came through town and showed them what a team made up of (surreptitiously paid) talent recruited from a wider geographical base was capable of, Wright began importing players to join his Red Stockings, enticing them with various forms of under-the-table compensation. In 1868, nearly half of Cincinnati's players were Eastern recruits, including third baseman Fred Waterman, lured from the New York Mutuals; catcher Doug Allison, from Philadelphia; and pitcher Asa Brainard, previously of the Brooklyn Excelsiors and the famed Nationals. When the NABBP officially opened the door to professionalism a year later, Wright built a full ten-man roster of professionals.

In addition to Allison, Brainard, and Waterman, Cincinnati signed Cal McVey from Indianapolis; Charlie Sweasy and Andy Leonard, both originally from New Jersey but who had relocated to Cincinnati in 1868 to play for the rival Buckeye club; Pennsylvanian Dick Hurley, who had also joined the Buckeyes in '68; and, most notably, Harry Wright's younger brother, George Wright. The younger Wright, who got his start in organized baseball as a teenager in New York, had established himself as one of the best players in the country. Rounding out Cincinnati's "First Nine" were local boy Charlie Gould, who had been with the team since 1867, and Harry Wright himself, who had played for the Knickerbocker and Gotham clubs in New York before joining the maiden Red Stockings squad in 1866 as a pitcher. He assumed the managerial and general managing duties as well.

Compensation for the players ranged from $600 (paid to substitute/utilityman Hurley) to $1,400 (shortstop George Wright's salary) for the season. George earned his high pay by leading the team in every hitting category in 1869, including a .633 batting average and 49 home runs in 57 games against Association foes. The team went undefeated in those 57 matches, plus 8 more against nonleague competition.

Cincinnati's impressive run continued into the following season. The team notched victories in its first 24 games of 1870. Counting the final 8 games of 1868, the Red Stockings had compiled an impressive and unprecedented run of 89 consecutive wins; some estimates put the streak even longer with the additional victories against amateur and nonleague clubs.

On June 14, 1870, the Red Stockings arrived at Capitoline Grounds to play the Brooklyn Atlantics, the dominant team of the previous decade and still one of the best. With an estimated 15,000 fans on hand, the Atlantics and Red Stockings played to a 5–5 tie after nine innings. The Brooklyn team was prepared to end it in a draw, but Wright insisted on extra innings to determine a winner, as was his right under the rules. Cincinnati scored two runs in the first half of the 11th, but Brooklyn rallied for three of its own in the bottom half of that inning. The Red Stockings were defeated, 8–7. The Atlantics' shocking victory was achieved by virtue of the "fairest, staunchest, skillfullest, pluckiest playing on record," or so reported the *Brooklyn Daily Eagle* the following day.

In a telegram back to Cincinnati, Red Stockings president Aaron Champion wrote: "The finest game ever played. Our boys did nobly, but fortune was against us. Eleven innings played. Though beaten, not disgraced."

The undisgraced Cincinnatians rebounded to go undefeated in their next 19 games, but enthusiasm was waning and the crowds grew thinner. The team's financial backers began withdrawing their support. Following the 1870 season, the executive

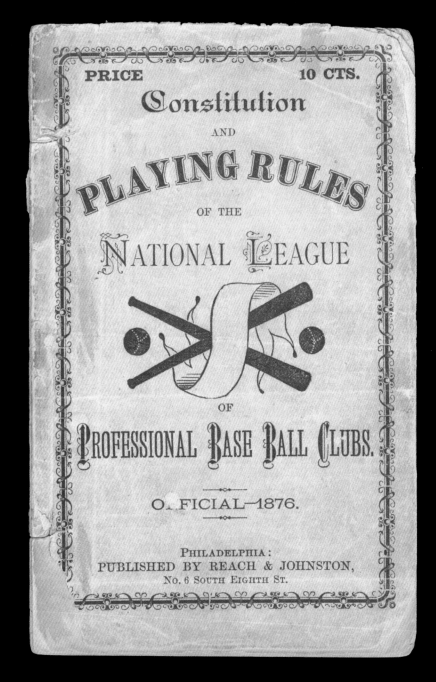

PRICE   10 CTS.

Constitution

AND

PLAYING RULES

OF THE

NATIONAL LEAGUE

OF

PROFESSIONAL BASE BALL CLUBS.

OFFICIAL—1876.

PHILADELPHIA:
PUBLISHED BY REACH & JOHNSTON,
No. 6 SOUTH EIGHTH ST.

13

"Constitution and Playing Rules of the National League of Professional Base Ball Clubs," 1876

THE RISE OF THE NATIONAL LEAGUE

The National League of Professional Base Ball Clubs was not the first organized baseball league when it formed in 1876. But whereas the National Association of Base Ball Players (NABBP) and the National Association of Professional Base Ball Players (NA) failed to establish a foundation for longevity, the National League celebrates its 140th anniversary in 2016—the longest-running professional sports league in the country's history.

The entire five-year life of the NA (1871–1875) was fraught with instability. Clubs were responsible for arranging their own games, which led to inconsistent and unreliable schedules; players regularly revolved to different clubs; rowdiness, drunkenness, and gambling were rampant at ballparks, as well as in some clubhouses; and teams frequently failed to complete seasons due to lack of funds. Any club could join the National Association simply by paying a $10 membership fee, and there was no screening process to ensure that a team would be financially viable or competitive on the field. Even successful clubs barely turned a profit in the face of rising player salaries.

Following another rocky year for the Association in 1875, William Hulbert, president of the Chicago White Stockings, engineered what some described as a "coup" to disband the NA and replace it with a new league that would be more stable and, ideally, more profitable. The result was the National League of Professional Base Ball Clubs.

Following a secret meeting with representatives from the top clubs from the western reaches of the National Association—Cincinnati, Louisville, and St. Louis, in addition to his own Chicago club—Hulbert invited representatives from the strongest

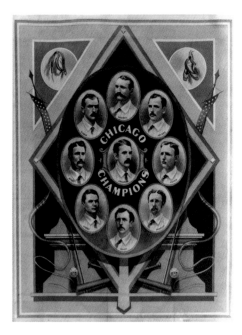

The NL's initial campaign was not without its controversies, however. Late in the season, once they had fallen out of championship contention, both the New York and Philadelphia clubs declined to travel to play late-season games against western opponents and complete their schedule. This had been common practice under the old National Association, but it would not be tolerated in the new order. Both clubs were expelled from the National League.

With the league reduced to six teams in 1877, a season-ending pennant race between the Boston Red Stockings and the Louisville Grays was tainted by rumors that Louisville players had thrown games down the stretch to hand the championship to Boston. Hulbert, as league president, barred four Grays players from the league. The shorthanded Louisville team then dropped out of the NL. Both St. Louis and Hartford soon departed as well. Teams from Providence, Indianapolis, and Milwaukee were brought in to fill out the league for 1878. Neither Indianapolis nor Milwaukee made it to the 1879 season.

Despite its best efforts, such fluidity characterized the early years of the National League. Chicago and Boston were the only two of the original eight NL teams to last more than five seasons—and these franchises remain to this day, as the Chicago Cubs and the Atlanta (nee Boston) Braves, respectively. By the end of the nineteenth century, the NL would host teams in Baltimore (1892–1899); Buffalo (1879–1885); Cleveland (1879–1884 and 1889–1899); Detroit (1881–1888); Troy, New York (1879–1882); Worcester, Massachusetts (1880–1882); and Washington, D.C. (1886–1889 and 1892–1899). One-season wonders popped up in Kansas City and Syracuse. Replacements for failed clubs emerged in the original NL cities of Cincinnati, Louisville, St. Louis, New York, and Philadelphia—the latter still in existence as the Philadelphia Phillies, and the New York club now functioning as the

San Francisco Giants. The three westernmost cities secured new clubs by poaching from the American Association, which had formed as a rival league in 1882.

In all, the National League would absorb eight teams from the American Association: Pittsburgh, Cleveland, Cincinnati, Brooklyn, Baltimore, Louisville, St. Louis, and Washington. The latter four came over in 1892 with the merging of the two leagues into the National League and American Association of Base Ball Clubs. The Cincinnati, Pittsburgh, and St. Louis franchises can all still be seen in their same cities to this day. Brooklyn, which first formed as the Atlantics in 1884, would be known by several different nicknames before becoming the Brooklyn Dodgers and, eventually, moving to Los Angeles.

The National League contracted back to eight teams for the 1900 season, eliminating Baltimore, Cleveland, Louisville, and Washington. The eight franchises that would compose the National League for the next 70 years were all in place by 1892, and all in the same eight cities through 1952. The eight-team composition would not change until the first expansion in 1962.

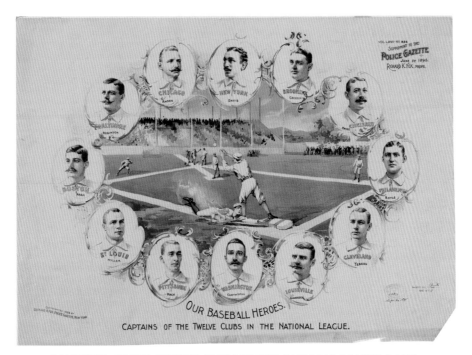

"CAPTAINS OF THE TWELVE CLUBS IN THE NATIONAL LEAGUE," 1895.

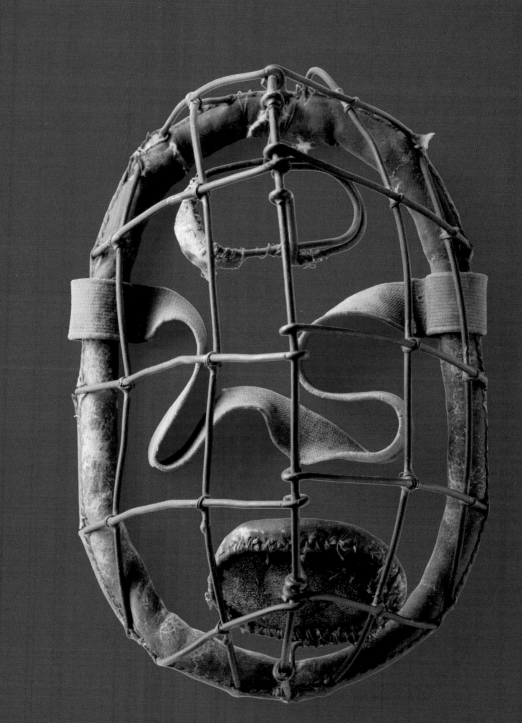

FRED THAYER'S CATCHER'S MASK, CIRCA 1876.

14

Fred Thayer's Catcher's Mask, circa 1876

THE "TOOLS OF IGNORANCE"

In the mid-1870s most baseball players were still playing bare-handed, and while catchers, the ones most vulnerable to errant pitches and foul tips, were among the first to adopt protection for their hands, they had to worry about their face and head as well. Some catchers took to wearing mouth guards to protect their teeth, at least, a move believed to have been pioneered by Red Stockings star George Wright. Even though catchers in those days stood farther back from the plate—in part because of the lack of protection and in part because, at the time, they were permitted to catch a foul tip or third strike on a bounce—broken noses, black eyes, and other facial injuries were increasingly common as pitchers got more inventive with their deliveries.

The innovation for a catcher's face mask came from Fred Thayer, captain of the Harvard University baseball team in 1876. Inspired by the masks worn by the school's fencing team, Thayer's mask was a basic wire cage with padding around the edges where it rested against the face. He asked a local tinsmith to make one and gave it to Harvard catcher James Tyng, who first donned it for a game in April 1877. As with those early souls who dared to wear gloves in the field, Tyng was met with ridicule and jeering from the crowd. Some critics called it a "rat-trap" and questioned why such an odd piece of equipment was necessary. The *Harvard Crimson*, however, lauded the invention: "The new mask was proved a complete success, since it entirely protects the face and head and adds greatly to the confidence of the catcher, who need not feel that he is every moment in danger of a life-long injury. To the ingenious inventor of this mask we are largely indebted." Henry Chadwick, the same man who chastised "childish" fielders for catching a ball on a bounce rather than

The potential dangers from closer proximity to swinging bats and less predictable pitches made face protection a virtual necessity.

on the fly, argued that the catcher's mask was only a sensible response to the alternative of "broken cheek bones, dislocated jaws, a smashed nose or blackened eyes."

Thayer patented his "bird-cage" mask in 1878. It was still used almost exclusively in the amateur ranks; most professional catchers had the same reservations about challenges to their "manhood" that delayed universal acceptance of fielding gloves.

The A. G. Spalding Sporting Goods Company began offering the "Thayer Catcher's Mask" for $3 in late 1878. Other sporting goods manufacturers—such as Wright & Ditson, A.J. Reach, and Draper & Maynard—began producing their own versions of catcher's masks as well.

Rule changes helped to spur wider adoption of this now-vital piece of equipment. Beginning in 1880, a catcher had to catch a third strike on the fly to register the out. This change meant that catchers had to position themselves closer to the batter. In addition, sidearm and overhand pitching deliveries were legalized in 1883 and 1884, respectively, increasing the velocity and movement on pitches as they hurtled toward the plate. The potential dangers from closer proximity to swinging bats and less predictable pitches made face protection a virtual necessity.

Improving on the light materials used in the early incarnations, masks soon were made with sturdier, interconnected mesh wires and better padding. George Bernard patented the "open view" mask in 1888 to provide greater visibility for the catcher, which developed further with the "wide-sight" masks of the 1910s, eliminating the vertical bar across the catcher's line of vision. Additional evolutions in the materials and construction continued over the decades, and better shock-absorbing mesh of carbon-steel wire ultimately became the standard. The next major, widespread structural change didn't come until the 1970s, when the throat protector was introduced, although this feature had been experimented with in the late nineteenth century.

With the ever-increasing velocity of pitches and of the impact of home-plate collisions, many catchers have turned to helmets that protect the entire head, similar to modern-day hockey goalie masks. In addition to providing further protection to the back and sides of the head, they offer greater peripheral vision as well. Invented by Toronto-based Jerry Van Velden, this style of mask was first worn in a game by Charlie O'Brien when he was with the Blue Jays in 1997.

As early catchers became more conscious of their personal safety and well-being and less concerned about appearing "soft" by wearing protective gear, they gradually adopted more and more of what were pegged the "tools of ignorance." Padded vests and homemade cork-padded chest protectors were worn by some catchers in the early 1880s. Commercially produced inflatable protectors soon followed, and these were eventually replaced by foam-filled protectors. Shin guards were also being worn by some catchers by the 1880s and '90s. Roger Bresnahan, who caught nearly 1,000 games behind the plate and would later be inducted into the Baseball Hall of Fame in Cooperstown, was among the first prominent backstops to regularly wear leg protection. In about 1908, he donned shin guards that were adapted from the leg guards worn by cricket players.

With the increased protection provided by masks and other equipment, catchers could be more aggressive in receiving pitches, fielding bunts, throwing out base stealers, and tagging out runners at the plate. Improved fielding and better control of the area around home plate dramatically changed the role of the catcher in the game.

ROGER BRESNAHAN,
CIRCA 1908.

EARLY FIELDER'S GLOVE, 1880S.

15

Early Fielder's Glove, 1880s

EVOLUTION OF THE FUNDAMENTAL FIELDER'S TOOL

As much as baseball was presented as a civilized, gentlemanly game in its earliest incarnations, the sport required a certain ruggedness and physical toughness, especially given the rudimentary nature of the equipment. To help protect players from bodily harm, the Knickerbocker Rules were thoughtful enough to eliminate the practice of plugging runners with the ball to get them out. That same set of rules also allowed fielders to catch a ball on a bounce ("first bound") to record an out, a welcome option for bare-handed fielders attempting to gather up a hard-hit ball.

The "first bound" rule was a contentious one, however, and many considered it "unmanly" to let a ball bounce rather than catching it on the fly. After the National Association of Base Ball Players officially eliminated the first-bound rule and required that balls be caught on the fly, the potential beating on a player's bare hands increased significantly.

As unmanly as it may have been to catch a ball on the first bounce, a similar stigma was attached to wearing any sort of protection on one's hands. Gradually, however, players looked for ways to protect their valuable appendages. Simple leather work gloves, often with the fingers cut off, began making their way onto ball fields. Catchers were most vulnerable, of course, given the number of pitches they received. Doug Allison, catcher for the Cincinnati Red Stockings, is believed to have donned a buckskin mitten to protect his hand in 1870. First baseman Charles Waitt of the St. Louis Brown Stockings is the earliest confirmed fielder to wear gloves, which he did (on both hands) during a game in about 1875—and he was mocked for it by opponents, fans, and teammates alike. He wore flesh-colored gloves in the hope that they would go unnoticed.

The earliest versions of gloves had minimal padding over the palms and lower knuckles. These gloves were worn to protect the hands, not to offer any aid in fielding.

Only a few years after Waitt called his own manliness into question by putting on a glove, Albert Spalding, first baseman for the Chicago White Stockings, began wearing a black glove (not flesh-colored) in the field. Not only did Spalding's status as a star player bring legitimacy to the practice, but as owner of a prominent sporting goods store in Chicago, he was able to expand the market for this new equipment. A. G. Spalding & Brothers began offering its own fielding gloves in 1877, and by the turn of the century, the Spalding catalog listed multiple varieties and styles of gloves. The company remains one of the leading producers of baseball gloves to this day.

Arthur Irwin, a shortstop with the Providence Grays, was another pioneer in the evolution of the baseball glove. After injuring his hand during a game in 1882, Irwin added padding to a leather driving glove and wore it the next game to protect his injured hand. Inspired by his innovation, he went to Draper & Maynard, a glove manufacturer in New Hampshire, and asked if they would manufacture a glove based on his design. The company took up the project and began producing high-quality, padded buckskin, fingerless gloves specifically for baseball use. By the early twentieth century, Draper & Maynard was a leading supplier of many styles of gloves and other sporting goods. A company advertisement in the 1920s claimed that more than 90 percent of major league players at the time used D & M gloves.

Today's major leaguers wear gloves produced by a number of different manufacturers,

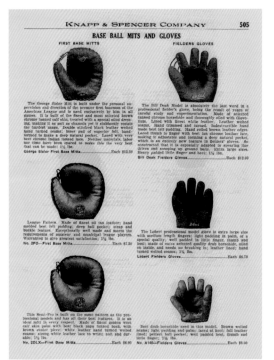

CATALOG PAGE OF
BASEBALL GLOVES, FEATURING
THE BILL DOAK MODEL
(TOP RIGHT), 1924.

MODERN RAWLINGS GLOVE WITH
"EDGE-U-CATED HEEL."

but Rawlings is the leader, owning nearly 50 percent of the market. The company was founded in 1887 as a sporting goods retailer in St. Louis, and like Spalding, it soon expanded into manufacturing. Rawlings was at the forefront of a major glove transformation in 1919 when the company began producing the Bill Doak model. Proposed by Cardinals pitcher Bill Doak, the glove included a built-in pocket and webbing between the thumb and index finger to help fielders snare the ball.

Even as gloves became more flexible and effective for fielding, players still needed two hands to secure the ball due to the open heel at the glove's wrist. The introduction of the "Edge-U-Cated Heel" by Rawlings in 1959, with a flexible closing at the heel, allowed players to catch balls one-handed. This advancement in glove design opened the door to more acrobatic catches; players could now fully extend their glove hand out to make one-handed catches on balls that would be out of reach if both hands were required.

Bid McPhee, second baseman for Cincinnati in the 1880s and '90s, is believed to have been the last major league position player to go bare-handed. McPhee didn't wear a glove until about 1896, 15 years into his career. But despite the occasional holdout, gloves had become standard equipment for players at all positions by the early 1890s. Specially designed gloves or mitts for different positions were also developed, particularly for catchers. By 1895, the National League had instituted a formal rule regulating glove sizes: "The catcher and the first baseman are permitted to wear a glove or mitt of any size, shape or weight. All other players are restricted to the use of a glove or mitt weighing not over ten ounces, and measuring in circumference around the palm of the hand not over fourteen inches." Today the Official Rules of Major League Baseball includes several pages of detailed regulations on the dimensions and construction of gloves, with specific clauses relating to catchers, first basemen, and pitchers.

TOLEDO BLUE STOCKINGS TEAM PHOTO WITH FLEET WALKER
(STANDING CENTER), 1884.

16

Toledo Blue Stockings Team Photo, 1884

MAJOR LEAGUE BASEBALL'S
FIRST INTEGRATED TEAM

After winning the 1883 Northwestern League Minor League championship, the Toledo Blue Stockings entered the major league ranks the following year. The Blue Stockings finished in eighth place in the 13-team American Association in 1884, when their roster featured a pair of brothers from Ohio: catcher Moses Fleetwood "Fleet" Walker and outfielder Weldy Walker. The older Fleet debuted with the Blue Stockings on May 1, 1884, and went on to hit a respectable .263 in 42 games. Weldy joined the team in mid-July but saw only limited action, collecting 4 hits in 18 at-bats. What makes these two Blue Stockings noteworthy, however, is not their on-field prowess but rather the color of their skin. The Walker brothers were among the first African Americans to play for a major league baseball team, and they would be the last for more than 60 years.

Fleet Walker had long been considered the first African American to play major league ball, but researchers in 2004 uncovered the story of William Edward White, who appeared in one game as an injury replacement at first base for the Providence Grays in 1879. White is believed to have been the son of a Georgia slaveowner and one of his black servants.

Even before White and the Walker brothers, other African Americans played organized professional baseball at the minor league level. Bud Fowler began playing in the early 1870s, and in 1878 he appeared in an exhibition game against the Boston Red Stockings as a member of the Lynn Live Oaks of the Northwestern League. Born John W. Jackson near Cooperstown, New York, Fowler continued to

UMPIRE'S BALL-STRIKE INDICATOR, 1887.

17

Umpire's Ball-Strike Indicator, 1887

FOUR STRIKES AND YER OUT . . . ?

In a game of numbers like baseball, three strikes and four balls are as integral to our understanding of the sport as any rule. The tradition of three missed pitches by a batter resulting in an out has been around since before the Knickerbocker Rules of 1845. (The called strike did not come into play until 1858; a foul tip was not counted as a strike until 1895, and only then if it was caught in the air by the catcher.) Bases on balls were introduced in 1879, when it took nine balls before a batter was permitted to take his base. The number of balls for a walk was reduced to eight in 1880, then to seven in 1881, six in 1884, and five in 1886.

During the 1887 season, from which this ball-strike indicator comes, walks were still granted on five balls, but for the one and only season in major league history, a strikeout required four strikes. Presumably this change was instituted to restore the balance between pitchers and batters, which began to shift in the former's favor with the removal of restrictions on a pitcher's delivery in 1884. Prior to 1883, the pitcher was required to deliver the ball from below the waist; this was extended to below the shoulder in 1883, and then eliminated altogether in 1884. The leaguewide strikeouts-per-game average hit 4.7 that year—the highest mark until 1957—and it again topped 4 per game (4.36) in 1886.

Not surprisingly, the addition of a fourth strike led the number of strikeouts per game to drop below three (2.8) in 1887, and scoring increased by nearly a run per game (from 5.2 to 6.1). In addition, bases on balls were counted as hits in 1887—the only year this rule was applied—causing batting averages to skyrocket. (Most record books retroactively omit walks from batting average calculations from this season.)

Another pivotal change in 1887, which may seem odd to modern fans, was that batters could no longer request the placement of pitches. Prior to that, batters would indicate to the pitcher whether he wanted a high pitch or a low pitch, and the ball had to be within that zone in order for it to be called a strike. (The batter could not change his call in the course of an at-bat.) Beginning in 1887, a single strike zone was created, extending from the batter's knees to his shoulders, where it remained for the next six decades. In 1950 the strike zone was redefined as the area between the batter's armpits and the top of his knees. The official designation of the upper limit of the zone was altered again in 1988 to be defined by a "horizontal line at the midpoint between the top of the shoulders and the top of the uniform pants." The lower limit dropped from the top of the knees to the "hollow beneath the kneecap" in 1996.

From the time of the Knickerbocker Rules through the end of the nineteenth century, major league baseball regularly tweaked the rules in an effort to maintain a balance of excitement and fair play. Some rules lasted only a season or two; others went back and forth a few times.

Strikeouts were back to three strikes in 1888, and four balls equaled a walk beginning in 1889. And those numbers have remained unchanged ever since, making this 1887 ball-strike indicator a relic of a brief moment in baseball history.

18

World's Series Championship Trophy, 1888

BASEBALL'S FIRST POSTSEASON CHAMPIONSHIPS

Following the 1888 baseball season, the champions of the National League faced the champions of the American Association in a best-of-ten-games exhibition series to determine the world championship of baseball. The NL's New York Giants defeated the AA's St. Louis Brown Stockings in six games to earn the right to bring home the Hall Trophy, shown here, the oldest existing baseball championship trophy.

When William Hulbert orchestrated the exodus of top teams from the National Association to form the National League in 1876, he sought to establish the premier organized league and attract the best baseball talent from throughout the country. The new league's constitution proclaimed that whichever club won the greatest number of games in the season would be declared "Champion Base Ball Club of the United States."

Just as the modern "World Series" does not, really, reflect any global achievement beyond the United States and one Canadian city, the determination of a "champion of the United States" in the 1870s excluded countless quality baseball teams throughout the land. The establishment of the eight-team National League left many top players and teams out in the cold.

The first group of clubs to present an organized alternative to the NL was the International Association of Professional Baseball Players. Created in 1877, the seven-team league was based in cities that lacked an NL club, including two Canadian cities—hence the designation "international." Though there was never an attempt to play a championship series between the two leagues, IA and NL teams met regularly in exhibition contests. The NL clubs used these matches not only as an opportunity

WORLD'S SERIES CHAMPIONSHIP TROPHY, 1888.

to earn additional revenue between league games, but also to poach players from the rival league. The poaching of players as well as entire teams ultimately contributed to the IA's demise in 1880.

The American Association, on the other hand, survived as a legitimate challenger to the National League for a full decade. The AA provided a viable alternative to the NL by establishing teams in cities unoccupied by the elder league and in catering to a more working-class clientele. The AA rejected the NL's ban on Sunday games and, again in contrast to the NL, permitted the sale and consumption of alcohol in its ballparks—earning it the nickname the "Beer and Whiskey League." The AA also set its minimum ticket prices at 25 cents, half of what NL teams charged.

The maiden season of the American Association featured the Baltimore Orioles, the Cincinnati Red Stockings, the Louisville Eclipse, the Philadelphia Athletics, the Pittsburgh Alleghenys, and the St. Louis Brown Stockings. The Cincinnati club—which had been expelled from the National League in 1880 for selling beer and allowing a semipro team to use its ballpark on Sundays—won the AA title handily in 1882.

Meanwhile, the Chicago White Stockings finished atop the 1882 NL standings. Although the leagues were engaged in a bitter battle over players and fans, the

two champion clubs agreed to play an exhibition series following their respective seasons. The two-game series concluded with each team winning one game. There was no intention to play a rubber match to determine a winner.

Peace between the leagues was achieved prior to the 1883 season with the signing of the Tripartite Agreement (later known as the National Agreement) by the NL, the AA, and the minor Northwestern League. The main focus of the agreement was

REAR OF WORLD'S SERIES
CHAMPIONSHIP TROPHY, 1888.

to ensure a mutual respect for each league's contracts and reserve clauses. There was no discussion of an interleague championship series.

Following the 1883 campaign, the AA-champion Philadelphia Athletics backed out of plans for a postseason meeting with the NL-champion Boston Red Stockings after the Athletics embarrassingly lost an exhibition series with the crosstown Philadelphia Quakers, who had finished dead last in the National League with a dismal 17–81 record.

In 1884, the New York Metropolitans claimed the title in the 13-team American Association, and following that season, Metropolitans manager Jim Mutrie issued a challenge to the NL-champion Providence Grays. Providence manager Frank Bancroft accepted, declaring that the winner would "fly a pennant next year as champion of America." Each team agreed to put up $1,000 in prize money.

All three games were played at New York's Polo Grounds, and the series was played under American Association rules. In those days, teams typically used one pitcher throughout a season, and the 1884 "World's Series" pitted future Hall of Famers Charles "Old Hoss" Radbourn of Providence against Tim Keefe of New York. Radbourn, winner of 59 games that season, led the Grays to victory in the first two contests. The two wins clinched the series for Providence, but the teams played a third game anyway, hoping to generate additional gate revenue. With an estimated 300 people in attendance, Providence busted out to a 12–2 lead before the game was called after six innings due to cold weather. Interestingly, and highlighting the exhibition nature of these games, Keefe stepped out of the pitcher's box to serve as umpire in the series finale—as selected by the Grays.

Sporting Life magazine reported the next day, "The long-standing question of superiority between [National] League and American Association clubs has been finally settled by a regular series of games between the champions of the respective organizations. The Providence and Metropolitan clubs [competed] in New York last week for the world championship . . . and the result clearly proclaims the Providence Club 'Champions of the World.'"

Even though the series held no official status, and attendance had been sparse, an interleague postseason series continued for six more seasons. The St. Louis Browns represented the American Association in each of the next four championships, taking on the Chicago White Stockings in 1885 and '86, the Detroit Wolverines in '87, and the New York Giants in 1888. St. Louis claimed victory in only one of them (1886), although the 1885 series was hotly disputed. After playing to a 5–5 tie in the opener in Chicago, the Browns stormed off the field during the second game in protest against a call by the umpire. The White Stockings were awarded the win by forfeit. St. Louis won the next two games at home, and then Chicago won Games 5 and 6, played in Pittsburgh and Cincinnati, respectively. When the Browns won the Game 7 finale, they chose to ignore the Game 2 forfeit and claimed series victory, but they never received the winners' purse. The series has gone down in history as a 3–3–1 tie.

After securing the Association's lone victory of the seven-year championship series in a rematch with Chicago in 1886, St. Louis met Detroit in a 15-game postseason series in 1887. The games were played in 10 different cities over the course of 16 days. The Wolverines effectively clinched the series in Game 11, but the teams played out the rest of the matches. Detroit won 10 games to St. Louis's 5. Following the series, Detroit was given the Dauvray Cup, a trophy commissioned and donated by actress

TEAMS AND TROPHIES FOR THE WORLD'S SERIES OF BASEBALL, 1888.

JOHN MONTGOMERY WARD POLITICAL CARTOON, DAILY GRAPHIC, 1888.

players were "injuring their own interests" by insisting on "exorbitant prices." Hulbert claimed that players' salary demands were forcing out of business clubs that could not cover such bloated salaries. Most clubs were operating at a loss or at the slimmest of margins, and salaries were by far their greatest expense.

The solution, for Hulbert and the other owners, was to assert that a team could unilaterally reserve the rights to a contracted player for the following season. Clubs could exercise this right indefinitely, effectively giving a player no choice but to re-sign with his current club and locking him into that team for the duration of his playing career, unless or until those rights were sold or traded to another club. The "reserve clause" effectively left a player with no room to negotiate for higher pay or to decide for himself where he wished to be employed. Any club that violated this agreement by signing a player reserved by another club was subject to severe sanctions, including expulsion from the league; players who attempted to circumvent it would be blacklisted.

In 1883, the National League brass got together with representatives of the new American Association (AA) and the Northwestern League, a minor league, in order to bring peace among the competing leagues and an end to player poaching. The result was the Tripartite Agreement. Each league agreed to honor the contracts and reserve clauses of the others, thus further limiting a player's opportunities. (When the AA first formed in 1882, it did not include a reserve clause in its contracts, which sparked a minor exodus of players from the NL to the new league.) The 1883 agreement also increased the number of reservable players to 11 per roster, up from 5 in the 1879 agreement; this soon was extended to entire rosters. The reserve clause became a mandatory element in every player contract.

Just as the National League had been formed, in part, as a way to stem the problem of players revolving to new teams, which had plagued the National Association, the expansion of the reserve clause led to the formation of a new league founded

> ... The reserve clause was used "as a handle for the manipulation of a traffic in players, a sort of speculation in livestock, by which they are bought, sold, and transferred like so many sheep."

Banquet tendered by
The Citizens of Chicago
to

Mr. A. G. Spalding and his Associates,

upon their return from their
Tour of the World.

WHITE STOCKINGS VS. ALL-AMERICAS, AT THE PYRAMIDS IN EGYPT, FEBRUARY 1889.

The White Stockings and the All-Americas then worked their way through Europe, beginning in Naples and across Italy, through France, and to the British Isles. According to the *London Times*, a match at London's Kensington Oval was attended by about 6,000 spectators, who "appeared to take only a lukewarm interest in the play itself." In particular, although the fielding was "very brilliant. . . . [i]n the batting department the form was rather disappointing and failed altogether to arouse any general enthusiasm." The tour departed for home in late March 1889.

Returning to the States on April 6, Spalding and the players were feted with a banquet at New York's grand Delmonico restaurant. In attendance were such luminaries as Theodore Roosevelt, Mark Twain, and the mayors of Brooklyn and Jersey City. In his speech, Twain called baseball the "very symbol, the outward and visible expression of the drive, and push, and rush and struggle of the raging, tearing, booming nineteenth century!"

The tour did not end with that celebration. The players picked up the series with exhibitions in Baltimore, Philadelphia, Boston, Washington, Pittsburgh, Cleveland, and Indianapolis before finishing where it started, at Chicago's West Side Park on April 20. Final tally: 29 wins for the All-Americas, 23 for the White Stockings, and 4 ties. Upon the tour's arrival back in Chicago, a lavish banquet was held for Spalding and his entourage on April 19 at the Palmer Hotel. This silk-covered, fringed program featured illustrations depicting the tour as well as the menu and musical selections for the banquet.

SPALDING WORLD TOUR BANQUET PROGRAM, 1889.

TEMPLE CUP, 1897.

held the league's best regular-season record in 1894 but was swept in the seven-game cup series by the second-place New York Giants. The Orioles finished atop the standings again in 1895 only to be bested by the Spiders, four games to one, again denying them the championship despite the best regular season. Baltimore won 90 games in '96, 10 more than second-place Cleveland. This time the O's followed through in the postseason, getting revenge with a four-game sweep of the Spiders. Another 90-win season put Baltimore back in the Temple Cup Series, this time as a second-place finisher to the Beaneaters. The Orioles stayed hot in October, defeating Boston in five games.

A general lack of interest among the players, combined with fading attendance, led to the demise of the Temple Cup Championship Series after 1897. In its four-year history, the second-place finisher won three times. Baltimore was the only repeat winner but fell short of earning permanent possession of the cup. William Temple's Pirates never finished higher than sixth place during the Temple Cup era.

Even if the Temple Cup failed to generate much enthusiasm as a postseason series, it does underscore the dominance of the Baltimore Oriole club in the 1890s. They were not major league baseball's first dynasty—the Beaneaters became the NL's first back-to-back champions in 1877–1878 and had the best record in four of five seasons from 1889 to 1893, and the Chicago White Stockings topped the NL five times between 1880 and 1886. But the Orioles' dominance was about more than the number of wins or championships. They brought a distinctive attitude and approach to the game.

The nineteenth-century Baltimore club (no relation to today's Orioles franchise) originated as a founding member of the American Association in 1882. The team struggled through most of its AA years. After a disastrous 100-loss, last-place finish in their first season as a member of the NL in 1892, the Orioles soon fought their way to the top—with an emphasis on the word "fought."

Led by player-manager-president Ned Hanlon, the Orioles of the mid-1890s epitomized a scrappy, some might say dirty, style of play.

TEMPLE CUP FINAL GAME,
BALTIMORE, 1897.

They embraced what has come to be known as "small ball" or "inside baseball," emphasizing the importance of getting on base and making ample use of the bunt, the hit and run, the stolen base, and their patented Baltimore Chop (hitting the ball hard into the ground so that it bounces high in the air).

The club's top hitter was outfielder "Wee Willie" Keeler, who famously coined the phrase, "Keep your eye clear and hit 'em where they ain't." Keeler posted a .388 batting average in five seasons with the Orioles, including a .424 mark in 1897, aided by a 44-game hitting streak. Fellow outfielder Joe Kelley was a career .351 hitter in seven Baltimore seasons, and shortstop Hughie Jennings batted .401 in 1896 and hit over .300 in every one of his full seasons there. All three are in the Hall of Fame.

The player that best represented Baltimore's aggressive attitude was John "Muggsy" McGraw, the club's plucky third baseman. A career .334 hitter who would go on to a legendary managerial career with the New York Giants, McGraw was best known for his grit, his mouth, and occasionally his fists.

Beyond perfecting and exploiting game strategies like sacrifices and daring base running, the Orioles were known for less savory ploys as well. They had their groundskeeper keep the infield grass long to help slow their bunts and keep them fair. The dirt in front of home plate and on the base paths was packed hard to accentuate the Baltimore Chop and to give their aggressive base runners better footing. Oriole runners sometimes even bypassed second base on their way from first to third if the umpire was looking elsewhere; Baltimore set an all-time major league record with 150 triples in 1894. McGraw allegedly would grab opposing players' belts as they attempted to tag up from third. Catcher Wilbert Robinson threw his mask in the path of oncoming runners. Rumor was that Oriole players would sharpen their spikes with files and were not shy about digging them into the legs of opponents, often leading to all-out brawls. Umpire baiting, and occasionally umpire beating, were particularly favored tactics. And the Orioles were known as the most foul-mouthed group of ballplayers around, although the Cleveland Spiders gave them a run for their money—in fines, that is. To be sure, 1890s baseball was characterized by a general lack of decorum, one that was only slightly mitigated by the expansion of an umpire's authority to levy fines on players, but the Orioles perfected the art.

In the end, the brawlin', cussin' Orioles brought a new approach to baseball with their innovative "small ball" and occasionally extralegal methods. And it worked, as evidenced by their name being etched on the (not-so-coveted) Temple Cup championship trophy four years running.

PART III

THE DEAD-BALL ERA

· · · ·

We, the undersigned, desiring to re-organize The American League of Professional Base Ball Clubs, which expires by limitation November 20th, 1900, and to protect and promote the mutual interests of professional base ball clubs and professional base ball players, and representing the following cities, to-wit:

Cleveland, O.   Chicago, Ill.

Milwaukee, Wis.   Washington, D.C.

Baltimore, Md.   Detroit, Mich.

hereby covenant and agree each with the other as follows:

1st.   That the name of this organization shall be "THE AMERICAN LEAGUE OF PROFESSIONAL BASE BALL CLUBS", said name having been adopted at a regular meeting of said League held in the city of Chicago, Ill., October 11th, 1899.

2nd.   That this organization shall continue and all obligations herein and hereafter entered into, shall be in force and binding upon the parties hereto subscribing, for the period of Ten (10) years, subject to the conditions and provisions of the Constitution governing the termination of membership which is to be hereafter adopted and made a part of and subject to this agreement.

3rd.   That the cities named in this agreement shall, through their accredited representatives, prescribe conditions, determine, award and dispose of rights and franchises and elect to full or limited membership such other cities as may be necessary to promote the best interests and success of this League.

4th.   That the parties named in this agreement shall deposit with the Treasurer of the League, to be held by him in trust until the termination of this agreement, the sum of One Thousand ($1000) Dollars as a guarantee for the faithful performance of all contractual obligations under this agreement, and Constitution pursuant

---

(2)   ($1000 00)

thereto, and they shall require a further deposit of One Thousand Dollars from such other cities as may be admitted to membership, subject to the provisions of the Constitution and this agreement.

5th.   We hereby mutually covenant and agree each with the other to work under and according to a National Agreement of Professional Base Ball Associations to be hereafter formulated, adopted and agreed upon by this and all other professional base ball associations that may desire to become a part thereto, providing the same be possible and advisable under this our agreement.

6th.   And it is further mutually agreed by and between the parties hereto that until such time as a National Agreement shall be formulated that will be equitable and agreeable to the parties hereto we are to proceed under this our agreement as an organization independent of, but not antagonistic to any other Professional Base Ball organization in accordance with the conditions herein set forth.

7th.   It is further agreed by and between the parties hereto that in the event of any party to this agreement breaking or violating any of the conditions herein set forth then and in that event the franchise, rights, property and players of the party or parties so violating or breaking the conditions herein set forth shall revert to and become the absolute property of the American League of Professional Base Ball Clubs to be disposed of as the President of said League to be hereafter elected may direct. And it is agreed by and between the parties hereto that the said President be, and he hereby is empowered to take charge of and dispose of, for the best interest of the American League of Professional Base Ball Clubs the franchise, property and players of the party or parties violating

---

(3)

and of the covenants or conditions of this agreement.

8th.   That the admission to membership other than named in this agreement shall be determined in the following manner: All applications for membership in the American League of Professional Base Ball clubs must be made in writing to the Secretary of the League according to the Constitutional rule governing the same. After due consideration by all parties to this agreement the acceptance, or rejection of an applicant shall be determined by ballot in the following manner: First-If the applicant be accepted by a unanimous vote then he may, upon unanimous agreement, be accepted for a longer period than one year, and the election shall carry with it full rights with the parties hereto, provided it be not prolonged beyond the life of this agreement. If there be two adverse votes then the applicant for membership shall only be elected for one year, and it shall require a two thirds vote to elect to membership.

9th.   That the Constitution to be hereafter adopted shall not be in conflict with this agreement.

10th.   That upon the signing of this agreement by the accredited parties in interest a President, Secretary and Treasurer shall be elected and one man can be elected to all three of said offices.
ACCEPTED and SIGNED this 20th day of November, A.D. 1900.

The Cleveland Ball Club Co   Detroit Ball Club
by _____   by Jas D Burns
Representing Cleveland, O.   Representing Detroit, Mich.

American League Ball Club   American League Base Ball Club
by _____   by Chas. A. Comiskey
Representing Milwaukee, Wis.   Representing Chicago, Ill.

American League Base Ball Club   American League Base Ball Club
Phila _____   Boston Mass
by C. McGillicuddy   by _____

---

(4)

The Baltimore League   The Washington Base Ball
by _____   by James H Manning
Representing Baltimore, Md.   Representing Washington, D.C.

The Baltimore Base Ball Club Athletic Company
Sydney S. Frank President

22

Contract for the Formation of the American League, 1900

A NEW MAJOR LEAGUE

As the nineteenth century came to a close, a new challenger to the National League's major league monopoly was emerging. In November 1893, Byron Bancroft "Ban" Johnson was named president of the Western League, a regional minor league that had undergone several reorganizations in the preceding years. Johnson wanted to put the Western League on solid footing while offering a clean, wholesome baseball alternative to the rowdy and unruly National League.

At the time Johnson took over, the Western League had teams in Detroit, Grand Rapids, Indianapolis, Kansas City, Milwaukee, Minneapolis, Sioux City, and Toledo. Following the 1894 season, Johnson's close friend, Charles Comiskey—who had initially recommended Johnson to the league—left his post as manager of the NL's Cincinnati Reds and purchased the Sioux City club, which he relocated to St. Paul, Minnesota. Two years later, Johnson brought in Connie Mack, recently dismissed as player-manager of the Pittsburgh Pirates, to manage the Milwaukee team. The trio of Johnson, Comiskey, and Mack were pivotal to the growth of the league, and baseball as a whole, in the new century.

Johnson and his cohorts took a major leap forward at the annual league meeting following the 1899 season. They announced that the Western League was being disbanded and would re-form as the American League of Professional Base Ball Clubs—a clear shot across the bow of the National League in asserting a nationwide element in its name. Further, with approval from the NL, Comiskey moved his St. Paul club to Chicago. The league also established a team in Cleveland, which had been vacated when the NL contracted from 12 to 8 teams. The disbanding of four NL teams not

only opened up new markets for the American League, it also left a whole bunch of major leaguers without jobs. Many were promptly swooped up by the new circuit.

After the 1900 season, Johnson approached the National League in a peace offering of sorts. He promised that his league would respect the other's contracts and would not venture into certain NL cities, provided that the NL accepted the AL as a fellow major league and allowed it into certain other cities. The National League rebuffed Johnson's offer. So Johnson launched an all-out war on the rival organization.

At the annual meeting in November 1900, league representatives signed a contract, effectively asserting the American League's place as a veritable major league. They promptly rejected the standing National Agreement, stating that the league would operate "independent of, but not antagonistic to any other Professional Base Ball organization." In addition to freeing itself from respecting the NL's reserve clause, the AL also was not tied down by the salary cap that its adversary had adopted. Raids on NL rosters began. Abandoning the smaller markets of Buffalo, Indianapolis, Kansas City, and Minneapolis, the AL established teams in Boston and Philadelphia, both currently occupied by the NL, and in the former NL enclaves of Baltimore and Washington.

Among the star players lured away from the NL were Clark Griffith, Nap Lajoie, Joe McGinnity, and Cy Young. Lajoie jumped across Philadelphia from the Phillies to join the Athletics and earn a $6,000 salary (well above the NL's $2,400 maximum at that time), and then went on to lead the AL in runs, hits, doubles, homers, RBI, batting average, and slugging percentage in 1901. Young, making the leap from the St. Louis Cardinals to the Boston Americans (later the Red Sox), won the AL pitching Triple Crown, leading in wins, ERA, and strikeouts. "Iron Man" McGinnity lived up to his nickname by topping the circuit in games and innings pitched as Baltimore's ace. Formerly of Chicago's NL club, then known as the Orphans, Griffith helped lead the Chicago White Sox to the AL crown in 1901 as its manager and its winningest pitcher.

In perhaps the most unlikely flip-flop, John McGraw was also wooed by Johnson. McGraw, the man who during his Oriole playing days most exemplified the "incivility" of the NL, which Johnson abhorred, was brought in to head Baltimore's new AL franchise as player-manager. Still irked at the NL for folding his original Orioles, McGraw was more than willing to go head to head with his old nemeses. (He lasted less than a season and a half before returning to the NL as manager of the New York Giants.)

The AL's full-on assault paid off. Although the NL's total attendance was greater in 1901, the AL won the battle for fans in Chicago, where the Sox outdrew the

Orphans, and attendance levels in former-NL cities Washington, Cleveland, and Baltimore exceeded what the National League was able to draw in prior years. Johnson and company stepped things up in 1902, moving the Milwaukee Brewers to St. Louis to become the Browns, who proceeded to outdraw the Cardinals. The Boston Americans had better attendance than the Beaneaters by a nearly three-to-one margin, and the Philadelphia Athletics welcomed a major-league-high 420,000 fans in 1902 while the Phillies could only attract a league-low 112,000. In 1902, total American League attendance exceeded 2.2 million; the National League dropped from its 1901 levels to just under 1.7 million.

Star players continued their exodus as well. In 1902 and 1903 the NL said goodbye to future Hall of Famers Willie Keeler, Ed Delahanty, Sam Crawford, Jack Chesbro, Jesse Burkett, and others who made the move to the younger, higher-paying league.

Lawsuits and legal injunctions by the National League owners failed in the courts. Finally, they had had enough. Following the 1902 season, a peace was reached. Johnson and the AL turned down the NL's offer to merge; instead the two leagues would coexist as independent major leagues. A three-man national committee was formed to rule on interleague disputes. It consisted of Johnson, NL president Harry Pulliam, and August Garry Herrmann, the owner of the Cincinnati Reds, who had been an influential peacemaker during the negotiations.

By the terms of the National Agreement of 1903, the reserve clauses of all current contracts on both sides were to be honored. The AL was permitted to install a franchise in New York, but Johnson relented on his plan to place a team in Pittsburgh.

As the 1903 season got underway, the makeup of the two parallel major leagues was set with eight teams per side, including five cities—Boston, Chicago, New York, Philadelphia, and St. Louis—hosting a club from each league. Only one of the original

Western League cities, Detroit, was represented. The eight franchises of the 1903 American League remained unchanged for the next half century.

THE NATIONAL COMMISSION:
HARRY PULLIAM, AUGUST
HERRMANN, BAN JOHNSON, AND
SECRETARY J. E. BRUCE, 1909.

WORLD SERIES PROGRAM AND SCORECARD, 1903.

23

World Series Program and Scorecard, 1903

THE "FALL CLASSIC" IS BORN

Even after the National and American Leagues made peace under the 1903 National Agreement, some NL stalwarts were reluctant to recognize the junior sibling as an equal partner in Major League Baseball. Others saw opportunity in the newfound alliance.

Pittsburgh Pirates owner Barney Dreyfuss, whose club had emerged relatively unscathed from the war between the leagues in 1900–1902, fell into the latter camp. In midsummer of 1903, with his team sitting comfortably atop the National League standings, Dreyfuss issued a challenge to Harry Killilea, owner of the AL-leading Boston club. "The time has come," Dreyfuss wrote, "for the National League and American League to organize a World Series. It is my belief that if our clubs played a series on a best-out-of-nine basis, we would create great interest in baseball, in our leagues, and in our players. I also believe it would be a financial success."

After meeting with AL president Ban Johnson, and assuring Johnson that his club could prevail, Killilea accepted the challenge.

The two owners laid out a set of rules for the postseason competition. It was to be a best-of-nine series, ending as soon as one side won five games. The series would begin on October 1 in Boston, which would host the first three games. The teams would travel to Pittsburgh for four games before returning to Boston for the final two, if necessary. One umpire from each league would officiate during the series: Hank O'Day from the National League and Tom Connolly from the American League (both Hall of Famers). World Series rosters would be limited to players who were members of their teams prior to September 1.

With more than 16,000 in attendance at Boston's Huntington Avenue Grounds, the visiting Pirates defeated Cy Young and the Americans 7–3 in the opener. Boston bounced back with a 3–0 shutout by Bill Dinneen in Game 2. Pittsburgh's Deacon Phillippe claimed his second victory of the series in Game 3 with a crowd of nearly 19,000 on hand. Phillippe came through with another complete-game win when the Pirates won 5–4 on their home turf at Exposition Park. Boston then rallied to win the next three in Pittsburgh. The teams returned to Boston with the Americans holding a four-games-to-three edge. In front of fewer than 7,500 fans, the lowest turnout of the series, Dinneen delivered a 3–0 shutout victory over Phillippe. The Boston Americans were world champions.

The American League had proven itself a worthy competitor to the senior National League. The agreement between Dreyfuss and Killilea, however, only addressed a series between those two teams for that October. There was no long-term commitment by the leagues to engage in a regular postseason contest.

When the New York Giants climbed to a 10-game lead in the NL midway through the 1904 season, owner John T. Brush made it clear that his club would

WORLD SERIES GAME 1 AT HUNTINGTON AVENUE
BASEBALL GROUNDS, BOSTON, 1903.

not participate in a postseason series with the champion of the "inferior" league. Manager John McGraw asserted that, as winners of the "only real major league," his Giants were already world champions, and there was no need for any further games to prove that.

Writers and fans alike accused Brush and McGraw of arrogance and cowardice. Stung by the criticism, early in 1905 Brush helped formulate an official agreement for a postseason interleague World Series. The "Rules and Regulations Governing the Contest for the Professional Base Ball Championship of the World"—also known as the "Brush Rules"—were approved by both leagues and the National Commission in February 1905. It established an annual series between the league champs and included a guarantee that the pennant-winning clubs would "faithfully carry out all of the provisions" of the rules and would not "exercise an arbitrary right or privilege of abandoning the series until it has been completed or the Championship determined."

According to the Brush rules, "Seven games shall constitute a series." The seven-game series has been the standard ever since, with the exception of the years 1919–1921 when the World Series was extended to a best-of-nine competition.

The 1905 agreement established that each city would host at least three games, and the location of the first three games was to be determined by lot. In fact, given the geographical proximity of the champion clubs in 1905 (New York and Philadelphia), the series alternated ballparks for each game. The same was true in 1906, when the series jumped back and forth between Chicago's West Side Grounds and Chicago's South Side Park, when the Cubs and White Sox faced off. The travel schedule between host cities followed no consistent pattern until the mid-1910s, when 2-2-1-1-1 was the norm. The 2-3-2 format was introduced in 1924 and has been the tradition ever since—with the exception of the war years of 1943 and 1945. The privilege

Even though the inaugural World Series competition of 1903 was mostly an unofficial challenge between pennant winners, it has been an annual rite of autumn every year since.

NEW YORK GIANTS' "WORLD'S CHAMPIONS" JERSEY, 1906.

after spitting tobacco juice in the face of an umpire in 1901 and inciting an on-field brawl. Although his nickname originated from his work at an iron foundry during the offseasons, McGinnity earned a reputation as an iron man for his durability on the mound. He led the NL in games pitched every year from 1903 to 1907 and set a post-1900 National League record with 434 innings pitched in 1903. He also led the circuit in wins five times, including while wearing the "World's Champions" jersey in 1906. Although his major league career lasted only 10 years, during which he won 246 games, McGinnity had a lengthy minor league career, bookending his career in the majors, that began when he was 22 and ended when he was 54.

McGinnity's mound-mate Christy Mathewson was simply one of the greatest pitchers of all time. He still ranks as the all-time winningest pitcher in National League history with 373 victories (tied with Grover Cleveland Alexander) and holds the post-1900 NL record for wins in a season (37 in 1908). Matty won more than 20 games every year from 1903 to 1914, topping 30 wins four times during that stretch. His 2.13 career ERA ranks ninth all-time, and his 1.14 in 1909 is the fourth-best single-season mark since 1900. He won the pitching Triple Crown for the World Champion Giants of 1905, leading the league in wins, ERA, and strikeouts—a feat he repeated in 1908. Mathewson had masterful control of his fastball, off-speed pitches, and various curveballs, including his revolutionary "fadeaway" (forerunner to the screwball). The college-educated Mathewson was also known as a gentleman

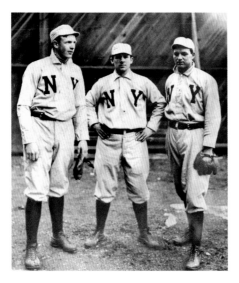

in an era of baseball rowdies, and his name was used to endorse a wide range of products, from baseball equipment to underwear. After 17 seasons with New York, Mathewson was traded to the Cincinnati Reds midway through the 1916 season, where he finished out his career as a player-manager. He took over full-time managerial duties for 1917

CHRISTY MATHEWSON, JOHN MCGRAW, AND JOE MCGINNITY OF THE NEW YORK GIANTS, 1905.

FROM·THE·BALL·PLAYERS·OF·THE
AMERICAN·LEAGUE
TO·SHOW·THEIR·APPRECIATION·OF
CY·YOUNG
AS·A·MAN·AND·AS·A·BALL·PLAYER
AUGUST·13·1908

CY YOUNG TROPHY, 1908.

CY YOUNG OF THE BOSTON AMERICANS, 1908.

Despite Young's struggles, the decision by the American League's Boston club to sign the star pitcher, for $3,500, during the great raid on NL players before the 1901 season, was a major coup for the junior league. More than just securing one of the game's biggest names, Boston acquired perhaps the best pitcher of the next several years.

In the AL's first season as an avowed major league, Young led the circuit with 33 wins, a 1.62 ERA, 158 strikeouts, and five shutouts, while walking just 37 batters in more than 371 innings. He repeated as the AL wins leader in 1902 and 1903. Save for a subpar 1906, Young finished among the league's top six in ERA every season he was with Boston. In 1908, at age 41, he posted a career-best 1.26 ERA.

The greatest single-game performance of his career came on May 5, 1904, when he pitched a perfect game against the Philadelphia Athletics. It was just the third perfect game in major league history and the first ever in the American League—and the first since the pitcher's mound was moved back to 60 feet, 6 inches.

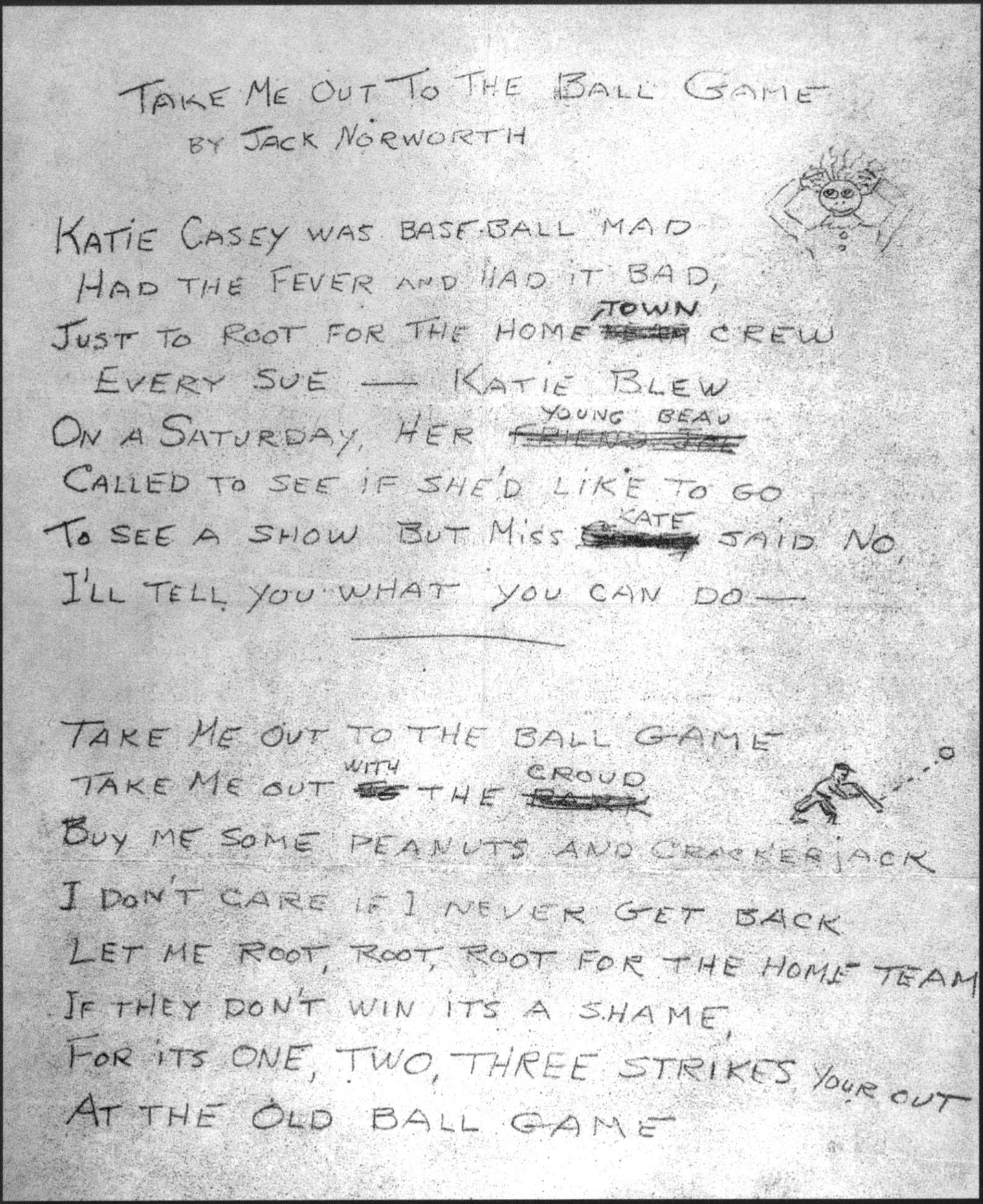

TAKE ME OUT TO THE BALL GAME
BY JACK NORWORTH

KATIE CASEY WAS BASE-BALL MAD
HAD THE FEVER AND HAD IT BAD,
JUST TO ROOT FOR THE HOME TOWN CREW
EVERY SUE — KATIE BLEW
ON A SATURDAY, HER YOUNG BEAU
CALLED TO SEE IF SHE'D LIKE TO GO
TO SEE A SHOW BUT MISS KATE SAID NO,
I'LL TELL YOU WHAT YOU CAN DO —

TAKE ME OUT TO THE BALL GAME
TAKE ME OUT WITH THE ~~BALL~~ CROUD
BUY ME SOME PEANUTS AND CRACKERJACK
I DON'T CARE IF I NEVER GET BACK
LET ME ROOT, ROOT, ROOT FOR THE HOME TEAM
IF THEY DON'T WIN ITS A SHAME,
FOR ITS ONE, TWO, THREE STRIKES YOUR OUT
AT THE OLD BALL GAME

"TAKE ME OUT TO THE BALL GAME" LYRICS, 1908.

26

"Take Me Out to the Ball Game" Lyrics, 1908

BASEBALL'S UNOFFICIAL ANTHEM

It is played at approximately 2,430 regular-season games, anywhere from 20 to 33 postseason games, and upwards of 400 spring training games. And that's just for Major League Baseball. Throw in hundreds of minor league and college games, and countless other amateur contests, and the song "Take Me Out to the Ball Game" is heard, and sung, by fans at thousands of baseball games every year. After the National Anthem and "Happy Birthday," it is perhaps the most frequently played song in the United States.

When vaudevillian entertainer and songwriter Jack Norworth penned the lyrics to this now-iconic song in 1908, he had never been out to a ball game himself. While riding the subway one day, he was inspired by a sign advertising, "Ballgame Today—Polo Grounds." He jotted down some lyrics, allegedly in just 15 minutes, and gave them to fellow Tin Pan Alley songwriter Albert Von Tilzer—who also had never seen a game—to set the words to music.

The song was first sung by Norworth's wife, singer-actress Nora Bayes. One of the first recordings of "Take Me Out to the Ball Game" was made in October 1908 by the Edison National Phonograph Company and sung by Edward Meeker. A recording by the Haydn Quartet singers hit number one on the music charts that year. Since then there have been more than 100 recordings of the song, including versions by Frank Sinatra, the Andrews Sisters, Dr. John, Carly Simon, the Goo Goo Dolls, and others.

Most fans are familiar only with the chorus of the song, which is what is sung at games. In fact, Norworth's original lyrics featured two full verses that told the story of a young woman, Katie Casey, pleading with her "young beau" to take her to a game:

HOT-DOG VENDOR'S BUCKET, EARLY 1900S.

27

Hot-Dog Vendor's Bucket, *early 1900s*

A STAPLE OF BALLPARK FARE

Although Jack Norworth's musical ode to baseball makes reference to "peanuts and Cracker Jack," the food most closely associated with going out to the ball game is undoubtedly the hot dog. Believed to have been introduced to American taste buds around the 1880s, the sausage-in-a-bun delicacy first became a regular ballpark offering in about 1901 at New York's Polo Grounds, thanks to pioneering concessionaire Harry M. Stevens.

Born in England, Stevens emigrated to the United States in the 1880s and became enamored of baseball. He got his start in the business producing and selling scorecards at a ballpark in Ohio, and he soon branched out to snacks and refreshments like peanuts, ice cream, and soft drinks. Over the next few years he secured agreements to sell scorecards and refreshments at major league parks. According to legend, the innovation to bring hot dogs into the mix came to him on a cold day at the Polo Grounds, when fans had no interest in buying ice cream or cold soda. He told his vendors to go to neighborhood stores to buy frankfurters, which they boiled and served piping hot on rolls to spectators. The "red hot sausages" caught on and soon spread to more ballparks.

Harry M. Stevens Inc. grew into the leading ballpark concessions operation during the twentieth century. Family-owned for more than 100 years, the business was sold in 1994 to international concessions empire Aramark, which has been in the concessions business since 1966.

The metal hot dog bucket shown here featured an open-flame to keep the hot dogs hot. Later generations of vendors sold dogs from wicker baskets with separate

SHIBE PARK ENTRANCE ROTUNDA, 1909.

FORBES FIELD,
PITTSBURGH, CIRCA 1909.

In addition to providing a safer and more luxurious environment in which to watch baseball, Shibe Park's sturdy construction allowed for a much larger seating capacity. Whereas the Athletics' previous home, Columbia Park, had a wooden grandstand that could accommodate fewer than 10,000 spectators, Shibe Park had a capacity of about 23,000 in its original incarnation—an estimated 30,000 were on hand for the grand opening on April 12, 1909. Some 675,000 fans walked through the Shibe Park turnstiles during that first season, the largest attendance in the American League in 1909.

The success of Shibe's innovation, and that of Barney Dreyfuss in Pittsburgh, led to a full-on ballpark revolution in the ensuing years. The St. Louis Browns replaced the wooden grandstand at Sportsman's Park with one of steel and concrete in 1909 and then replaced the remaining wooden bleachers a few years later. The Indians upgraded Cleveland's League Park with new steel-and-concrete grandstands in 1910. Then came a wave of all-new steel-and-concrete facilities in Chicago (Comiskey Park, 1910; Wrigley Field, 1914), Boston (Fenway Park, 1912; Braves Field, 1915), Cincinnati (Crosley Field, 1912), Detroit (Navin Field/Tigers Stadium, 1912), and Brooklyn (Ebbets Field, 1913). The New York Giants and the Washington Senators completely rebuilt their old wooden ballparks—the Polo Grounds and Griffith Stadium, respectively—after fires in 1911, this time employing the fireproof materials then in vogue.

By the end of the 1910s, the only teams without brand-new or thoroughly refurbished homes of their own were the St. Louis Cardinals, who moved in with the Browns at Sportsman's Park in 1920; the Philadelphia Phillies, who held on at the partially steel-and-concrete Baker Bowl until they became tenants of the A's at Shibe Park in 1938 (Shibe Park was renamed Connie Mack Stadium in 1953); and the New York Highlanders (not yet known as the Yankees), who paid rent to the Giants at the Polo Grounds from 1913 to 1922.

Growing weary of seeing their tenant-team and its megastar, Babe Ruth, get all the attention from the New York fans and media, the Giants booted the Highlanders from the Polo Grounds and off the island of Manhattan. Highlander owners Tilling-hast L'Hommedieu Huston and Jacob Ruppert had the last laugh, however. On a Bronx site directly across the river from the Polo Grounds, the rechristened Yankees opened a huge, 58,000-capacity stadium with three decks of seating—and featuring the home-run prowess of Ruth and Murderer's Row. Truly a stadium and not a park, Yankee Stadium could accommodate 18,000 more fans than the second-largest ball-park at the time, Braves Field. Whereas Shibe Park was built for a then-unheard-of sum of $315,000 in 1909, Yankee Stadium carried an astronomical price tag of $2.5 million, plus an additional $600,000 simply to purchase the site's land.

As Shibe Park had done, Yankee Stadium changed the way baseball facilities were perceived. But while teams did continue to expand and upgrade their existing ballparks, no new stadiums were constructed specifically for major league baseball for nearly 40 years after Yankee Stadium opened. The 80,000-seat Cleveland Stadium was built in 1932, but it was a multipurpose facility meant to serve both the Indians and the NFL's Browns. (The Indians also continued to play some home games at the smaller League Park from 1934 to 1946.) After leaving Boston in 1953, the Braves moved into Milwaukee County Stadium, which was originally built for a minor league team with the hopes of someday attracting a major league resident. It was a similar story for Minnesota's Metropolitan Stadium, which became major league only after the Washington Senators relocated to become the Minnesota Twins in 1961, after five years as the home of the minor league Millers. Baltimore's Municipal Stadium had been a longtime minor league park, built in 1922, when the St. Louis Browns moved to town and became the Baltimore Orioles in 1954; same with Kansas City's Municipal Stadium before it became the home for the relocated A's in 1955. Even when the Giants and Dodgers boldly headed across the continent to usher in Major League Baseball on the West Coast, they had to make do in converted minor league facilities for their first few years in San Francisco and Los Angeles until new ballparks could be completed.

When the Philadelphia Athletics broke ground on their steel-and-concrete masterpiece in April 1908, Ben Shibe could not have known the ballpark renaissance that would follow. Over the next 15 years, baseball would be graced with a collection of "jewel boxes" that, in many cases, served their teams well into the second half of the century and, in a few cases, even into the next century.

29

Ty Cobb's "Honey Boy Evans" Trophy, 1909

BASEBALL'S GREATEST HITTER

When the 1909 season got underway, Ty Cobb was just 22 years old, and he already had two batting titles under his belt. In addition, he had led all American Leaguers in hits, runs batted in, slugging percentage, and on-base plus slugging (OPS) in both 1907 and '08; in stolen bases in 1907; and in doubles and triples in 1908.

By the end of the 1909 season, the Detroit Tigers center fielder had not only secured a third consecutive batting crown with a .377 mark—for which he received this ornate cup—but he sat atop the AL in home runs (9) and RBI (107) to claim his league's Triple Crown, just the fourth player in baseball history to accomplish such a feat. Adding to his achievements, he was the AL leader in runs, hits, stolen bases, on-base percentage, and slugging. And he helped Detroit win a third straight American League pennant.

George "Honey Boy" Evans was a Welsh-born musician and entertainer who had developed a great love for baseball. Beginning in 1908, he commissioned a trophy to be awarded to the player with the highest batting average in Major League Baseball. Pittsburgh's Honus Wagner won the inaugural trophy. Ty Cobb took home the next four.

Cobb won the 1910 trophy by edging out Cleveland's Nap Lajoie in a controversial race for the AL batting crown. Playing in just his sixth major league season, Cobb had already established a reputation as an irascible, aggressive, and at times downright-nasty player who rubbed teammates and opponents the wrong way. With a seemingly comfortable lead in the batting race, Cobb sat out the Tigers' last two games of the season. Cleveland, meanwhile, was scheduled to play a doubleheader against the last-place St. Louis Browns on the final day. Browns manager Jack O'Connor instructed his third baseman to play deep, on the edge of the outfield grass, whenever Lajoie came to bat. This enabled Lajoie, a popular and admired

TY COBB'S "HONEY BOY EVANS" TROPHY, 1909.

star, to drop easy bunt singles down the third-base line. He went 8 for 8 that day.

Despite the obvious collusion, league president Ban Johnson declared Lajoie's hits valid. In the end, though, when the final averages were calculated, Cobb eked out the top batting average—.385 to Lajoie's .384.

The controversy did not end there. Many decades later, a researcher found that, due to a clerical error, Cobb had received credit twice for a game in which he went 2 for 3, giving him two more hits than he actually got. Not only did this lower his long-revered career hit total from 4,191 to 4,189, it also dropped his 1910 season average to .383, making Lajoie the true, if tainted, batting champ. (Major League Baseball still officially credits Cobb with the title.)

Cobb followed the controversial 1910 season with perhaps his greatest year in a career that would last 24 seasons in all. He earned a fifth straight batting title with a .420 average to go along with a league- and career-best .621 slugging percentage. He posted career highs in runs (147), hits (248), doubles (47), triples (24), RBI (127), and on-base plus slugging (1.088), all tops in the AL in 1911. He also led the circuit with 83 stolen bases and belted 8 home runs, which in those days was good enough to tie him for second most in the league.

That year, the Chalmers Automobile Company sponsored an award for the "most important and useful player to the club and to the league," to be voted on by a committee of baseball writers. Cobb was the unanimous selection for the 1911 American League Chalmers Award. Although it was only given for four years, the Chalmers is considered baseball's first Most Valuable Player Award.

When Cobb first joined the Tigers in 1905 as an 18-year-old out of rural Georgia, he was the youngest player then in the majors. The hazing from his teammates put him at odds with many of them right off the bat. As Davy Jones, Cobb's teammate from 1906 to 1912, put it in Lawrence Ritter's *The Glory of Their Times*, Cobb was "a very complex person—never did have many friends. Trouble was he had such a rotten disposition that it was damn hard to be his friend. . . . He antagonized so many people that hardly anyone would speak to him, even among his own teammates."

On the field, he was aggressive on the base paths, often sliding in spikes first, and he did what he could to rattle the opposition. Cobb also had altercations with fans and others. In 1912 he was suspended for going into the crowd to fight a heckling fan at New York's Hilltop Park. Three years earlier he had been arrested for getting into a fight with a night watchman at a Cleveland hotel. The watchman was black. It was not the only

TY COBB SLIDING HARD INTO
AN OPPOSING CATCHER.

incident in which Cobb, known as a notorious racist, had run-ins with African
Americans.

Despite such incidents, Cobb continued to perform otherworldly feats on
the diamond. Following his incredible
1911 output, he posted another .400-plus
season (.409) and began a string of four more batting titles. After finishing second to
Tris Speaker in 1916 while hitting .371, Cobb won three more titles from 1917 to 1919,
giving him 12 titles in 13 seasons, including nine in a row from 1907 to 1915 (counting
the disputed 1910 title). Although he did not win the batting crown, his .401 average
in 1922 made him one of only three people in major league history, along with Ed
Delahanty and Rogers Hornsby, to bat over .400 three times. Following his 41-game
rookie campaign of 1905, Cobb never hit lower than .316 in a season, including a .323
mark at the age of 41 in his final year in the majors, 1928. His .366 career average still
stands as the best in history.

Although many contend that the value of batting average as a statistic has long been
overstated, Cobb more than proved his worth through other statistical measures—not
to mention through the accolades and observations of his contemporaries. He led the
AL in slugging percentage eight times and in OPS 10 times. Cobb scored more than
100 runs in a season 11 times and drove in more than 100 seven times. He even ranked
among the league's top 10 in homers in 11 seasons. His 897 career stolen bases placed
him first among post-1900 players until Lou Brock surpassed him in 1977. More than
85 years after his retirement, Cobb still stands in the all-time top 10 in hits (2nd), runs
(2nd), triples (2nd), doubles (4th), stolen bases (4th), total bases (5th), RBI (8th), and
on-base percentage (9th). He was one of the best fielding center fielders of his day, and he
ranks with the all-time leaders in assists, putouts, and double plays among all outfielders.

When the voting was held for the inaugural Hall of Fame class in 1936, Cobb
received more votes than anybody, more than Babe Ruth, who surpassed Cobb as
the game's biggest star in the 1920s, and more than Honus Wagner, Cobb's main
contemporary challenger for the label of the greatest hitter of the Dead-Ball Era.

30

Honus Wagner T206 American Tobacco Company Baseball Card, 1909

THE HOLY GRAIL OF BASEBALL CARDS

Few objects of baseball memorabilia are as famous, mysterious, or valuable as the Honus Wagner tobacco card from 1909. Only an estimated 50 to 200 of these were produced by the American Tobacco Company (ATC) for its T206 series of 1909–1911, and only a few dozen are known to have survived to today. Given the rarity and mystique that surrounds them, Wagner T206 cards sold at auction or in private deals have carried price tags in the millions.

Only a small number of cards were produced because Wagner denied the company the right to use his likeness and ordered ATC to cease production. Popular legend is that Wagner did this because he did not want to be associated with the company's tobacco products and did not want to encourage kids to smoke. The more likely story is that Wagner, who had previously promoted cigars and other tobacco products, was not happy with the compensation he was offered by ATC.

The T206 series included cards for more than 500 major leaguers, with card backs promoting a range of cigarette brands. Packaging baseball cards with tobacco products had been going on for decades prior to 1909. Allen & Ginter, of Richmond Virginia, was one of the first to include cards featuring baseball players (as well as other athletes) in its cigarette packs in the 1880s. The New York–based Goodwin & Company's Old Judge series of 1888 featured sepia-toned photos of players in action poses—sliding, swinging, throwing—in a studio setting. In addition to hundreds of players, the series also offered cards picturing managers and owners.

HONUS WAGNER T206 BASEBALL CARD, 1909.

Innovation in baseball cards, by tobacco companies and increasingly by candy and confectioner companies, accelerated after the turn of the twentieth century. In 1911, ATC introduced its so-called Gold Borders set. Featuring gold edges around the player portraits, these cards were the first to provide biographical and statistical information on the backs. The National League cards from this series also included facsimile autographs on the front.

The 1930s saw a new wave of manufacturers bring card production to another level. By this time card collecting had gone from a largely adult-oriented hobby to one geared to kids. In 1933, the Goudey Gum Company packaged cards with sticks of chewing gum. Goudey manufactured baseball cards from 1933 until 1941, when production virtually ceased with the outbreak of World War II.

Baseball cards made a comeback in postwar America in the late 1940s, led by the Bowman Gum and Leaf Candy companies. Leaf ceased producing cards in 1950. The Topps Chewing Company entered the fray in 1952.

Topps and Bowman operated as the leading card companies until Topps purchased Bowman in 1956. Over the next quarter century, Topps had a virtual monopoly in the field, possessing exclusive rights to the likenesses of most major leaguers. Notwithstanding occasional promotional cards inserted in cereal boxes and other snack foods during the 1970s, Topps's corner on the market came to an end in 1981, when the Fleer Corporation successfully sued to challenge its monopoly. Fleer, a candy company that first began producing sports cards in the 1920s, was joined by Donruss, another long-established candy company, as Topps's main competitors. Topps retained its monopoly on cards sold with gum, so Fleer packaged cards with team-logo stickers and Donruss introduced puzzle piece inserts.

Card collecting had become a big business. Annual price guides charted the fluctuating market values of each card, and vintage cards were bought and sold for thousands of dollars. New manufacturers like Score and Upper Deck expanded the market in the late 1980s, and the "Big Three" of Topps, Fleer, and Donruss continued to create new and different series and limited-edition runs—bringing further market confusion and a glut in the marketplace. Over the subsequent decades, smaller brands came and went, existing brands were merged and consolidated, and the collectible value of cards began to recede.

Despite this decline, however, the T206 Wagner card continued to garner interest among collectors. One particular specimen followed a notable path. Purchased

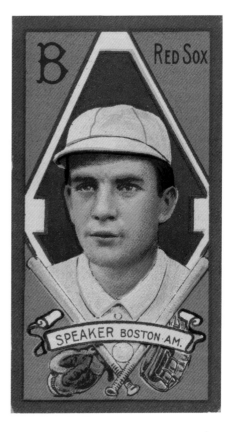

by memorabilia dealer Bill Mastro from a private owner for $25,000 in 1985, the card was resold to collector Jim Copeland for $110,000 two years later. When Copeland put his massive collection up for auction in 1991, the Wagner card was bought for $451,000 — by hockey legend Wayne Gretzky. Gretzky then sold it in 1995 for $500,000. By 2000, the price of this card was $1.27 million, in a sale to collector Brian Siegel. In February 2007, an anonymous collector paid Siegel $2.35 million before turning around and selling it to another collector for $2.8 million later that year. Other copies of the Wagner T206 card are held at the New York Public Library, the Metropolitan Museum of Art, and in various private collections.

While the Honus Wagner card from 1909 is widely known for being the "Holy Grail" of baseball card collecting, what may be less well known among some fans today is that Honus Wagner also happened to be one of the greatest baseball players of all time. A member of the first group inducted into the Hall of Fame in 1936, Wagner batted .300 or better in 15 consecutive seasons (1899–1913), during which time he collected a National League–record eight batting titles (later tied by Tony Gwynn). Wagner led the league in RBI and stolen bases five times each, in slugging percentage six times, and in doubles seven times. In 1908 alone, he was tops in hits, doubles, triples, RBI, stolen bases, batting, slugging, and on-base percentage; he finished second in home runs. Over 21 major league seasons, 18 of them with the Pittsburgh Pirates, Wagner collected 3,420 career hits, which ranks him seventh on the all-time list. He was arguably one of the greatest all-around shortstops the game has ever seen. These days, that is worth more than the $2.8 million paid for his baseball card.

31

Bill Klem's Ball-Strike Indicator, circa 1910

THE OLD ARBITRATOR

If a baseball fan were asked to list the people who had the greatest impact on the sport during the first half of the twentieth century, he or she might bring up names like Cobb, Ruth, Mathewson, Grove, McGraw, and Mack, among others. Few would probably think to mention Bill Klem. But during his 46 years in Major League Baseball, this Hall of Famer was on the field for 18 World Series, two All-Star Games, five no-hitters, and many memorable moments on the diamond.

Bill Klem was an umpire, wielding this ball-strike indicator to keep tabs on the game action. His career as an on-field umpire in the National League extended from 1905 until 1940 (he worked a few games during the 1941 season), and then he served as the chief of NL umpires until his death in 1951.

In addition to his longevity, Klem was instrumental in elevating the authority and integrity of the umpire position. He was also an innovator. Although not the first to employ hand signals, Klem was known for adding flourishes to his calls. In addition, while umpires had been wearing chest protectors since the late 1880s, Klem was the first prominent umpire to wear one underneath his shirt, which allowed him to sit closer to the catcher than with the bulky "balloon" style protector worn on the outside.

The "Old Arbitrator" had a reputation for being both tough and fair. He stood up to the most volatile protests and originated the practice of drawing a line in the dirt in front of irate players and managers, telling them that if they crossed that line, they would be ejected. Over the course of his long career, Klem issued more than 250 ejections for a variety of infractions.

BILL KLEM'S BALL-STRIKE INDICATOR, CIRCA 1910.

Asserting control and discipline on the diamond did not always come easy to umpires. Still, the need for an irrefutable third-party arbiter to settle disputes is as old as the game itself. The Olympic Ball Club of Philadelphia determined, in its 1837 club constitution, that the team's recorder should serve as the umpire "in the event of a disputed point of the game, and from his decision there shall be no appeal." The sanctity of umpires' decisions was echoed in the rules of the Knickerbocker Club of 1845: "All disputes and differences relative to the game, to be decided by the Umpire, from which there is no appeal." By 1876, the National League Constitution decreed that this deference to umpires extended to fans as well: "The umpire is the sole judge of play, and is entitled to the respect of the spectators, and any person hissing or hooting at, or offering any insult or indignity to him, must be promptly ejected from the grounds." Suffice it to say, despite this warning, hissing, hooting, and insulting umpires have long been popular pastimes among baseball's rabid crowds.

The umpire's primary function in the nascent years of the sport was to ensure fair play and honorable conduct by the participants. It wasn't until the 1860s that the role went beyond settling disputes to one of making regular rulings on plays, especially with the introduction of called strikes and balls.

A consequence of this greater involvement in determining the outcome of plays was an increase in the amount of abuse heaped on umpires from players and spectators. This, in turn, made it increasingly difficult to convince "distinguished and respected" members of the community to take on this thankless (and unpaid) job. Early on, umpires were typically chosen from among the members of the club or from the hometown crowd, on mutual agreement of both captains. A more structured system of creating an umpire pool was established by the National Association in 1871. Per the NA constitution, the visiting club would submit the names of five "acknowledged and competent men" from which the home team would select an umpire for a match. Beginning in 1874, teams were permitted to pay umpires, as long as both sides shared equally in the compensation.

Shortly after its founding, the National League established a pool of "gentlemen of repute" in each league city from which the umpire would be selected by the visiting team. The league subsequently took over the responsibility for hiring a staff of umpires and assigning them to games. Umpires were paid for their service—$5 per game—beginning in 1878.

"The umpire is the sole judge of play, and is entitled to the respect of the spectators, and any person hissing or hooting at, or offering any insult or indignity to him, must be promptly ejected from the grounds."

The added expense of hiring umpires meant that owners were reluctant to have more than one work each game, but it soon became clear that more than one pair of eyes was needed. Players would take advantage when the lone umpire was looking elsewhere on the field, such as base runners skipping bases if the umpire's gaze was fixed on the ball or on another runner. Until 1882, an umpire was permitted to consult with spectators if his view was obstructed.

The professional leagues all experimented with two-umpire crews during the 1880s and '90s, one stationed behind the plate and the other in the field. It became increasingly common after the turn of the twentieth century but was not mandated until 1911. A third umpire was occasionally on hand beginning in the late 1910s, especially for important games. By the late 1940s, each league employed enough umpires to have three present for most contests. Four-man crews were instituted for World Series games beginning in 1909. It became standard for all regular-season games in the early 1950s. Six umpires have been present for World Series games since 1947.

No matter the number of umpires, managers and players continued to challenge the authority—even the humanity—of those arbiters. As early as the 1840s, umpires were given the authority to fine and, later, eject players on the spot for infractions ranging from swearing to fighting to betting on the game. As the game got rougher, verbal assaults on umpires became more frequent, and in the rough-and-tumble years of the 1890s, physical assaults were not unheard of, particularly in the National League. Spitting on, kicking, spiking, or punching of umpires could be dealt with by fines, ejections, and suspensions, but it nevertheless left umpires feeling vulnerable and even fearing for their personal safety. The league tried at various times to crack down. Ban Johnson made protecting the umpires a foremost goal of his newly created American League around the turn of the twentieth century.

BILL KLEM (THIRD FROM LEFT) WITH OTHER UMPIRES
AND MANAGERS AT THE 1913 WORLD SERIES.

As a result of the agreement forged by the National and American Leagues in 1903, and a drive by owners and league presidents to clean up the game, incidents of excessive verbal and physical attacks on umpires were less common by the time Bill Klem suited up in 1905. Not to say that he and generations of umpires since haven't been subjected to violent rants and even the occasional shove or expectoration—but it's surely a safer world for the men in blue than it was in the late 1800s.

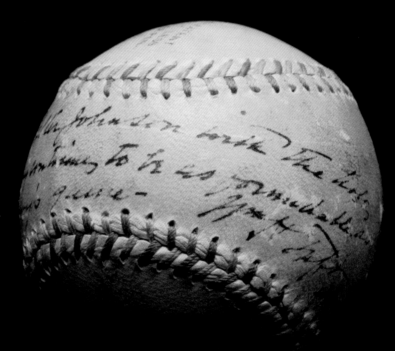

PRESIDENT TAFT'S FIRST-PITCH BALL, 1910.

32

President Taft's First-Pitch Ball, 1910

THE FIRST FAN OF THE UNITED STATES

In the spring of 1910, American League president Ban Johnson sent an invitation to the White House requesting U.S. President William H. Taft's presence at the Opening Day of the Washington Senators' season at Griffith Stadium. The president accepted and was given a seat near the home team's dugout. The story goes that presidential participation in the Opening Day ceremony was not planned, but Senators team owner Clark Griffith handed a ball to President Taft and invited him to throw out a ceremonial first pitch. From his front-row seat, Taft tossed the ball to Senators pitcher Walter Johnson, who then led Washington to a 1–0 victory over the Philadelphia Athletics on April 14, 1910.

The ball was inscribed by the president and kept in a commemorative box by Johnson. The box with the ball and pens used for the signatures was later donated by the Johnson family to the Baseball Hall of Fame in Cooperstown.

Taft continued this rite of spring in 1911, but he was absent the next year when the sinking of the *Titanic* earlier in the week forced him to miss the game. Vice President James S. Sherman filled in for Taft at the Senators' home opener on April 19, 1912.

Since then, every U.S. president, with the exception of Jimmy Carter, has delivered an Opening Day first pitch at least once during his presidency. (Carter did throw out a first pitch at the 1979 World Series.)

Herbert Hoover attended Opening Day at Griffith Stadium in all four years of his presidency (1929–1932). Franklin D. Roosevelt did it eight times—skipping 1939 and then the World War II years of 1942–1945—and his successor, Harry S. Truman, was present for seven Opening Days. In 1950, the southpaw commander-in-chief threw two first pitches: one righty and one lefty.

The final season of the original Senators franchise in Washington was 1960, and Dwight D. Eisenhower performed the first-pitch ceremony at the season opener on April 18. When the expansion Washington Senators franchise was established the following year, John F. Kennedy threw out the last first pitch at Griffith Stadium. The new Senators moved to brand-new D.C. Stadium in 1962—later renamed RFK Stadium in honor of JFK's brother—and President Kennedy delivered the first-ever pitch in that stadium's debut. Richard Nixon, in 1969, became the last president to throw a first pitch at a Senators game before the team moved to Texas, following the 1971 season.

With no team in the nation's capital from 1972 until the Washington Nationals came to town in 2005, presidents took the show on the road. Nixon threw out the first pitch at Anaheim Stadium in his home state of California for the Angels' 1973 opener. Gerald Ford went to Arlington Stadium in Texas in 1976, and Ronald Reagan's ceremonial tosses in 1984 and 1986 took place at Memorial Stadium in Baltimore.

George H. W. Bush delivered Opening Day first pitches in four different stadiums: Memorial Stadium, Toronto's SkyDome, Arlington Stadium, and Oriole Park at Camden Yards. The SkyDome toss was the first Opening Day presidential first pitch outside the United States. Bill Clinton followed suit with a traveling show to Camden Yards (1993 and '96), Cleveland's Jacobs Field (1994), Shea Stadium in New York (1997), and Pac Bell Park in San Francisco (2000). In 1993 Clinton became the first to throw from the pitcher's mound, rather than a box seat.

George W. Bush, who had previously been a part owner of the Texas Rangers, was on hand for the first game at Milwaukee's Miller Park in the 2001 opener, and he later threw first pitches at Busch Stadium in St. Louis (2004) and Cincinnati's Great American Ball Park (2006). The return of Major League Baseball to the Beltway in 2005 brought POTUS back to RFK Stadium, where Bush opened the Nationals' first season. He returned three years later for the inaugural game at the newly constructed Nationals Park in 2008.

Through the first six years of his presidency, Barack Obama has participated in only one Opening Day first-pitch ceremony, delivered at Nationals Park in 2010. Obama was, however, on hand for a first pitch at the 2009 All-Star Game in St. Louis.

FDR was the first president to attend the Midsummer Classic, in 1937. Nixon and Ford also attended All-Star Games and delivered ceremonial first pitches while in office. Presidential first pitches have been a tradition at the Fall Classic for a century. Woodrow Wilson was the first president to attend a World Series game, and he threw

PRESIDENT TAFT THROWING OUT
A FIRST PITCH, CIRCA 1910.

out the first pitch for Game 2 at Philadelphia's Baker Bowl in 1915. Calvin Coolidge is the only resident of the White House (to date) to throw out a World Series first pitch for the hometown team. In 1924, he kicked off the Senators' first-ever postseason game at Griffith Stadium. Washington lost that game—with Walter Johnson on the mound—but won the series in seven games. The Senators were back in the World Series the following year, and Coolidge was back at Griffith Stadium for Game 3.

Hoover traveled to Philadelphia to throw ceremonial pitches at back-to-back Philadelphia Athletics' championships in 1929 and '30. Eisenhower kicked off the epic 1955 World Series between the Brooklyn Dodgers and the New York Yankees, which ended with Brooklyn's first world championship. It would be nearly a quarter century before another president was on hand for a World Series first pitch—Carter in Game 7 of the 1979 series—and then another two decades after that.

On October 30, 2001, George W. Bush threw out the ceremonial first pitch for Game 3 of the World Series at Yankee Stadium, in the first World Series game in New York following the September 11 terrorist attacks. He was the first president to throw from the mound in a World Series, and despite wearing a heavy bulletproof vest under his FDNY jacket, Bush delivered a strike to Yankees catcher Jorge Posada.

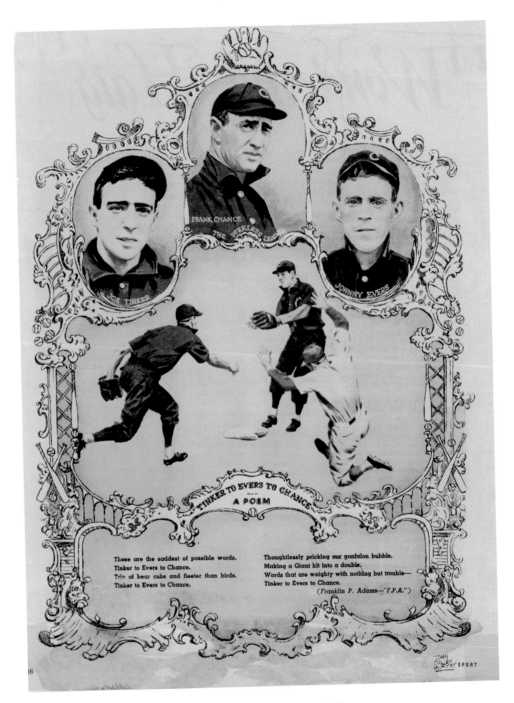

TINKER TO EVERS TO CHANCE
A POEM

These are the saddest of possible words,
Tinker to Evers to Chance.
Trio of bear cubs and fleeter than birds,
Tinker to Evers to Chance.

Thoughtlessly pricking our gonfalon bubble,
Making a Giant hit into a double.
Words that are weighty with nothing but trouble—
Tinker to Evers to Chance.

(Franklin P. Adams—"F.P.A.")

"BASEBALL'S SAD LEXICON," 1910.

33

"Baseball's Sad Lexicon," 1910

BEFORE THEY WERE "LOVABLE LOSERS"

Baseball experts will debate where the Chicago Cubs double-play combination of shortstop Joe Tinker, second baseman Johnny Evers, and first baseman Frank Chance rates in the annals of history. Few can deny, however, that Franklin Pierce Adams's ode to this infield trio ranks among the best-known baseball poems.

> These are the saddest of possible words:
> "Tinker to Evers to Chance."
> Trio of bear cubs, and fleeter than birds,
> Tinker and Evers and Chance.
> Ruthlessly pricking our gonfalon bubble,
> Making a Giant hit into a double—
> Words that are heavy with nothing but trouble:
> "Tinker to Evers to Chance."

The verse first appeared in Adams's "Always in Good Humor" column in the *New York Evening Mail* on July 12, 1910. It was written in response to a game-saving double play turned the day before by the Cubs trio during a defeat of Adams's home-town New York Giants at the Polo Grounds; the win put Chicago up by 1 1/2 games over the Giants in the standings. The poem appeared with the title "That Double Play Again." The *Evening Mail* reprinted it on July 18 with the now-familiar title of "Baseball's Sad Lexicon."

The Cubs went on to win the National League pennant that year, finishing 13 games ahead of the second-place Giants. Their 104 wins in 1910 marked the fourth time in five years that Chicago won more than 100 games in a season and the fourth time they won the pennant—all with Tinker, Evers, and Chance patrolling the infield.

UNDERWOOD MODEL NO. 5 TYPEWRITER, C. 1910.

of new media. From the 1930s to the 1970s, Red Smith was one of the most celebrated baseball writers, the bulk of his career spent at the *New York Herald-Tribune*. Ernest Hemingway called him the "most important force in American sportswriting." Smith won a Pulitzer Prize in 1976. The Associated Press named its annual sportswriting award, given for outstanding contribution by writers and editors, the Red Smith Award. Smith was presented with the first Red Smith Award in 1981.

The words of Jim Murray, another Pulitzer Prize– and Red Smith Award winner, graced the pages of the *Los Angeles Times* for nearly four decades beginning in 1961. Shirley Povich spent more than 50 years on the staff of the *Washington Post* and then continued to write for another quarter century after his "retirement." In Povich's first year as a *Post* reporter, 1923, Babe Ruth was still four years away from his historic 60-homer season; in the year Povich typed his final column for the *Post*, 1998, Mark McGwire and Sammy Sosa were engaged in a frenzied chase of baseball's single-season home run record.

Dick Young, who got his start with the *New York Daily News* in the early 1940s and continued writing into the 1980s, broke ground in the tactics used by sportswriters to get a story. He approached the clubhouse, previously considered a sanctuary of sorts for the players, as a vital source of information and scoops. He wasn't afraid to expose the private lives and personal faults of the athletes. Young's abrasive and confrontational style put him at odds with many players, managers, executives, and fellow journalists, but it set a new tone in sports journalism.

In the final decades of the twentieth century and the first years of the twenty-first, Dave Anderson, Murray Chass, Peter Gammons, Bill Madden, and Roger Angell were among the leading writers who continued the revered baseball writing tradition that Grantland Rice and others helped bring to maturity in the early 1900s. Beat writers and columnists throughout the country continue to push the envelope in sports journalism while offering fans unprecedented insight into the world of baseball.

The J. G. Taylor Spink Award, named for the longtime publisher of the *Sporting News*, is given annually by the Baseball Writers Association of America for "meritorious contributions to baseball writing." Spink Award winners are honored in a special wing at the Baseball Hall of Fame. Spink was the first to receive the award, shortly after he died, in 1962.

"SHOELESS" JOE JACKSON'S SHOES, 1919.

1919 with a 1.82 ERA. Fellow White Sox hurler Lefty Williams won 23 games and struck out more than twice as many batters as he walked.

When Chicago was set to take on the NL-champion Cincinnati Reds in that year's World Series, the smart money was on the White Sox to win another title. Chicago was so heavily favored that New York gambler, racketeer, and gangster Arnold Rothstein saw an opportunity to make big bucks off a Cincinnati victory. To help ensure that he won that bet, Rothstein sent his associates to pay the White Sox to throw the series.

The mobsters had a receptive audience in the Chicago players, who nearly to a man reviled the team's notoriously cheap owner, Charles Comiskey. With Gandil and Risberg as the ringleaders, a total of eight White Sox players (according to a grand jury's findings in September 1920) were in on the fix. The Reds won the 1919 Fall Classic, five games to three.

In the wake of the grand jury deliberations and in an effort to clean up the game's image, federal judge Kenesaw Mountain Landis was brought in to serve as commissioner of baseball. Although the eight White Sox players were acquitted in a civil trial in the summer of 1921—in part a result of the disappearance of some key evidence, including signed confessions by Jackson and Cicotte—Landis used his newfound power to ban the conspirators from baseball. Those placed on Landis's "ineligible list" were Cicotte, Felsch, Gandil, Jackson, Fred McMullin (a little-used bench player who demanded a piece of the action after learning of the plot and threatening to expose the other players), Risberg, Weaver, and Williams. Weaver did not accept any money or participate in the fix, but he was involved in the early meetings and failed to disclose it to the team or the league.

Landis also banned St. Louis Browns infielder Joe Gedeon for his knowledge of the fix and for placing bets on the series. Hal Chase, who had been out of baseball since 1919, was also given a lifetime ban by the new commissioner. Chase had been unofficially blackballed from the majors because of his known association with gamblers and for suspicion of fixing games dating back to 1910 when he was with the New York Highlanders and later as a member of the New York Giants.

The relationship between gambling and baseball has a long history that goes back to the game's early years. Indeed, in his exploration of the birth of the sport in *Baseball in the Garden of Eden*, John Thorn asserts that gambling was one of the "essential ingredients" that helped facilitate the growth of baseball in the 1840s by providing added interest in the young sport among spectators. Some early ballparks

COMMISSIONER KENESAW LANDIS WITH
MEMBERS OF THE "BLACK SOX," 1921.

included special sections for gamblers, isolating them from the rest of the crowd while recognizing wagering as an integral part of the baseball experience.

The players, meanwhile, being initially unpaid and later underpaid, were ripe for corrupting, and many were eager for a piece of the gambling action. The prevalence of gambling and corruption in the final years of the National Association played a big role in the move to establish a new, cleaner major league—the National League—in 1876. League president William Hulbert and his cohorts went to great lengths to keep gambling from the ballparks and out of the game as a whole.

Still, incidents of players being paid to throw a game did not disappear altogether. In 1877, the second year of the NL's existence, four Louisville Grays players were expelled for fixing games. Like his teammate Hal Chase, Giants infielder Heinie Zimmerman was banned for various allegations relating to game fixing and betting. None, however, was as big a star as Joe Jackson (until Pete Rose, 70 years later; see **Object #78**).

Jackson long asserted his innocence in the so-called Black Sox scandal of 1919, and several other players implicated in the scandal later claimed that Jackson had not been involved. He hit a series-best .375 against Cincinnati, collected a World Series–record 12 hits, drove in a team-high six runs, and committed no errors in the eight games. All efforts to clear his name were unsuccessful, however, and to this day Jackson is ineligible for induction in the National Baseball Hall of Fame.

BABE RUTH AND THE BIRTH OF THE LIVELY BALL ERA

◆ ◆ ◆ ◆

UNIFORM AGREEMENT

FOR TRANSFER OF A PLAYER

NOTICE.—To establish uniformity in action by clubs when a player, released by a major league club to a minor league club, or by a minor league club to a major league club, refuses to report to and contract with the club to which he is transferred, the Commission directs the club securing him to protect both parties to the deal from responsibility for his salary during his insubordination by promptly suspending him.

Payment, in part or in whole, of the consideration for the release of such player will not be enforced until he is reinstated and actually enters the service of the purchasing club.

TO OR BY A

Major League Club

WARNING TO CLUBS.—Many contentions that arise over the transfer of players are directly due to the neglect of one or both parties to promptly execute and file the Agreement. The Commission will no longer countenance dilatory tactics, that result in appeals to it to investigate and enforce claims which, if made a matter of record, as required by the laws of Organized Base Ball, would not require adjustment. In all cases of this character, the complaining club must establish that it is not at fault for delay or neglect to sign and file the Agreement upon which its claim is predicated. (See last sentence of Rule 10.)

This Agreement, made and entered into this 26th day of December 191 9 by and between   Boston American League Baseball Club
(Party of the First Part)
and   American League Base Ball Club of New York
(Party of the Second Part)

Witnesseth: The party of the first part does hereby release to the party of the second part the services of Player   George H. Ruth   under the following conditions:

(Here recite fully and clearly every condition of deal, including date of delivery; if for a money consideration, designate time and method of payment; if an exchange of players, name each; if option to recall is retained or privilege of choosing one or more players in lieu of one released is retained, specify all terms. No transfer will be held valid unless the consideration, receipt of which is acknowledged therein, passes at time of execution of Agreement.)

By herewith assigning to the party of the second part the

contract of said player George H. Ruth for the seasons of 1919,

1920 and 1921, in consideration of the sum of Twenty-five Thous-

and ($25,000.) Dollars and other good and valuable considerations

paid by the party of the second part, receipt whereof is hereby

acknowledged.

The parties to this Agreement further covenant to abide by all provisions of the National Agreement and by all Rules of the National Commission, regulating the transfer of the services of a player, particularly those printed on the reverse side of this Agreement.

In Testimony Whereof, we have subscribed hereto, through our respective presidents or authorized agents, on the date above written:

Witness: BOSTON AMERICAN LEAGUE BASEBALL CLUB

(SEAL)

(Party of the First Part)   President

AMERICAN LEAGUE BASE BALL CLUB OF NEW YORK

Corporate name of Company, Club or Association of each party should be written in first paragraph and subscribed hereto. (See Rule 10.)

(Party of the Second Part)

Club officials are cautioned to carefully read the provisions of the National Agreement and the rules of the National Commission, printed on the back of this Agreement, for their information and guidance.

AGREEMENT TO TRANSFER BABE RUTH FROM THE RED SOX TO THE YANKEES, 1919.

37

Agreement to Transfer Babe Ruth from the Red Sox to the Yankees, 1919

BIRTH OF A DYNASTY—AND A CURSE

The sale of George Herman "Babe" Ruth from the Boston Red Sox to the New York Yankees, for the then-princely sum of $100,000, in December 1919 was a watershed moment for both American League clubs. But more than sending one franchise on a path to dynasty and domination and the other on a path to long-lasting disappointment, the transfer proved to be a watershed moment for baseball as a whole.

From 1915 to 1917, Ruth had established himself as one of the most dominant left-handed pitchers around. He posted a combined record of 65–33 and a 2.02 ERA in those three seasons. During those years he also hit nine home runs in just under 400 plate appearances, and the Red Sox brass saw something in how he handled the bat. In 1918, manager Ed Barrow gave Ruth just 19 mound starts (he won 13 of them), but the Babe was in the lineup as a starting outfielder or first baseman in 70 other games, in addition to a few as a pinch hitter off the bench. In 382 plate appearances that year, he hit a major-league-high 11 homers. He also led the AL in slugging percentage and on-base plus slugging, and finished among the league's top 10 in batting average, doubles, triples, RBI, and walks—as well as in ERA, winning percentage, and complete games as a pitcher.

The Boston Red Sox went on to win the World Series in 1918. Ruth was the starting pitcher in the series opener against the Chicago Cubs and led the Sox to victory with a complete-game shutout. He also earned the "W" in Game 4 and drove in two runs with a triple, his only base hit of the series.

The victory marked the Red Sox's third title in four seasons and their fifth since 1903. (They also won the AL pennant in 1904 but were denied a chance to defend their 1903 World Series triumph when John McGraw and the New York Giants refused to participate in the postseason contest.) Two years prior to Ruth's arrival, Boston won a franchise-record 105 games in 1912, led by an all-star outfield of Tris Speaker, Duffy Lewis, and Harry Hooper. The club defeated McGraw's Giants, four games to three, in an epic World Series. Twenty-two-year-old pitching phenom Smoky Joe Wood topped off a 34-win regular season by defeating the Giants three times in October.

When the 19-year-old Ruth came to town in 1914, he joined a deep pitching staff that included the still-dangerous-but-injury-plagued Wood; Ray Collins, a 20-game winner in 1914; lefty Dutch Leonard, who went 19–5 and led the universe with a 0.96 ERA; Rube Foster (14 wins, 1.70 ERA); and rookie Ernie Shore.

The young Ruth started only three games for the second-place Sox in 1914, but the following season he went 18–8, joining Foster, Shore, Leonard, and Wood as winners of 15 or more games. Boston won 101 games in 1915 and defeated the Philadelphia Phillies to claim another World Series title. Ruth's only appearance in the series came as a pinch hitter in the ninth inning of Game 1; he grounded out.

Despite trading away their top hitter and future Hall of Famer Tris Speaker, and losing the 25-year-old Wood to injury, the Red Sox were back on top in 1916. Ruth led the squad with 23 wins and led the league with a 1.75 ERA. Along with Leonard (18 wins), Shore (16), Foster (14), and Carl Mays (18), Boston once again had the game's best pitching staff and once again won the World Series, defeating the

Brooklyn Dodgers (then known as the Robins). In the second game, Ruth allowed an inside-the-park home run in the first inning and then held Brooklyn scoreless for the next 13 innings.

BOSTON PITCHERS RUBE FOSTER, CARL MAYS, ERNIE SHORE, BABE RUTH, AND DUTCH LEONARD AT THE 1915 WORLD SERIES.

After he tied the game 1–1 with an RBI groundout in the third, Boston finally won in the bottom of the 14th. Ruth pitched all 14 innings.

Although their 90 wins in 1917 were only good enough for second place in the AL, Ruth did his part by winning 24 games and posting a 2.01 ERA. He also batted .325 and hit two homers in 123 at-bats.

In 1918, in a season abbreviated due to World War I, Ruth's shift from pitcher to position player was underway. In addition to his league-leading 11 homers, Ruth's 13 wins as a pitcher were supplemented by 21 from Mays, 16 from "Sad Sam" Jones (acquired from Cleveland in the Speaker trade), and 15 from "Bullet Joe" Bush, a former ace for Connie Mack's Philadelphia Athletics. Additional windfalls from Mack's Philadelphia clearinghouse (see **Object #35**) were the acquisition of first baseman Stuffy McInnis and catcher Wally Schang.

After capping off a fourth World Series win of the decade in 1918, the dismantling of the Red Sox began—a process that would leave the team struggling, and perhaps cursed, for decades to come.

In November 1916, New York theater owner and producer Harry Frazee had purchased the Red Sox and their ballpark for upwards of $1 million. As declining attendance at Fenway Park and the struggles of his Broadway productions left Frazee financially strapped, he began to unload many of the team's best—and highest-paid—players.

When Duffy Lewis and Ernie Shore returned after missing the 1918 season to military service, Frazee promptly shipped them to the Yankees, along with Dutch Leonard, for four inconsequential players and $15,000 cash. In July 1919, Frazee traded Carl Mays to the Yanks for two players and $40,000. Five months later, the Red Sox owner agreed to the notorious sale of Ruth to New York—in response to which Ed Barrow warned, "You ought to know you're making a mistake." In December

> After capping off a fourth World Series win of the decade in 1918, the dismantling of the Red Sox began— a process that would leave the team struggling, and perhaps cursed, for decades to come.

RAY CHAPMAN'S GRAVESTONE.

The first change in the wake of the tragedy was a new rule requiring umpires to substitute a new ball whenever the ball in use became dirty or scuffed. (Prior to this, team and league officials had complained that umpires were too generous in replacing used balls, thus running up expenses.) Scuffed and soiled balls were not only more difficult for batters to see, but the uneven surface made the pitched ball more unpredictable in its flight.

Pitchers had long been aware of the effects of scuffing or otherwise tampering with a baseball, including the addition of foreign substances. The originator of the "spitball" is difficult to trace, but the man most responsible for popularizing it was Jack Chesbro. A Hall of Famer, Chesbro used the spitball with great effectiveness in 1904, setting a post-1900 record by winning 41 games that season. Other pitchers followed suit, and within a few years, most staffs featured a pitcher who included the spitball in his repertoire. Its popularity was on the wane during the 1910s, however, as batters adjusted to the pitch and few hurlers were able to master it.

On February 9, 1920—six months before Chapman's death—the Joint Rules Committee declared the spitball, as well as the emery ball, mudball, licorice ball, grease ball, and other variations, illegal. Seventeen active spitballers were grandfathered in and could continue to use the pitch. Burleigh Grimes, a five-time 20-game winner whose career spanned 19 seasons with seven different clubs, was the last to *legally* pitch a spitball when he retired in 1934. To be sure, Grimes was not the last to pitch a spitball, as numerous pitchers in subsequent decades have been suspected of and punished for throwing doctored pitches, among them Hall of Famers Don Sutton and Gaylord Perry.

There is nothing to indicate that Carl Mays's fateful pitch to Ray Chapman was a spitter. Rather, this incident highlighted the dangers of the "brushback" pitch, another popular and controversial tactic in the pitcher's arsenal. Mays was known to be an enthusiastic employer of the brushback, regularly throwing high and tight to intimidate batters and keep them on their heels. The Yankee hurler was widely disliked for his "headhunting." Following Chapman's death, Mays was vilified by players and journalists, and many called for him to be banished from the league. Mays always asserted that he had no intention of hitting Chapman, and immediately after the play, before he or anyone knew how badly Chapman was hurt, Mays reportedly showed the ball to the umpire and pointed out a scuff that had caused it to sail off course.

KDKA RADIO ANNOUNCER HAROLD ARLIN STANDS IN FRONT
OF A MICROPHONE, CIRCA 1921.

The Cincinnati Reds bucked that trend, however. Harry Hartman of WFBE in Cincinnati did play-by-play commentary regularly for Reds games beginning around 1930. "Radio," Hartman argued, "is the best advertiser that baseball could want." With the Great Depression putting ticket prices out of the reach of many fans, radio could keep baseball in the consciousness of everyday Americans.

Cincinnati continued as a leader in this arena following the hiring of Larry MacPhail as general manager in 1933. MacPhail (who later pioneered night baseball in Cincinnati; see **Object #46**) hired a young broadcaster named Red Barber from WRUF in Florida. Barber provided the play-by-play commentary for the Reds–Cubs game on Opening Day of the 1934 season. It was the first baseball game he ever attended in person.

Barber spent five years as the Reds broadcaster until MacPhail, recently hired by the Brooklyn Dodgers, brought him east to be the Dodgers broadcaster in 1939. Before then, all the New York teams had agreed to prohibit radio broadcasts of baseball games. Barber soon became a Brooklyn institution, beloved by fans and cherished for his catchphrases infused with Southern charm.

Barber was part of a long line of memorable radio men whose distinctive voices, phrases, or vocal tics helped bring a vividness to the game while broadening baseball's appeal among the radio-listening public. Other radio legends that emerged during the Golden Age of Radio in the 1940s and '50s include Mel Allen (Yankees), Ernie Harwell (Giants, Orioles, and Tigers), Harry Caray (Cardinals, White Sox, and Cubs), Russ Hodges (Giants), Vin Scully (Dodgers), Curt Gowdy (Red Sox), and Jack Buck (Cardinals). Former players—like Dizzy Dean, Pee Wee Reese, Jerry Coleman, Ralph Kiner, Bob Uecker, and others—followed up their playing careers by entering the broadcast booth; some became as well known for their malapropisms as for their baseball insights.

Most owners feared that, if fans could follow the action of their favorite team on the radio from the comfort of their own home, they would stop coming to the ballpark.

Although it was the first such literal crown he received, Ruth earned a fourth straight home run title in 1921. Prior to that, the last player to lead a league for four consecutive years was the aptly nicknamed Frank "Home Run" Baker from 1911 to 1914—a stretch in which Baker hit a *combined* 42 homers. From 1918 to 1931, Ruth was the American League's top home run hitter in 12 of 14 seasons. The only times he fell short were 1922, when he missed nearly a third of the season because of suspensions, but still hit 35 homers in 110 games; and an injury-plagued 1925 campaign, when he hit 25 in 98 games. He finished third and second in those years, respectively.

The home run pinnacle for Ruth, and for the first 85 years of major league baseball, came in 1927. The 60 in '27 stood as a hallowed number for decades. When fellow Yankee Roger Maris finally broke Ruth's record in 1961, he needed 162 games to do it, whereas Ruth's total came in the 154-game season.

Ruth followed with 54 home runs in 1928 and then hit more than 40 in each of the next four seasons, before dipping to 34 in 1933, when he was 38 years old. He retired in 1935 following a brief turn with the Boston Braves. His 714 career home runs stood as the major league record until Hank Aaron broke it four decades later. And don't forget that Ruth reached his number while spending the first four years of his career as a pitcher, appearing in only every fourth or fifth game.

Ruth's fame and influence are most closely tied to his home-run hitting prowess, but he was a true all-around talent. In a 14-year span from 1919 to 1932, he led the league in on-base percentage 10 times, a category in which he ranks second on the career list (behind Ted Williams) with a .474 mark. The rotund Ruth recorded double-digit stolen bases in five different seasons and four times hit more than 10 triples. His .690 career slugging percentage still ranks as the highest of all time. He was the AL's top RBI man five times, and although he led the league only once between 1926 and 1931 (Lou Gehrig, who had the privilege of batting behind Ruth in the Yankee lineup, earned that honor in four of those seasons), Ruth averaged 156 RBI during that stretch. His career total of 2,214 RBI has been surpassed by no one but Hank Aaron. And while Ruth won just one batting title (.378 in 1924), his career average of .342 is the 10th best of all time; Ted Williams is the only player to come after Ruth to surpass him in that category.

BABE RUTH WEARING HIS HOME RUN CROWN, 1921.

BABE RUTH SWINGING FOR THE FENCES, CIRCA 1927.

Although it seems an almost-comical suggestion today, many contemporaries criticized Ruth's obsession with the home run. Players, managers, writers, and fans alike argued that such a bombastic show not only sullied the game's integrity, but it was actually a less effective strategy. Ty Cobb, the poster child for the "scientific" approach of using placement and precision to get on base, was one of the most vocal detractors of Ruth and the rise of slugging. Cobb and others suggested that trying to hit the ball as hard as possible to send it over the fences did not require the same level of skill as place hitting did. As Ruth's celebrity grew, Cobb set out to show that hitting home runs wasn't all that hard and that any hitter worth his salt could do it if he set his mind to it. To prove his point, during a game in May 1925, Cobb eschewed his normal choked-up grip and swung for the fences. He connected for three home runs (along with a double and two singles in a 6-for-6 performance). The next day he belted two more. To this day, nobody has hit more than five home runs over two consecutive games (many, though not Ruth, have tied it).

Despite the naysayers, fans quickly came around to embrace the excitement of the home run. Players, too, followed suit. By the time Ruth retired, guys like Jimmie Foxx, Mel Ott, Hank Greenberg, Chuck Klein, Hack Wilson, and fellow Bronx Bomber Lou Gehrig had picked up the mantle of home run slugger.

Ruth was a larger-than-life figure who pursued a carefree lifestyle. With affable charm to go along with his otherworldly talents, Ruth captured the imagination of fans everywhere and became a veritable national celebrity. His name and likeness were used to promote all sorts of products, from breakfast cereal and candy to underwear and cigarettes. Ruth and the Yanks drew record numbers of fans not only to Yankee Stadium but to visiting ballparks as well. He did much to restore interest in baseball after the dark years of World War I and the Black Sox scandal of 1919.

Of course, it wasn't all about the number or the distance of his home runs. Ruth's Yankees were winners, too. They captured seven pennants and four World Series in his 15 seasons with the club. And that winning tradition continued long after he hung up his pinstripes. Babe Ruth not only changed the way the game was played, but he helped to build the most successful franchise in professional sports. He was indeed "King Ruth."

ROGERS HORNSBY MVP AWARD, 1925.

41

Rogers Hornsby's MVP Trophy, 1925

RAJAH RULES THE NL

In 1924, the National League bestowed a Most Valuable Player Award for the first time since the Chalmers Award of 1911–1914. That year the honor went to Brooklyn's Dazzy Vance, who won the pitching Triple Crown (28–6, 2.16 ERA, 262 strikeouts). The second-place finisher was St. Louis Cardinals second baseman Rogers Hornsby, who had an astronomical .424 batting average. That mark not only set him 50 points ahead of the second-place finisher in the batting race, but it ranks as the highest single-season average in post-1900 National League history.

The 1925 following year, Hornsby left no doubt that he was the league's Most Valuable Player. For that distinction, he took home the medallion pictured here. He earned it by posting his third .400 season since 1922 and winning the NL Triple Crown (39 homers, 143 RBI, .403 average) for the second time in four years. His .756 slugging percentage was the highest in NL history to that point, and it remained the NL record until 2001 (when Barry Bonds broke it).

The MVP season capped off an amazing six-year run for Hornsby that is unmatched in baseball history. From 1920 to 1925, "Rajah" won six consecutive batting titles and led the league in hits, doubles, and RBI four times each. He also had the most home runs twice in that period and the most runs scored three times. Not only did he become one of only two players ever to win two Triple Crowns (Ted Williams, in 1942 and 1947, is the other) and one of only three to bat over .400 three times (joining Ed Delahanty and Ty Cobb), but Rajah became the only person in major league baseball history to lead a league in batting average, on-base percentage, *and* slugging percentage in six consecutive seasons. His combined batting average over this period was .397, and he averaged 118 runs scored and 115 runs driven in. If you drop the 1920 season out of the equation, the numbers jump to .402, 123 runs,

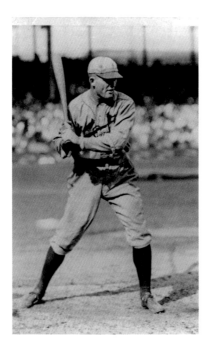

ROGERS HORNSBY AT THE PLATE, 1920S.

and 120 RBI, to go along with 29 homers, 41 doubles, and 13 triples per season.

As the emergence of Babe Ruth signaled the end of the Dead-Ball Era in 1919, Hornsby stood out as the dominant hitter in the National League for the better part of the next decade. After averaging .310 through his first five seasons (1915–1919), Rajah busted out with a league-best .370 in 1920. He also topped the NL in hits, doubles, RBI, slugging, and on-base percentage. His nine home runs, though not quite a Ruthian total, ranked him sixth in the senior circuit.

Hornsby improved across the statistical board in 1921, batting .397 and again leading in nearly every major offensive stat, adding runs and triples to his title categories from the previous year. He also jacked up his home run total, driving 21 long balls, two behind the NL leader (New York's George Kelly).

The 1922 season marked a true breakthrough. By belting 42 home runs and driving in 152 runs—both career bests for the future Hall of Famer—to go along with a .401 batting average, Hornsby became the first National Leaguer in 44 years to win the Triple Crown. He was also the only player ever to bat .400 and hit more than 40 homers in the same season. That year he tallied 250 base hits, setting a new NL record (which stood for seven years), and again outpaced his league mates in most stats.

Despite injuries that limited him to 107 games in 1923, Hornsby led the way with a .384 average and .627 slugging percentage. In addition to his phenomenal .424 average and 1.203 OPS in 1924, he finished second in the league in homers (25) and seventh in RBI (94)—failing to win those categories may be what denied him the MVP Award. That, or the fact that Hornsby's surly attitude didn't endear him to the voting committee of baseball writers (not to diminish Dazzy Vance's accomplishments that year, however).

Following his MVP campaign of 1925, the 30-year-old second baseman struggled in 1926—by his standards, anyway. He failed to lead the league in any major category and posted his lowest average (.317) since 1918. But his attentions were focused elsewhere. After taking over as the Cardinals' skipper early in the 1925 season, player-manager Hornsby led St. Louis to its first World Series in 1926. The Cards defeated the mighty New York Yankees in a seven-game series.

Just over three months after bringing the franchise its first championship trophy since its American Association days, Hornsby was traded away over a salary dispute. Long coveted by manager John McGraw, he was sent to the New York Giants for Frankie Frisch in a swap of Hall of Fame second basemen. Hornsby batted .361 and led the NL with 133 runs and a .448 on-base percentage, but it would be his only season as a Giant. He was shipped to Boston to join the Braves, where he once again posted a trifecta of league highs in average, slugging, and on-base percentage. And once again it was a brief, one-year stay for the now-seven-time batting champ.

Hornsby took his talents to the Windy City and donned a Chicago Cubs uniform. Although his impressive .380 average, 39 homers, and 149 RBI were each only good enough for third best in the NL during the offensive explosion of 1929, Hornsby won his second MVP trophy. He also helped the Cubs claim their first pennant in more than a decade.

Appearing in only 42 games as a player in an injury-plagued 1930, the second baseman took the managerial reins for the final four games of that season. In 1931, Hornsby put himself in the lineup for 100 games and led the third-place Cubs in homers, RBI, and average. The 36-year-old player-manager spent considerably more time on the bench in 1932 (making only 70 plate appearances), and after 99 games, the team was sitting in second place. Then he was fired, and Chicago went on to win the pennant without him.

The MVP season capped off an amazing six-year run for Hornsby that is unmatched in baseball history.

Hornsby re-signed with the Cardinals following the 1932 season but was released in late July 1933. His next stop wasn't far away, as he was hired as player-manager of the lowly St. Louis Browns, who shared the same ballpark with the Cards. He remained with the Browns through 1937, without much success, and after bouncing around as a manager in the minor leagues and doing some broadcasting, he briefly returned to manage the Browns in 1952 before finishing out his managerial career with the Reds in 1952–1953. The following decade, he worked as a scout and coach for the expansion New York Mets, but died after the team's first season, at the age of 66.

A baseball man to the end, Rajah got his start in organized ball as a 15-year-old in Texas. He went on to become one of the greatest hitters of all time. Like Ty Cobb, the arrogant and abrasive Hornsby didn't win many popularity contests—Bill James tagged him as the greatest "horse's ass" in baseball history—but his numbers on the field and his drive to succeed put him at the top of the game for more than a decade. His .358 career average is second only to Cobb's .366. No National Leaguer hit more home runs, hit for higher average, or drove in more runs than Hornsby during the 1920s. Today he is celebrated with a statue outside of St. Louis's Busch Stadium and a plaque in Cooperstown.

42

Heinie Groh's "Bottle Bat," circa 1925

VARIATIONS ON THE HITTER'S MOST IMPORTANT TOOL

Heinie Groh spent 16 years in the major leagues, nearly all with the Cincinnati Reds and the New York Giants. A master at drawing walks and laying down bunts, he twice posted the highest on-base percentage in the National League and batted over .300 four times in a five-year span (1917–1921). Groh was a key member of four pennant winners. He led the 1919 world champion Reds in homers and runs scored, and helped the Giants win the 1922 World Series by batting .474 in the five-game series. Groh was also a superior glove-man at third base, leading the league in fielding percentage at his position five times and in double plays six times.

Although Groh had several All-Star-caliber seasons, he finds a place in this book less for what he did with his bat than for what he did *to* his bat.

Groh's first major league manager, John McGraw, encouraged him to try a bat with a large barrel. But the 5-foot, 8-inch-tall Groh had trouble gripping the large handles of large-barreled bats, so he took it to the Spalding Sporting Goods Company to have it modified. As he explained to Lawrence Ritter in the book *The Glory of Their Times*: "What I wanted was a bat with a big butt end but with a skinny handle, so I could get a good grip and swing it. We whittled down the handle of a standard bat, and then we built up the barrel, and when we were finished it looked like a crazy sort of milk bottle or a round paddle." Groh choked up to get better control of the weighty, top-heavy bat.

Groh's adaptation was one brief sidestep in the evolution of arguably the sport's most important tool. In the earliest days of the game, batters would step to the plate with rods of ash, maple, or pine in varying sizes, including, according to Henry

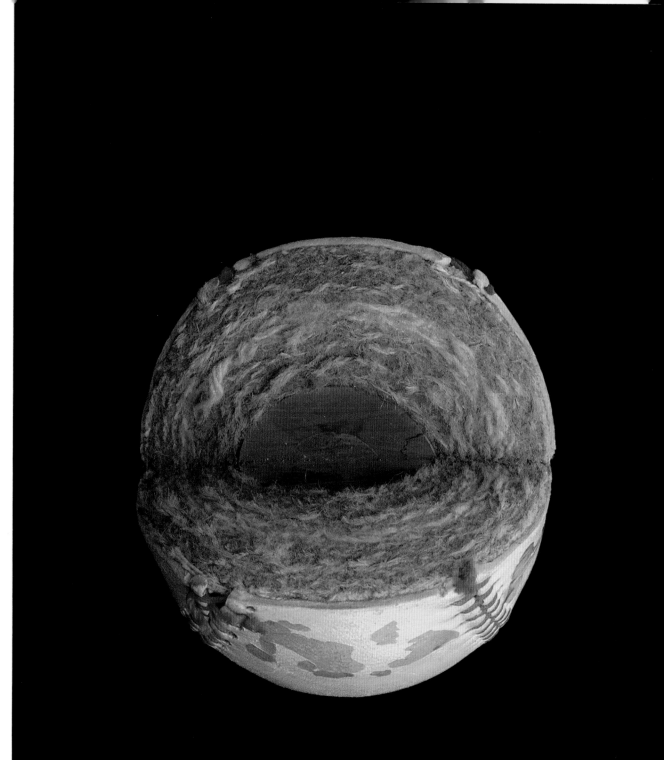

CROSS-SECTION OF A BASEBALL, CIRCA 1950.

baseballs, caused a slight increase in scoring in the years 1911–1913, but scoring was back down to pre-1910 levels in the latter half of the decade. A cushioned cork center (basically, a different type of rubber surrounding the cork) was introduced in 1925. Although scoring jumped to over 5.0 runs per game for the first time in the century that year, there was no sustained period of inflated scoring, and the average dropped back to 4.6 in 1926.

In 1930, however, the official balls for Major League Baseball reportedly included an extra layer of rubber around the cork center, in an effort to make them more resilient. The result was the greatest offensive explosion since the turn of the twentieth century. Teams scored an average of 5.6 runs per game. The leaguewide batting average was .296, the second highest of all time, after 1894. A total of 1,565 home runs were hit, 2 1/2 times the number that were hit a decade earlier. Chicago Cub Hack Wilson set new National League records with 56 homers and 191 RBI; the former held as the NL high-water mark until 1998, while the latter remains a major league record in 2014. Bill Terry of the Giants hit .401, the last .400 season in the National League. Philadelphia Phillie Chuck Klein collected 107 extra-base hits, a number matched only one time since (Barry Bonds, in 2001).

Rumors of juiced or lively balls have circulated at other times as well, but for the most part the makeup of the ball has remained unchanged since 1925. (Wartime restrictions led to the use of a synthetic rubber center for a period during World War II.)

The current requirements for the circumference (9.0–9.25 inches) and weight (5.0–5.25 ounces) of baseballs have been in place since 1872. Horsehide was the standard cover material since the earliest days of organized baseball; cowhide was added to the rule book as an acceptable material in 1974. To cushion the hard cork-and-rubber center, a combination of wool and cotton yarn is wound around the core. A two-piece leather cover is then hand-sewn together with exactly 108 stitches.

After many decades of teams providing their own balls from a variety of manufacturers, the quality and content of baseballs used in league games was standardized in 1877, when A. G. Spalding & Brothers became the official and exclusive provider of baseballs for the National League. The A. J. Reach Company served that role for the American League upon that league's birth in 1900. The Rawlings Sporting Goods Company has been Major League Baseball's official source of balls since 1977.

Before being stamped as an MLB "official" ball, every single one goes through rigorous testing to make sure it meets the basic requirements. A few overly tightly wound or too loosely packed balls might slip through now and again, but the leagues have endeavored to maintain consistency in the "bounce" or liveliness in their balls for many decades.

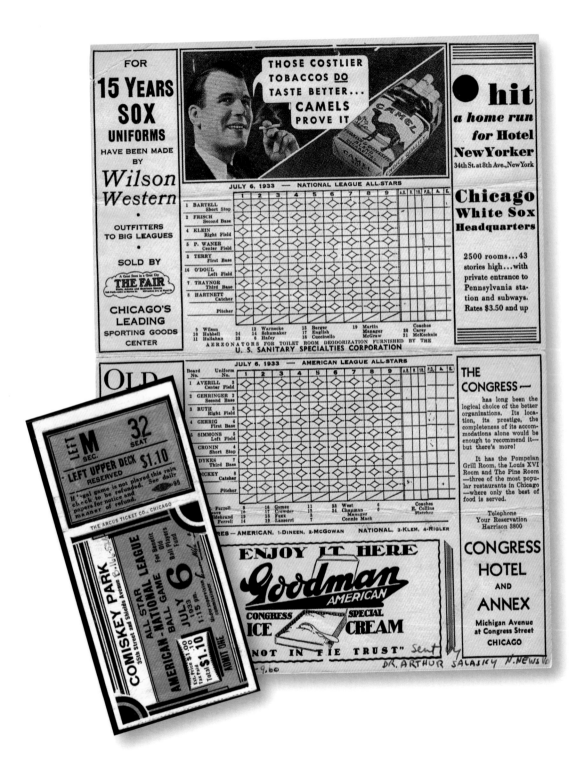

44

All-Star Game Scorecard and Ticket Stub, 1933

THE MIDSUMMER CLASSIC IS BORN

On July 6, 1933, St. Louis Cardinals pitcher Bill Hallahan had to face a batting order that included six future Hall of Famers: Charlie Gehringer, Babe Ruth, Lou Gehrig, Al Simmons, Joe Cronin, and Rick Ferrell. He walked away from the experience having allowed three runs and two hits while walking five batters in two innings of work, earning the loss.

Fortunately, Hallahan—as well as his replacements Lon Warneke of the Cubs and Giants lefty Carl Hubbell—had to face that formidable lineup for only one afternoon and for a game that did not count in the standings or against their individual stats. And these pitchers had some pretty impressive hitters backing them up as well, including reigning MVP and 1933 Triple Crown winner Chuck Klein, former .400 hitter Bill Terry, 1931 NL MVP Frankie Frisch, and future Hall of Famer Chick Hafey, among others. Heck, the two teams had seven future Hall of Fame hitters sitting on the bench when the game got underway.

This scorecard for the 1933 All-Star Game had the expected starting lineups printed on it, but the managers on both sides made some last-minute adjustments. Considering that the skippers for the contest were the legendary Connie Mack and John McGraw—the latter coming out of retirement to head the NL squad—you can excuse some lineup tweaking.

Mack led the American Leaguers to a 4–2 win. Yankee pitcher Lefty Gomez earned the win as the starter and helped his own cause with an RBI single in the second for the game's first run. Another "Lefty," Robert "Lefty" Grove of Mack's Athletics, shut the National Leaguers out through the final three innings to earn the

ALL-STAR GAME SCORECARD AND TICKET STUB, 1933.

PITTSBURGH CRAWFORDS TEAM BUS, 1935.

45

Pittsburgh Crawfords
Team Bus, 1935

A VERY BRIEF HISTORY
OF THE NEGRO LEAGUES

The Pittsburgh Crawfords had one of the most talented lineups in all of organized baseball in the mid-1930s. Boasting Josh Gibson, James "Cool Papa" Bell, Oscar Charleston, Judy Johnson, and Satchel Paige—all members of the Baseball Hall of Fame—the Crawfords won back-to-back league titles in 1935 and 1936 and drew big crowds wherever they played. They were the elite of the Negro National League.

Founded by Pittsburgh numbers racketeer Gus Greenlee in 1931 as an independent team, the Crawfords were funded largely by Greenlee's gambling operations. This backing, along with the team's popularity among Pittsburgh's African-American community, allowed Greenlee to build his team its own ballpark, Greenlee Field, in 1932, when most black teams played at white-owned major or minor league parks. Greenlee also bought his Crawfords their own team bus, pictured here, in which they traveled in style from city to city during their championship seasons.

Greenlee was instrumental in organizing the new league for African Americans in 1933. His Negro National League was established in the wake of the demise of the original Negro National League, which operated from 1920 to 1931. The new league debuted in 1933 with eight teams, and over its 16-year history, as many as 18 different clubs held a spot in the NNL. Only the Elite Giants lasted the duration, moving from Nashville to Columbus to Washington to Baltimore during that time. Greenlee owned the Crawfords through 1938, when he sold the team due to financial troubles; the Craws then spent a season each in Toledo and Indianapolis before folding.

RUBE FOSTER, 1920S.

featured the Unknown of Weeksville (now part of Brooklyn) against the Henson Base Ball Club of Jamaica (now in Queens) in 1859.

In 1867, a black team from Philadelphia, the Pythians, applied for membership in the National Association of Base Ball Players. Their application was rejected, and the NABBP's nominating committee unanimously voted to bar admission to "any club which may be composed of one or more colored persons."

As the exclusion of African Americans from organized baseball became more entrenched, more independent black teams were being formed. The first attempt at organizing a league for such teams was the Southern League of Colored Base Ballists, in 1886. Comprising teams from Charleston, Savannah, Jacksonville, Memphis, and New Orleans, the league survived only a few weeks. Another attempt in 1887 included teams based in larger cities in the Northeast, the Mid-Atlantic, and the

Midwest. The National League of Colored Base Ball Clubs even agreed to adhere to the National Agreement that governed the white leagues, but alas it too collapsed within a month of its opening games.

Nevertheless, the number of black teams continued to grow after the turn of the twentieth century. Teams barnstormed across their states or regions, occasionally playing white clubs in exhibitions. With the successful establishment of the Negro National League in 1920, other owners followed suit in getting together to form leagues. The Negro Southern League, also established in 1920, was a minor league that lasted for more than two decades.

In 1923, the Eastern Colored League (ECL) emerged as a rival to Foster's league. The foundations for the new league were the Hilldale club, based outside of Philadelphia, and the Bacharach Giants of Atlantic City, both of which had been associate members of the Negro National League, meaning they could play other teams in the league but not compete for the championship. The owners of the Bacharach Giants and the Hilldale club decided to break away and form their own league, enlisting four other clubs for 1923 and two more in 1924. After two seasons of raiding each other's rosters for players, the rival leagues reached a peace, and they agreed to hold an annual Colored World Series. Hilldale, which featured Hall of Famers Judy Johnson and Biz Mackey, won the first three ECL titles and the 1925 Colored World Series. The Bacharach Giants won the ECL pennant in 1926 and 1927, but lost to the Chicago American Giants in the Colored World Series both years. Disputes over player contracts and between owners led to the demise of the Eastern Colored League midway through the 1928 season.

The various leagues that formed between 1920 and the integration of Major League Baseball in 1947 provided a rich showcase for the top African-American talent in the nation. Outside of league competition, teams would play assorted amateur, semipro, and professional squads, of either race. Exhibitions pitting Negro League All-Stars against Major League All-Stars also took place during baseball's segregated era, and the Negro Leaguers held their own against such elite white talents as Bob Feller, Dizzy Dean, Joe DiMaggio, and others.

With the void left by the collapse of the first Negro National League in 1931, Gus Greenlee was able to establish a new incarnation in 1933 that would survive into the late 1940s, when the integration of Major League Baseball siphoned off not only players from the Negro Leagues but also fan interest.

"RECOMMENDATIONS FOR LIGHTING," CROSLEY FIELD, 1935.

46

"Recommendations for Lighting," Crosley Field, 1935

NIGHT BASEBALL

On the evening of May 24, 1935, with just over 20,000 fans in attendance at Cincinnati's Crosley Field, President Franklin D. Roosevelt turned a switch at the White House in Washington, D.C., which sent a signal to Reds general manager Larry MacPhail standing along the third-base line in Cincinnati, who then flipped a switch turning on 632 lights that had been installed at the ballpark. Under the glow of artificial lights, the Reds and the Philadelphia Phillies played the first night game in major league baseball history. (The Reds won, 2–1.)

Prior to the season, the Westinghouse Electric Company presented this proposal for illuminating the ballpark sufficiently for players and fans. It included recommendations on the types of equipment, on ideal locations for light towers, and on floodlights and lamps.

Cincinnati hosted seven night games in 1935, one against each National League opponent. The team's attendance reached its highest level since 1928, even as the Reds finished in sixth place, 31 1/2 games out of first.

Despite the successful run in Cincinnati, many owners and executives remained skeptical, dismissing night baseball as a "gimmick" that would only hurt the sport. Detroit Tigers owner Frank Navin declared that night baseball would be "the beginning of the end of major league baseball." Ed Barrow of the New York Yankees saw no future in "electric-lighted play" and called night games a "wart on the nose of the game." The American League went so far as to impose a ban on night baseball.

But as teams struggled to bring in fans in the midst of the Great Depression, owners looked to night games as a way to attract a wider fan base. The Brooklyn

By the end of the 1941 season, 11 of the 16 major league clubs had lights installed at their home parks.

Dodgers, who hired MacPhail as team president in 1938, installed lights at Ebbets Field that very year. In the ballpark's first night game, on June 15, Cincinnati's Johnny Vander Meer pitched a no-hitter, his second in as many starts. A year later, on May 16, 1939, the Philadelphia Athletics became the first American League team to host night baseball.

By the end of the 1941 season, 11 of the 16 major league clubs had lights installed at their home parks. One club that was to begin construction of a lighting system that December was the Chicago Cubs. The Japanese attack on Pearl Harbor interrupted those plans, however, and the materials were given over to the War Department to support the war effort. It would be another 47 years before lights were installed at Chicago's Wrigley Field, the last of the original 16 teams to host night baseball—by a margin of 40 years. (The Tigers, then owned by Walter Briggs Sr., finally relented in 1948.)

The advent of World War II proved to be a stimulus, rather than a deterrent, for the expansion of night baseball. In his "Green Light" letter, reassuring baseball's owners that the game should go on in spite of the war, FDR suggested that more night games be played so that people working day shifts could attend games. The limit of allowable night games per team was doubled from 7 to 14, until the restriction was lifted completely.

MacPhail's efforts in Cincinnati ushered in night games as a regular part of baseball, but the first recorded night game at the amateur level took place decades earlier. That occurred on September 2, 1880—one year after Thomas Edison filed a patent for his incandescent lightbulb—when two department store teams played under lights at Oceanside Park in Hull, Massachusetts. To illuminate the field, the Northern Electric Light Company installed a system of massed lamps erected on wooden towers.

A handful of other night games were played at the amateur and minor league levels in the late 1800s and early 1900s, to

NIGHT GAME AT CROSLEY FIELD, 1935.

varying degrees of success. The first professional team to create a system of lights for regular night games was the Kansas City Monarchs of the Negro Leagues. First used in 1930, the lights were mounted on pickup trucks and could be taken on the road. The Monarchs' success inspired other minor league and Negro League teams to build their own ballpark lighting systems.

By late 1934, Larry MacPhail was able to convince a skeptical commissioner and group of owners to allow him to schedule night baseball under lights for his Reds. His efforts revolutionized how the game was experienced. These days, most regular-season games, and every World Series and All-Star Game, are played under lights.

NEW YORK YANKEES WORLD CHAMPION BATS, 1936–39.

47

New York Yankees World Champion Bats, 1936–1939

BASEBALL'S GREATEST DYNASTY

Beginning in 1934, the Hillerich & Bradsby Company, manufacturer of Louisville Slugger baseball bats, produced commemorative bats for the World Series champions from each year. The bats, produced in limited numbers for team members and executives, were adorned with the facsimile signatures of the players and manager.

Every year from 1936 to 1939, H&B's world champion bats were emblazoned with the signatures of the New York Yankees. These bats represent the first time one team ever won four consecutive World Series—and they represent one of baseball's greatest dynasties.

The Yankees of 1936–1939 were dominant from start to finish. In 1936 they took over first place on May 10 and never looked back. In 1939 New York held or shared first place for all but four game days. The Yanks won an average of 102 regular-season games over the four years. They scored the most runs and allowed the fewest in the American League in every one of those seasons. The closest any other team finished in the standings was 9 games back (Boston in 1938); twice New York's lead at season's end was 17 games or more.

The Yankees were just as dominating in the postseason. The New York Giants managed to win two games in the 1936 World Series, but the Yanks outscored them by a 43–23 margin over the six games. Their 18–4 victory in Game 2 stands as the most runs ever scored by one team in a World Series game. The following year, the Yanks beat the Giants in five games, winning the first three by a 21–3 combined score. The National League representative failed to win a single game against the Bombers in each of the next two Fall Classics. In the four-game sweep of the Cubs in 1938, the Yanks outscored their opponents 22–9. The Cincinnati Reds scored a total of eight runs in four games in '39.

Lou Gehrig, still in his prime at the tender age of 33, was named the American League's Most Valuable Player in the title year of 1936. His 49 homers, 167 runs, .478 on-base percentage, and .696 slugging average were all better than anyone else in the majors; he also drove in 152 runs and batted .354. In 1937 he finished among the AL's top three in homers, RBI, and batting average. He started to slip in 1938, and his average dropped below .300 for first time since 1925, his first full season. Yet, the "Iron Horse" still played in every game and scored and drove in more than 100 runs for the 13th consecutive year. He also appeared in his final World Series. A member of six world champion teams, Gehrig batted .361 and drove in 35 runs in 34 career World Series games.

Then tragedy struck in 1939. Although the source of his struggles wasn't clear at the time, he was suffering from ALS—better known as Lou Gehrig's disease—which dramatically affected his ability to play. On May 2, Gehrig informed manager Joe McCarthy that he would not be in the lineup that day. It was the first time he'd sat out since June 1925, a streak of 2,130 consecutive games. Gehrig, the team captain and a native New Yorker, remained on the bench through the spring but would not play again. On June 21, he officially announced his retirement. On July 4, the Yankees held "Lou Gehrig Appreciation Day," where the longtime first baseman was honored with gifts and accolades, and where he gave his famous "luckiest man" speech. The Yankees retired his uniform number, 4, making him the first baseball player so honored.

An all-time legend in his own right, Gehrig provided the transition out of the "Ruth Era" of Yankee history and into the "DiMaggio Era." "Joltin' Joe" DiMaggio was a rookie when the Yankees began their streak of four straight titles in 1936. The 21-year-old center fielder batted .323 with 29 homers and 125 RBI in 138 games. In the repeat-pennant season of 1937, he led the AL with 46 homers and 151 runs, while driving in 167 and upping his average to .346; he finished second in the MVP voting. DiMaggio was among the league leaders in homers, runs, RBI, and slugging in 1938.

Despite playing in only 120 games due to injury, and despite losing the protection of having Gehrig hitting behind him, DiMaggio was the AL MVP in 1939. He posted a career-best .381 average and a fourth straight season with at least 100 runs and 100 RBI. Through his first four major league seasons, the "Yankee Clipper" had a .341 batting average, a .622 slugging percentage, 137 home runs, more than 500 runs and RBI, and four All-Star Game appearances. And he was just 24 years old. (DiMaggio's later career exploits are explored with **Object #50.**)

Gehrig and DiMaggio may be the biggest names from this Yankee juggernaut, but they also had a Hall of Fame catcher in Bill Dickey, who put forth the best four seasons of his 17-year career from 1936 to 1939. He batted over .300, drove in at least 100 runs, and belted more than 20 homers in each of those seasons. Dickey was one of the best-fielding catchers of his or any day. In all, he was a member of seven Yankee world championship teams.

Dickey had the task of catching one of baseball's best pitching staffs as well. Although the Bronx Bombers are best remembered for their power at the plate, the Yanks of the late 1930s dominated from the mound as well. They led the American League in ERA every season from 1936 to 1939. Their 3.31 team mark in '39 was more than a full run lower than the league average (4.62). Lefty Gomez and Red Ruffing were the aces of the rotation, and both are in the Hall of Fame.

MANAGER JOE MCCARTHY WITH LOU GEHRIG, RED RUFFING, LEFTY GOMEZ, JOE DIMAGGIO, BILL DICKEY, AND RED ROLFE, 1938.

TELEVISION CAMERAS AT YANKEE STADIUM, CIRCA 1950.

certain teams. In late 1966, NBC bought the exclusive national television rights to Major League Baseball. The network paid just over $12 million to televise 25 *Games of the Week*, the All-Star Game, and the World Series in 1967.

From 1976 through 1989, ABC and NBC split the rights: ABC got the Monday night telecasts, NBC the Saturday afternoon games, and they alternated postseason coverage. In December 1988, CBS signed a contract worth about $265 million per year for the rights to the *Game of the Week*, the All-Star Game, and the entire postseason. Less than a month later, Major League Baseball agreed to a four-year, $400 million deal with ESPN for the cable rights to a specified number of regular-season games.

After a failed attempt at its own television network, the Baseball Network, as a joint venture with ABC and NBC in the mid-1990s, Major League Baseball introduced the 24-hour MLB Network in 2009. Between that and national deals with the Turner Sports networks TBS and TNT, ESPN, and FOX Sports—not to mention local network contracts with individual teams—nearly every major league game can be viewed on television today. The eight-year deals that MLB signed with ESPN,

RCA TRK-12 MODEL TELEVISION SET, 1939.

FOX, and TBS alone are worth $1.5 billion per year, beginning in 2014. The Los Angeles Dodgers signed a contract with Time Warner Cable that brings them $8.35 billion over 25 years, the largest local television deal.

Although Branch Rickey may have been onto something when he commented, in the early 1950s, that "once a television set has broken [people] of the ballpark habit, a great many fans will never reacquire it," there is little doubt that television has been an incredible financial boon to the sport.

PART V

WAR AND INTEGRATION

. . . .

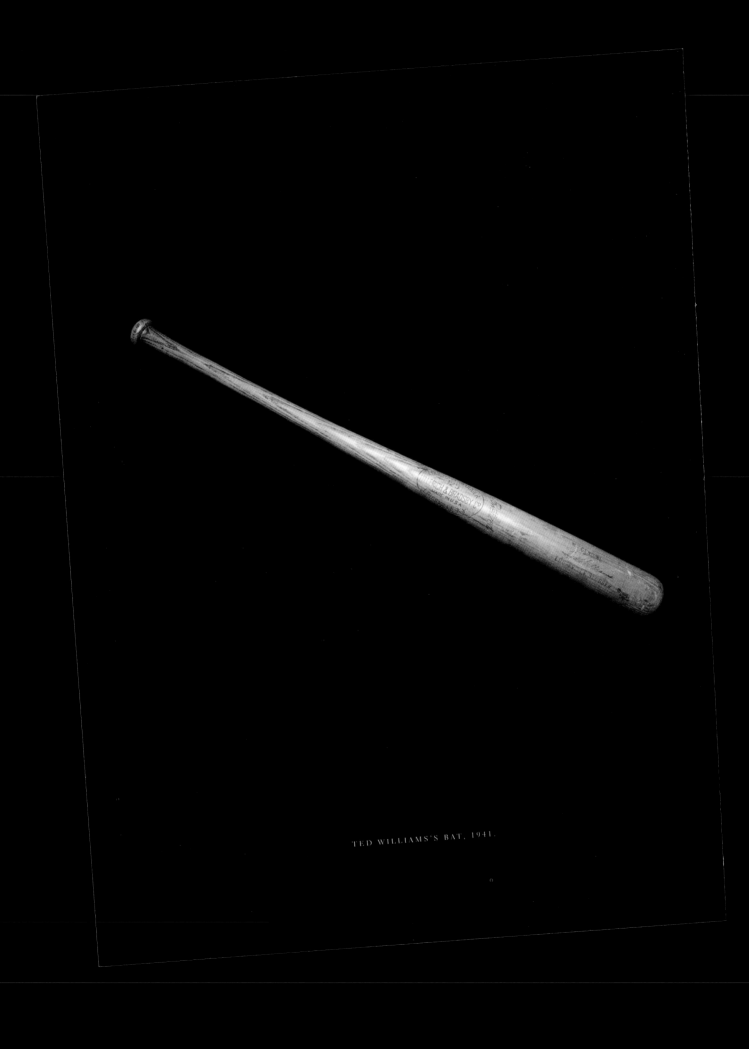

TED WILLIAMS'S BAT, 1941.

49

Ted Williams's Bat, 1941

THE "GREATEST HITTER THAT EVER LIVED" BATS .406

In any discussion of the greatest hitter in baseball history, the name Ted Williams will inevitably come up as a leading contender. In 1941, he wielded this 33-ounce hunk of ash to post a .406 batting average. It was only the 13th time since 1900 that anyone had hit better than .400 in a season and the first time in more than a decade. What nobody could know at the time was that it would also be the last time (to date) that any major leaguer broke the .400 plateau.

Williams began his career with the Boston Red Sox in 1939 at the age of 20. He batted .327 with 31 homers and a 1.045 on-base plus slugging percentage as a rookie. He ended his career, still with Boston, in 1960 at age 42. That year, he batted .316 with 29 homers and a 1.096 OPS. Although he was not selected for the All-Star Game in his rookie year, he was in every other active season of his career.

Beyond hitting .406 in '41, Williams also led the American League in home runs (37), runs scored (135), walks (147), and both on-base and slugging percentages. His 1.287 OPS ranks as the seventh best in history, bested only by Babe Ruth and Barry Bonds (three times each). His .553 OBP stood as the single-season record until Bonds broke it 61 years later.

Somewhat amazingly, Williams was not considered the Most Valuable Player in the American League that year. Instead, the award was given to Joe DiMaggio, with his 56-game hitting streak. Perhaps more amazingly, Williams failed to muster enough MVP votes to take home the trophy in either of his Triple Crown seasons. In 1942, he lost out to another Yankee, Joe Gordon, despite posting league-high numbers with 36 homers, 137 RBI, a .356 average, 141 runs, 145 walks, .499 OPB, and .648 slugging percentage. Five years later, another Triple Crown season ended with another MVP

PLAYERS	Pos.	1	2	3	4	5	6	7	8	9	10	11	12	AB	R	H	PO	A	E
Sturm	1b	43		8			4		4										
Rolfe	3b				K	43		4											
Henrich	rf			43			43												
Di Maggio	cf				8		63	43											
Gordon	2b		8	8					44										
Rosar	c		63		7	4		8											
Keller	lf		4		43			8											
Rizzuto	ss		43	K		63	53												
Gomez	p		K		K	4	K												
Murphy	p																		
Totals		0	0	0	0	0	0	1	0						4	0			

50

Yankees – Indians Scorecard, July 17, 1941

"JOLTIN' JOE" DIMAGGIO'S UNBEATABLE HITTING STREAK

On July 17, 1941, the New York Yankees' cleanup hitter grounded out three times and walked once against the Cleveland Indians. His team won, 4–3, in front of 67,468 fans at Cleveland Stadium.

What is notable about the 0-for-3 performance by Yankees center fielder Joe DiMaggio in this fairly inconsequential midseason game is that it was the first time since May 14—a span of 56 games—that the "Yankee Clipper" failed to collect a base hit.

On the morning of May 15, DiMaggio had a .306 average, and the Yanks were sitting in fourth place with a 14–14 record. By the morning of July 17, before his streak came to an end, DiMaggio's average had climbed to .375, and the Yankees had climbed into first place, six games up, with a 55–27 record. New York would go on to win the American League by a 17-game margin and win their fifth World Series in six seasons. DiMaggio would go on to bat .357 for the year and take home his second American League Most Valuable Player trophy.

The 56-game hitting streak is one of those storied records that most agree is unlikely to be broken. In the more than 70 major league seasons since DiMaggio's magical run, the closest any player has gotten is 44 games, achieved by Pete Rose in 1978. Going back through the 70 major league seasons prior to 1941, only Willie Keeler came within a dozen games of 56, when he hit safely in the first 44 games in 1897; adding in his final game of 1896, the streak ran a total of 45 games. Other than DiMaggio and Rose, only two players since 1900 have hit safely in as many as 40 consecutive games: Ty Cobb in 1911 (40) and George Sisler in 1922 (41). In the

STAN MUSIAL'S MVP AWARD, 1946.

52

Stan Musial's MVP Award, 1946

"STAN THE MAN" LEADS A
REDBIRD DYNASTY

As the United States, and the world, was recovering from the trauma and devastation of the Second World War, the left fielder/first baseman for the St. Louis Cardinals helped to restore some sense of normalcy in the first postwar baseball season. Stan Musial had been among the hundreds of major leaguers called to duty during the war. He spent 1945 with the U.S. Navy, and shortly after being discharged in March 1946, he rejoined the Cardinals for spring training.

When the regular season got underway, Musial picked up where he had left off prior to his naval service. "Stan the Man" hit safely in 15 of the first 17 games to start the 1946 season. He was batting .420 on May 7. He cooled off a bit—but not much. At season's end, the 25-year-old Musial won the second batting title of his career with a .365 average. He also led all National Leaguers in runs, hits, doubles, triples, slugging, and OPS. It was good enough to earn Musial his second Most Valuable Player trophy and send St. Louis to the World Series for the fourth time in five years.

Musial's first MVP season, 1943, was also his first as NL batting champ, when he also led in hits, doubles, triples, on-base percentage, and slugging percentage, in just his second full season.. He was no slouch as a rookie in 1942, either. At just 21 years of age, Musial batted .315—the first of 16 consecutive seasons in which he hit over .300—as the Cards claimed the pennant and won the World Series against the New York Yankees. Musial and St. Louis won the NL crown again in '43 (this time, they lost to the Yanks in the Fall Classic) and then made it three in a row in '44. They beat their ballpark mates, the St. Louis Browns, in the 1944 World Series.

Beyond being one of the greatest individual players of his or any generation, Musial was perhaps the greatest in the history of one of baseball's most storied franchises.

After defeating Ted Williams and the Boston Red Sox in the 1946 World Series, Musial would not see the postseason again, despite playing 17 more years with St. Louis. He did win a third MVP Award in 1948, compiling career-high totals in hits (230), runs (135), homers (39), RBI (131), average (.376), OBP (.450), and slugging percentage (.702). He added more batting crowns to his shelf in 1950–1952 and another in '57. Only Honus Wagner and Tony Gwynn have more NL batting titles than Musial's seven.

When Musial retired in 1963, he held the all-time record for base hits by a National Leaguer, with 3,630. At the time, Ty Cobb was the only player in major league history with more; as of 2015, Musial ranks fourth overall. Only Mel Ott had hit more home runs in NL history at the time of Musial's retirement. He never led the league, but Stan the Man knocked more than 25 homers in nine seasons between 1948 and 1957. To this day, he ranks in the all-time top 10 in both runs scored and RBI. With a .331 lifetime average, 475 career homers, 1,951 RBI, 1,949 runs, and a record 24 consecutive All-Star team selections, Musial was all but guaranteed a spot in Cooperstown. He was

STAN MUSIAL AT BAT, 1946.

inducted into the Hall of Fame in his first year of eligibility, garnering more than 93 percent of the vote.

Beyond being one of the greatest individual players of his or any generation, Musial was perhaps the greatest in the history of one of baseball's most storied franchises. Nobody has played more games in a Cardinals uniform than Musial, and he holds the all-time franchise record in nearly every major hitting category. In addition to winning four pennants during a five-year span in the 1940s, Musial's Cardinals had five second-place finishes in the decade, including 1941 (when a 19-year-old Musial appeared in only 12 games) and 1945 (when Musial was in the Navy). St. Louis struggled in the late 1950s, posting five losing seasons—the only sub-.500 seasons of Musial's long career—but the team rarely finished in the second division with Musial on hand. The Cards finished in second place in Musial's final season of 1963, before winning three of the next five NL pennants without him.

Widely admired and respected by teammates, opponents, fans, and the media, Stan was indeed the man during more than two decades of baseball.

JACKIE ROBINSON'S BROOKLYN DODGERS UNIFORM.

53

Jackie Robinson's Brooklyn Dodgers Uniform, 1947

BREAKING BASEBALL'S COLOR BARRIER

Few objects in baseball annals represent a more significant moment in the history of our national pastime than the uniform worn by the Brooklyn Dodgers' first baseman at Ebbets Field on April 15, 1947. After Jackie Robinson took the field in a major league uniform, baseball would never be the same. For the first time, the men playing the game could be chosen based on their abilities, not the color of their skin.

The jersey shown here is not the one worn by Robinson in his debut, but his Brooklyn number 42 is an iconic object in the evolution of the sport and the nation. Fifty years after Robinson's historic debut, in 1997, the number 42 was retired throughout Major League Baseball in his honor.

The decision by Dodgers president and general manager Branch Rickey to peg Robinson as the man to break baseball's "color barrier" was based not solely on Robinson's superior abilities on the diamond but also on the strength of his character. The player who was to take on this trailblazing role would have to display the psychological and mental fortitude to withstand the inevitable abuse from fans and fellow players, while resisting the urge to fight back.

JACKIE ROBINSON IN ACTION, CIRCA 1947.

251

Baseball's unofficial, unwritten ban on African Americans had held a firm grip for more than 60 years, since Moses "Fleet" Walker last played for the Toledo Blue Jackets in 1884 (see **Object #16**). In the subsequent decades, no major league owner or general manager put forth serious efforts to sign black players, despite the high level of talent on display in the Negro Leagues throughout the first half of the twentieth century.

Rickey began exploring the possibility of signing an African American shortly after he was hired as general manager by the Dodgers in 1942. On October 23, 1945, with the support of team ownership, he made the leap and officially signed Jackie Robinson to a contract with Brooklyn's minor league affiliate in the International League, the Montreal Royals. It was just a brief first step on the path to the big leagues.

Robinson had been a multisport star at UCLA, where he lettered in baseball, basketball, football, and track. After two years of service in the Army, he spent the 1945 season with the Kansas City Monarchs, one of the elite teams of the Negro Leagues. He joined Montreal the following spring and helped them to an International League championship. Robinson hit a league-best .349, scored 113 runs, stole 40 bases, and walked 92 times while striking out just 27 times in 124 games with the Montreal Royals.

With his team based in Montreal and the International League made up of mostly Northern cities, Robinson was relatively sheltered, although he did encounter plenty of harassment and racism during his time with the Royals. His performance on the field, along with the grace and cool-headedness with which he handled his experience in integrated baseball, proved to Rickey that Robinson was ready to move on to the majors.

And ready he was. Although he went 0 for 3 in his first game, Robinson got a base hit (a bunt single) the next day and went on to bat .297 and score 125 runs on the year. He also led the league in stolen bases. He was selected as the winner of baseball's first Rookie of the Year Award. The Brooklyn Dodgers won the NL pennant that year.

Robinson accomplished all this despite facing frequent abuse from players and fans, and receiving hate mail and other threats. Opposing players threatened to boycott any game against the integrated Dodgers. Philadelphia Phillies manager Ben Chapman was particularly persistent and offensive in the racist invectives directed at Robinson. Commissioner Happy Chandler and National League President Ford Frick both came out in strong support of Rickey and the Dodgers and threatened to punish any player who refused to play against Robinson.

Even some of Robinson's own teammates, led by outfielder "Dixie" Walker, signed a petition saying they would not play alongside a black man. Manager Leo Durocher would have none of it and openly reprimanded the players; Walker was traded at the end of the season. Others were openly supportive, most significantly Brooklyn's Kentucky-born shortstop Pee Wee Reese. During a game in Cincinnati, as Reds players heckled Robinson viciously, Reese put his arm around him on the field and made it clear to everyone that Robinson was their guy and he wasn't going anywhere.

Two years after his Rookie of the Year season, Robinson won the NL's Most Valuable Player Award. He won a batting title (.342), stole a league-high 37 bases, and led the pennant-winning Dodgers with 124 RBI. Robinson was chosen for the All-Star team every year from 1949 to 1954. Over those six seasons, he had a combined .327 batting average and a .933 OPS.

Robinson spent just 10 years in the majors, retiring after the 1956 season at the age of 37. In that time he played in six World Series, including Brooklyn's long-awaited victory in 1955. His speed, smarts, and aggressive base running allowed him to rank among the NL's top 10 base stealers in all but one season. A versatile and talented fielder, he played at least 150 games at four different positions—first base, second base, third base, and outfield—shifting around according to the needs of the Dodger lineups. He was elected into the Hall of Fame in his first year of eligibility, in 1962.

Even with Robinson's extraordinary performance on the field, the full integration of baseball did not happen overnight. By the end of the 1940s, only three other teams (the Cleveland Indians, the St. Louis Browns, and the New York Giants) had joined the Dodgers in opening up their rosters to black players. Ten years after Robinson's debut, the Philadelphia Phillies, the Detroit Tigers, and the Boston Red Sox still had not had any African Americans play for them. (Pumpsie Green debuted with Boston on July 21, 1959, making the Red Sox the last of the 16 major league teams to integrate.)

Even before Robinson made his first appearance in a Brooklyn uniform, Rickey had signed four more African Americans into the Dodgers system in 1946, including catcher Roy Campanella and pitcher Don Newcombe. In late August 1947, just a few months after Robinson's Dodger debut, Rickey signed Dan Bankhead from the Memphis Red Sox of the Negro American League. On August 26, Bankhead became the first black pitcher in a major league game when he came in in relief against the Pirates. He did not fare too well on the mound that day, but he did homer in his first at-bat. Bankhead spent the next two seasons in the minors before rejoining Brooklyn for 1950 and '51.

Campanella first played organized ball in the Negro Leagues when he was just 15 years old. He played nine seasons, mostly with the Baltimore Elite Giants, and after two years in the Dodgers farm system, he arrived in Brooklyn in April 1948. He was a mainstay on the great Dodgers teams over the next decade. A three-time Most Valuable Player, Campanella hit more than 30 homers in a season four times in his 10-year Hall of Fame career.

Newcombe got the call-up in 1949. Although he got hit hard in his debut, he went on to win a team-high 17 games for the NL champions. He was named National League Rookie of Year for 1949. Newcombe then won 19 games in 1950 and 20 in '51 before missing the next two years to military service. He was a 20-game winner again in the world champion season of 1955 and led the league with an impressive 27–7 record in 1956. It was good enough to earn Newk not only the NL MVP trophy but also baseball's first Cy Young Award.

The Dodgers continued to mine the Negro Leagues to bolster their roster. Joe Black pitched for the Elite Giants in the 1940s before joining the Dodgers farm system in 1951. He went 15–4 with a 2.15 ERA and 15 saves in 1952 to become the third Dodger to win the Rookie of the Year Award. Jim "Junior" Gilliam continued that tradition as Brooklyn's rookie second baseman in 1953. He played 13 more years with the Dodgers and was one of the few everyday starters on both the last (and only) Brooklyn title team and the first for the franchise in Los Angeles, in 1959.

Beyond Brooklyn, Larry Doby earned the distinction of being the first black player in the American League as a member of the Cleveland Indians in July 1947. Signed by another pioneering owner, Bill Veeck, Doby went on to a 13-year major league career. He was named to seven consecutive All-Star teams (1949–1955) and won two home run titles. With 32 in 1952, Doby became the first African-American home run king in the majors. For the 1954 AL-champions Indians, he led the league with 32 homers and 126 RBI. Doby was also the first African American to homer in the World Series, a feat he accomplished on October 9, 1948, against the Boston Braves. The following day, Doby's teammate Satchel Paige became the first black pitcher to pitch in a World Series game. He retired both batters he faced.

Twelve days after Doby's 1947 debut, Hank Thompson suited up for the St. Louis Browns. He later had a solid eight-year run with the New York Giants, where he teamed up with Willie Mays and Monte Irvin to form the first all-black outfield. Thompson also holds the distinction of being the only player to break the color barrier for two different teams. When he led off against the Dodgers on July 8, 1949, he became the first African American to see action in a Giants uniform (Irvin pinch hit later in that

ROY CAMPANELLA,
LARRY DOBY, DON
NEWCOMBE, AND JACKIE
ROBINSON AT THE ALL-STAR
GAME AT EBBETS FIELD,
JULY 12, 1949.

same game). On the mound that day for Brooklyn was Don Newcombe, marking the first time a black pitcher and a black batter faced each other on a major league diamond.

The immediate impact of integration on baseball in the late 1940s and early '50s is evident by, among other things, the fact that seven of the first ten Rookies of the Year for the National League were African American. In addition to the Brooklyn quartet of Robinson, Newcombe, Black, and Gilliam, the Braves' Sam Jethroe won the award in 1950, Willie Mays took it in 1951, and Frank Robinson won it with the Reds in 1956. Between 1949 and 1959, African Americans won 9 of 11 NL MVP Awards; five African Americans won the award the following decade, along with two Latinos.

Progress in the American League did not come as quickly. The first African-American MVP in the AL was Elston Howard of the Yankees in 1963. The AL's first American-born black player to win Rookie of the Year was Baltimore's Tommie Agee in 1966. After Larry Doby in 1950, the next time an African American was chosen as a starter for the American League All-Star team was 1962: left fielder Leon Wagner and catcher Earl Battey.

On September 1, 1971, the Pittsburgh Pirates made history by being the first major league team to field an all-black lineup in a game, including pitcher Dock Ellis. The Pirates would go on to win the game, 10–7, over the Phillies at Pittsburgh's Three Rivers Stadium.

The milestone of the first all-black lineup did not receive as much attention as Jackie Robinson's debut 24 years earlier, and many of the milestone "firsts" for African-American players had been reached by the end of the 1960s. There was—and still is—a long way to go, especially with regard to African Americans in major league front offices, but the appearance of Robinson in a Dodgers uniform in 1947 set baseball on a path to becoming a truly national game.

GIANTS–DODGERS PLAYOFF TICKET, OCTOBER 3, 1951.

54

Giants–Dodgers Playoff Ticket, October 3, 1951

BOBBY THOMSON AND THE "SHOT HEARD 'ROUND THE WORLD"

The walk-off home run holds a certain mystique in baseball, bringing a quick and dramatic end to a game. When that home run comes at the end of a long and thrilling season, in a contest of longtime rivals, for a chance to play in the World Series, it can take on mythic proportions. Bobby Thomson's "shot heard 'round the world," which won the 1951 National League pennant, was just such a thrilling, mystical, and mythic moment. To have had a ticket to that game is something that no fan would forget—on either side of the outcome.

The Brooklyn Dodgers, winners of pennants in 1947 and 1949, seemed poised for another one as the 1951 season entered the dog days of summer. Brooklyn climbed into first place on May 13 and held that spot for the next four-and-a-half months. The team was nearly unbeatable in July, going 21–7. The Dodgers' lead in the standings reached 13 games on August 11. They compiled a mediocre 19–13 record in August, yet they were still seven games up heading into the season's final month. A five-game winning streak in early September appeared to give Brooklyn breathing room, but after the team lost 9 of the next 15, things weren't so secure.

The New York Giants, meanwhile, began the year horribly. An 11-game losing streak in April put them at 2–12 to start the season. They were in the league's basement as late as May 15, but a strong month helped to right the ship. By mid-June, New York was entrenched in second place. Nine games back when the calendar flipped to August, the Giants would need to get hot if they wanted to catch Brooklyn

helplessly at the base of the wall near the 315-foot mark, Thomson's drive landed in the left-field seats.

As radio broadcaster Russ Hodges famously called—nay, yelled—on WMCA radio: "The Giants win the pennant! The Giants win the pennant! The Giants win the pennant! The Giants win the pennant! . . . The Giants win the pennant, and they're going crazy, they're going crazy!"

Employing more somber yet reverential terms, Tommy Holmes recapped the game in the following day's *Brooklyn Eagle:*

> This was a dynamic melodramatic climax in a great season that has no parallel in the entire history of major league baseball. The finish was unbelievable. Giant fans went wild with enthusiasm, and the Dodger rooters who all but died in their seats had to settle for the scant solace—they had seen their ball club go down to defeat in what certainly must have been one of the greatest ball games ever played.

It was the third time in five years that the Dodgers, "dem bums," had lost the pennant on the final day of the season.

Although the game does hold up, more than 60 years later, as one of the greatest ever played, there is an afterword to the story. In 2001, long-standing rumors were confirmed that the Giants employed a system, using a telescope and a buzzer, to steal signs from opposing catchers and notify batters at the plate what pitch was coming. Although Thomson himself always denied it, others insist that Thomson knew that Branca was coming at him with a fastball. This intrigue only solidifies the moment as one of the most mythic and memorable in baseball history.

55

"*Meet Your Braves*" *Magazine, 1953*
THE ERA OF FRANCHISE RELOCATION

In 1953, the citizens of Milwaukee were introduced to the city's first Major League Baseball team since the original Milwaukee Brewers of the American League played one season in 1901 before leaving town to become the St. Louis Browns. To help Milwaukeeans get to know their new hometown ballplayers, the *Milwaukee Journal* produced this publication of bios and profiles of the soon-to-be *Milwaukee* Braves. Among those coming to town were future Hall of Famers Eddie Mathews and Warren Spahn, and past and future all-stars Joe Adcock, Lew Burdette, Del Crandall, Sid Gordon, Johnny Logan, Andy Pafko, and others. Some were making the journey with the franchise from Boston; for others, their first experiences in a Braves uniform would be with the letter "M" stitched on their caps.

The city eagerly embraced its new team. The Braves drew a major-league-high 1.8 million fans to Milwaukee County Stadium in 1953. Mathews topped all National Leaguers with 47 homers, Spahn led with 23 wins and a 2.10 ERA, and the team won 92 games, the most since the *Boston* Braves' claimed their sole championship in 1914.

The arrival of the Braves in Milwaukee was not only a seminal moment for the Wisconsin city, it was a groundbreaking event for the sport as a whole. Over the previous 50 years, fans had witnessed baseball's first World Series, the dawning of the home-run era, night baseball played under artificial lights, integration, and along with the nation, two world wars and a Great Depression. Through all those momentous developments, one thing that had remained unchanged was the teams that made up Major League Baseball. In 1952, the same 16 teams played in the same 10 cities as in 1903. No new franchises, no franchise relocations. Then, in the six years between 1953 and 1958, five teams set up shop in new cities, all departing towns that housed more than one major league club and settling in ones that lacked a big league franchise.

Meet Your *Braves*

Brief biographies to help you know your Milwaukee Braves better

15c

Published by THE MILWAUKEE JOURNAL

The team that paved the way was the Boston Braves. The franchise had been based in Beantown since the birth of the National League in 1876, when their nickname was the Red Stockings, which later changed to the Beaneaters, then the Doves, then the Rustlers, before finally settling on the Braves in 1912, except for a few seasons in the late 1930s when they were known as the Bees. Whatever they were called, Boston remained their home city, which they shared with the AL's Red Sox since 1901.

A pennant in 1948 helped spark interest in the Braves and brought attendance over 1 million in each season from 1947 to 1949. But after three losing seasons in four years, fan support in Boston began to wane. In 1951, the Braves had a total attendance under 500,000, the worst in the National League. The next year, as rumors swirled about a possible move and as the team stumbled toward a seventh-place finish, the fans stayed home in droves. Attendance fell to 281,278, or just 3,653 per game.

Although Milwaukee had not hosted major league baseball since 1901, the city did have a popular minor league club, also known as the Brewers, which had been the Braves' farm team since 1947. In 1950, the city began construction of Milwaukee County Stadium in hopes of attracting a major league tenant. The stadium was completed by early 1953—just in time for Braves owner Lou Perini to announce that his team was moving to Milwaukee.

After their 92-win Milwaukee-coming-out party, the Braves' win total dipped to 89 in 1954, but their attendance exceeded 2.1 million, and it remained above 2 million for four years running. The '54 campaign also saw the arrival of slugger Hank Aaron. With Mathews and Aaron crushing the ball at the plate and Spahn and Burdette stymieing opposing hitters from the mound, the Braves would win back-to-back pennants in 1957 and '58, defeating the New York Yankees in 1957 for the second World Series victory in franchise history.

The Braves remained in Milwaukee for 13 seasons before relocating again, this time to Atlanta, in 1966.

The city of Milwaukee had been a desirable target for other teams looking for a fresh start in the early 1950s. Bill Veeck—whose St. Louis Browns had finished last in American League attendance in all but two seasons between 1926 and 1953—was eager to find a new home for his franchise. Prior to the 1952 season, he sought approval to move the club to Milwaukee. The other American League owners, perhaps resentful of Veeck's promotional "antics" and publicity stunts, rejected the request.

In the six years between 1953 and 1958, five teams set up shop in new cities, all departing towns that housed more than one major league club and settling in ones that lacked a big league franchise.

A year later, with the Braves poised to claim Milwaukee, Veeck turned his attentions east, to the city of Baltimore.

Baltimore, like Milwaukee, had been one of the original American League cities in 1901 but hosted only minor league ball (not counting the Terrapins of the Federal League in 1914–1915) after the original AL Orioles moved to New York in 1903 to become the Highlanders. Memorial Stadium, built in 1944 for the Orioles of the International League, was expanded to major league caliber in the early 1950s.

Just days before the NL approved the Braves' move to Milwaukee in 1953, AL owners again rejected Veeck's proposal to move the Browns. Only after Veeck sold his stake in the team did the league agree, in 1954, to the relocation to Baltimore. The franchise immediately changed its name to the Orioles, which had a legacy dating back to the National League team of the nineteenth century—and which served to distance the team from the somber history of the Browns.

Despite losing 100 games, the Orioles drew more than a million fans in 1954. By the middle of the next decade, Baltimore had established itself as a championship-caliber team.

Following the move of the Braves in 1953 and the Browns in '54, the Philadelphia Athletics were the next to abandon the city they had called home for more than half a century. (The struggles of the A's in the final years of Connie Mack's reign are addressed with **Object #35**.) Once the Browns were out of the picture, the A's were the lowest-drawing team in the majors in 1954.

The American League was pushing for new ownership for the A's, ideally one that would move the team out of Philadelphia. Arnold Johnson of Chicago owned Blues Stadium in Kansas City and offered to buy the team if he could move it to KC. As offers from Philadelphia-based ownership groups failed to gain traction, the league approved Johnson's purchase and relocation of the team in 1955.

Kansas City had never had a major league team, but the roots of minor league ball go back at least as far as the Western League, precursor of the American League, in the 1890s. Blues Stadium had been home to the American Association's Blues, as well as the Negro League Kansas City Monarchs, since the 1920s. The facility had to be rebuilt to upgrade it for major league capacity, but the renamed Municipal Stadium was ready for Opening Day 1955.

The A's set a new franchise record by attracting nearly 1.4 million fans that first year in Kansas City. They again topped a million despite losing 102 games in 1956. After 13 straight losing seasons in Kansas City, however, attendance suffered, and it was time to move once again. In 1968, the team headed to California to become the Oakland A's.

By the time the A's showed up, the state of California already had three major league teams, with one more to come in 1969. The precedent for baseball on the West Coast had been set just a couple of years after the A's left Philadelphia for the then-westernmost major league city, Kansas City. The move of the Dodgers to Los Angeles and the Giants to San Francisco was a pivotal moment in the nationwide expansion of the sport—and is discussed with **Object #58**.

finished first in the NL in 1962, after another thrilling pennant race and a three-game playoff with the rival Dodgers, now of Los Angeles. In the World Series, again facing the Yankees, the Giants trailed 1–0 in the bottom of the ninth inning of the decisive seventh game. With two outs, Mays stood on second base and Matty Alou was on third, 90 feet away from tying the game. Willie McCovey came up and crushed a screaming line drive—right to Yankee second baseman Bobby Richardson. One foot higher, and the Giants might have won the series.

The disappointment of that 1962 close call was exacerbated when the star-studded roster—featuring Mays, McCovey, Orlando Cepeda, Juan Marichal, Gaylord Perry, and others—could get no closer than second place for the rest of the decade, where they finished five years in a row. With the advent of divisions and an extra round of postseason play, Mays and the Giants reached the postseason in 1971 but lost the National League Championship Series to the Pirates.

By then, Mays was in his 40s and showing his age. Early in the 1972 season, the Giants traded this franchise icon back to the city where he first became a legend. As a member of the New York Mets, Mays had one more chance at the October spotlight, but the Mets lost the 1973 World Series in five games, the "Say Hey Kid" a shadow of his former self.

For his fans, though, the memories of such out-of-this-world plays as the 1954 World Series catch keep Willie Mays firmly entrenched as an all-time hero.

PART VI

EXPANSION

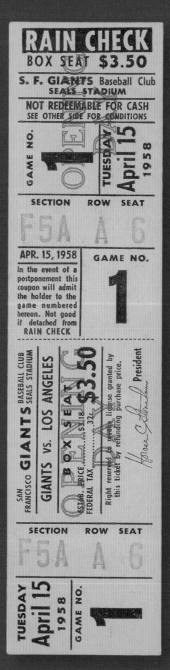

TICKET FROM GIANTS–DODGERS INAUGURAL WEST COAST GAME, APRIL 15, 1958.

58

Ticket from Giants–Dodgers Inaugural West Coast Game, April 15, 1958

BASEBALL HEADS WEST

A sellout crowd of 23,448 was on hand at Seals Stadium when the Giants opened the 1958 season by hosting their longtime nemeses, the Dodgers. The home nine knocked around Dodger starter Don Drysdale early and went on to win, 8–0, behind a complete-game shutout from Ruben Gomez.

The two teams had faced each other in nearly 1,400 regular-season matchups prior to this one. What makes this mid-April encounter in 1958 notable is that it marks the first time that an official major league game was played on the West Coast.

On August 19 of the previous year, New York Giants owner Horace Stoneham had announced that, after 75 seasons in Manhattan, the team would be moving to California to become the San Francisco Giants. Seven weeks later, Brooklyn Dodgers owner Walter O'Malley announced that his team would be heading to Los Angeles, after a 74-year history in Brooklyn.

The East Coast fan bases of the two organizations were devastated. Particularly for Brooklyn fans, the ball club and its players were an integral part of the community and its identity. But despite an extended period of success in the 1940s and '50s, Dodgers games were not selling out. O'Malley's efforts to build a new, up-to-date stadium in Brooklyn to replace the aging Ebbets Field were thwarted by city officials. So he decided to pick up and move to Los Angeles, where he would be able to build a suitable home for his team.

O'Malley then urged Stoneham to join him on the West Coast, rather than moving to Minneapolis, as had been Stoneham's plan. Stoneham was looking to get out of the Polo Grounds, where attendance at the crumbling ballpark had been steadily declining. After drawing nearly 1.2 million fans in the pennant season of 1954, the Giants were bringing in fewer than 8,500 per game in 1956 and 1957, the worst in the National League.

With advances in air travel and the expansion of national broadcasts, it was now feasible to have major league teams in cities from coast to coast. The success of previous moves by the Braves, Browns/Orioles, and A's (see **Object #55**) proved that there was opportunity in unclaimed markets. Plus, the cities of Los Angeles and San Francisco offered considerable enticements to O'Malley and Stoneham, respectively, including the construction of and/or land for new ballparks and control over concessions and other revenue streams.

WEST COAST OPENER AT SEALS STADIUM IN SAN FRANCISCO, APRIL 15, 1958.

The Giants initially moved into Seals Stadium, a minor league park that had been the home of the Pacific Coast League's Seals since 1931. Despite a seating capacity of under 23,000, the ballpark welcomed 1.27 million fans in 1958—the third highest total in franchise history to that point. Attendance jumped to 1.42 million in 1959, before the team moved into their very own, brand-new ballpark in 1960, Candlestick Park.

The Dodgers, too, set up shop in temporary digs until their new stadium could be completed. Los Angeles Memorial Coliseum—first built in 1921 for college football and then expanded in 1932 to host the Summer Olympics—was an odd setup for baseball. The left-field fence sat barely 250 feet from home plate, forcing the team to erect a 40-foot-tall screen to prevent cheap home runs; on the right-field side, the farthest seats sat about 700 feet from the plate. But it could accommodate more than 90,000 spectators, which allowed the Dodgers to draw nearly 2.1 million fans in 1959. Not only did they become the first National League team to draw more than 2 million in a season, but that year the Los Angeles Dodgers became baseball's first West Coast champion, after they defeated the Chicago White Sox in the World Series.

The Dodgers won another championship in 1963, in their second year in the new Dodger Stadium. Los Angeles won two more pennants in 1965 and 1966, with their rivals from up the coast finishing a close second in both years.

By this time, the West Coast success story had led to the establishment of a second team in southern California. The Los Angeles Angels entered the American League as an expansion team in 1961. After playing four years as tenants at Dodger Stadium, the renamed California Angels moved into Anaheim Stadium in 1966.

Two years after that, the Kansas City A's moved across San Francisco Bay from the Giants to become the Oakland A's. A year later, in baseball's second major expansion of the decade, a new team, the Padres, was installed in San Diego. Including the expansion Seattle Pilots (who would move to Milwaukee in 1970 and be renamed the Brewers), Major League Baseball had as many teams in the Pacific Time Zone as in the Central Time Zone in 1969.

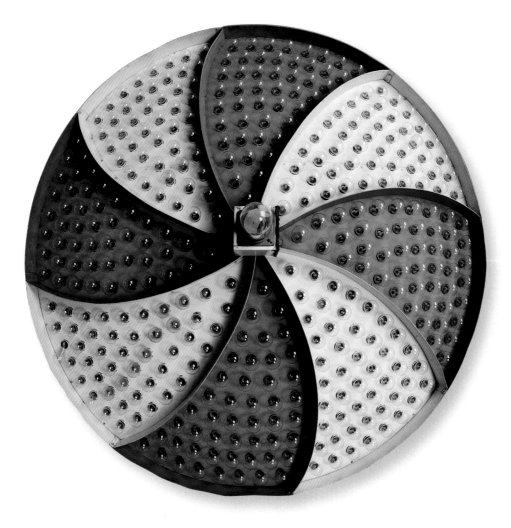

COMISKEY PARK SCOREBOARD PINWHEEL, 1960.

59

Comiskey Park
Scoreboard Pinwheel, 1960
MASTER OF PROMOTIONS, BILL VEECK

Bill Veeck Jr. was an innovator, pioneer, and marketing whiz over his four-decade span as a baseball executive and team owner. Some of his promotional ideas caught on; others did not.

In 1948, while owner of the Cleveland Indians, Veeck organized "Good Old Joe Earley Night" in response to a fan, Joe Earley, who wrote a letter to the local paper saying that there should be more ballpark nights honoring "average Joes" like him. More than 60,000 fans showed up at Cleveland Stadium on September 28, 1948, where Earley was showered with gifts, including a truck and some livestock, and odd prizes were handed out to random fans. In one of his most famous stunts, in August 1951 Veeck signed three-foot-seven-inch-tall Eddie Gaedel to a $100 contact with the St. Louis Browns. In his lone plate appearance, as a pinch hitter against the Tigers, Gaedel, wearing uniform number 1/8, walked on four straight pitches—all high balls—and was removed for a pinch runner. (Gaedel's contract was voided by the league president the next day.) Five days after Gaedel's debut, Veeck organized "Grandstand Managers Day" at Sportsman's Park, where fans received placards with the word "yes" written on one side and "no" on the other, which they were to hold up in response to cards held by the team's publicity director with questions like "Steal?" or "Bunt?" as regular manager Zack Taylor sat in a rocking chair smoking a pipe. The Browns won, 5–3. As owner of the Chicago White Sox, Veeck introduced short pants as part of the team's uniform in 1976, although they were only worn in a few games—much to the relief of the White Sox players.

in Baltimore was if Veeck was out of the picture. He sold his shares, and the Browns headed for Baltimore.

Undaunted, Veeck resurfaced a few years later when he took control of the White Sox in 1959. In Chicago, he stepped up his promotions, again giving away unusual prizes and organizing special days. The Sox set a new team attendance record in Veeck's first year as owner, and the "Go-Go Sox" won the franchise's first pennant since the Black Sox scandal of 1919. Attendance improved again in 1960, but health problems forced Veeck to sell off his piece of the team.

The Sox were searching for new ownership again in 1975, and Veeck returned to the city where he got his start. After having multiple bids rejected by the league, Veeck and his group finally got approval to purchase the club. The team was always short on cash, however, and Veeck had to find resourceful ways to bring in talent. Chicago mounted only one winning season in five during his second go-round as owner. Still, attendance was better than it had been in the first half of the decade.

One of Veeck's last and more infamous promotions took place in 1979. That July, the team collaborated with a local radio station to stage a "Disco Demolition Night." Fans who brought a disco record to the ballpark would gain entry for 98 cents, and the records were to be blown up between games of a doubleheader. An estimated 50,000 fans showed up—more than twice what the team expected. When the records were detonated after the first game, fans stormed the field, and all hell broke loose. The field was badly damaged, and the White Sox had to forfeit the second game. Chicago's promotions director at the time was Bill's son, Mike Veeck, who would later run the minor league St. Paul Saints (co-owned by actor-comedian Bill Murray), a team known for its fun and innovative promotions.

More than just a master of gimmicks, Bill Veeck was a maverick and a forward-thinking baseball mind. He infuriated other owners not simply by his "shenanigans" but by standing up for new ideas. In addition to being an early trailblazer for integration, he testified in support of Curt Flood during the player's court battle against baseball's reserve clause in 1970 (see **Object #67**). Veeck was not a baseball owner at the time, however, and the advent of free agency proved to be crippling for Veeck's White Sox later that decade.

60

Forbes Field Left-Field Wall, 1960

OCTOBER DRAMA

This book contains several objects that represent the great players and teams that have worn Yankee pinstripes over the years, for a franchise that has won more championships and produced more Hall of Famers than any other in major league history. The 1960 New York Yankees rank among the best, having won 97 games and sending seven players to the All-Star Game. Their 193 home runs as a team set a new American League record (which they surpassed a year later).

After securing yet another pennant, the Yanks were headed to the Fall Classic to take on the Pittsburgh Pirates, who were playing in their first World Series since getting demolished by New York's "Murderer's Row" in 1927. While New York racked up 10 AL pennants between 1947 and 1958, Pittsburgh finished last in the National League five times and second to last four times, managing just one winning campaign during that stretch. A 95-win season in 1960 helped them break out of that slump.

Not surprisingly, the Yankees were heavily favored to win the World Series. They backed up those predictions by winning games by scores of 16–3, 10–0, and 12–0. Pittsburgh, meanwhile, eked out victories by scores of 6–4, 3–2, and 5–2 through the first six games. Five different Yankees homered in the first six games; the Pirates had just one long-ball, by light-hitting second baseman Bill Mazeroski in the series opener.

Yet, outscored 46–17 to that point, the Pirates went into the deciding seventh game at Pittsburgh's Forbes Field with a clean slate. When they jumped out to a 4–0 lead after two innings, the Pirates appeared poised for a remarkable upset. But, in typical fashion, the Yanks rallied back. They took a 5–4 lead in the sixth on Yogi Berra's three-run homer and then added two more in the top of the eighth.

Pittsburgh countered in the bottom of the inning. Gino Cimoli led off with a single. On the next at-bat, the Pirates got a lucky break when a ground ball from Bill

FORBES FIELD LEFT-FIELD WALL, 1960.

Virdon took a bad hop on the infield dirt and struck Yankee shortstop Tony Kubek in the throat. Instead of a potential double play, the Pirates had their first two runners on; Kubek had to leave the game. A single by Dick Groat drove in Cimoli, and with two outs and two strikes, Roberto Clemente beat out an infield single to score Virdon and put Pittsburgh within a run, 7–6. With runners on the corners and two men out, catcher Hal Smith knocked a 2–2 pitch deep over the left-field wall. The Pirates had a 9–7 lead heading into the ninth inning.

Following two Yankee singles to open the ninth, Mickey Mantle delivered an RBI single. Berra then knocked in the game-tying run on a ground ball to first base. The score was knotted at 9–9.

With Ralph Terry on the hill for New York, Pittsburgh's number-eight hitter, Mazeroski, came to the plate to lead off the bottom of the ninth. Mazeroski drove a 1–0 pitch to left field, sending it over the red-brick wall for a game- and series-winning home run. As the Yankees stood stunned on the field, Maz danced and whooped around the bases. The crowd of 36,683 went wild. Despite getting outscored 55–27 and outhit 91–60 in the seven games, the Pittsburgh Pirates had defeated the mighty Yankees in one of the greatest World Series upsets, in the most dramatic way possible.

To this day, Mazeroski's blast is the only time in history that a World Series has been won with a walk-off home run in a winner-take-all Game 7. (Toronto's Joe Carter is the only other player to end a series with a homer, but that came in Game 6 of the '93 series.) That it came off the bat of a Gold Glove second baseman with only 138 lifetime homers in his 17-year career made it that much more extraordinary—and that much more painful for the Yankees of 1960.

In honor of that memorable moment, the portion of the left-field wall over which Mazeroski's home run flew was preserved when Forbes Field was demolished in 1971. It was relocated to the Pirates' new ballpark, PNC Park, in 2009. A plaque in the sidewalk on the original site, now part of the University of Pittsburgh campus, commemorates the exact spot where Mazeroski's blast cleared the fence.

ROGER MARIS'S 61ST HOME RUN BALL, 1961.

61

Roger Maris's 61st Home Run Ball, 1961

CHASING RUTH AND
CHALLENGING HISTORY

In the summer of 1961, the baseball world was mesmerized by a thrilling home run race between a duo of sluggers in New York. Yankee outfielders Mickey Mantle and Roger Maris were putting on a display of power that made many wonder if Babe Ruth's legendary single-season home run record might finally fall.

In the 33 seasons since Ruth's 60-homer output in 1927, only a handful of players had given serious chase to the record. Hack Wilson hit 56 homers in 1930, setting a new National League record, but ultimately couldn't make up the four-homer difference. In 1932, Jimmie Foxx had 29 homers by the end of June and then hit the same number in the final three months of the season, coming up short at 58. When Hank Greenberg matched Foxx's total of 58 in 1938, he had a record 11 multi-homer games in the season but needed a four-homer game on the final day if he hoped to pass Ruth. Willie Mays homered a then-record 31 times before the All-Star break in 1954 but dropped off significantly in the second half of the season, finishing with just 41. Mantle himself surpassed the 50-homer mark in 1956, falling 10 homers shy of the record—much to the relief of Yankee fans who viewed Ruth's record as sacred and had not yet warmed to the "hick" from Oklahoma.

When Roger Maris was traded to the Yankees before the 1960 season, he was not a particularly formidable home run threat. He had belted 28 for the Indians and Athletics in 1958, but his three-year career total when he arrived in New York was just 58. Maris went deep twice in his first game as a Yankee, and he finished the 1960 season with 39 homers, one fewer than the man who played alongside him in the

CY YOUNG AWARD

PRESENTED TO
SANDY KOUFAX

MOST VALUABLE PITCHER
NATIONAL LEAGUE
1963

SANDY KOUFAX'S CY YOUNG AWARD, 1963.

63

Sandy Koufax's Cy Young Award, 1963

DODGERS LEFTY DOMINATES THE GAME AND THEN LEAVES EARLY

In 1963, Sandy Koufax was voted the recipient of Major League Baseball's Cy Young Award. He was the award's first unanimous selection, and it came at a time when just one award was given for both leagues. He was also selected as the National League's Most Valuable Player for 1963, becoming the second man to win both awards in the same year (following teammate Don Newcombe, in 1956).

Koufax earned such distinction by winning the pitchers' Triple Crown with 25 wins, 306 strikeouts, and a 1.88 ERA. The Dodgers lefty was the first pitcher in two decades to record an ERA under 2.00, and his 11 shutouts were the most by any pitcher since Grover Cleveland Alexander's 12 in 1915. On May 11, facing a powerful San Francisco Giants lineup, Koufax pitched the second no-hitter of his career. That October, he helped the Los Angeles Dodgers wrap up a World Series title by defeating the New York Yankees twice in a four-game October sweep. He struck out a World Series–record 15 batters in the opener. Koufax added to his rapidly growing trophy room by taking home the World Series MVP award.

The 1963 season was a true breakout for the Jewish lefty from Brooklyn. Koufax had first signed with his hometown Dodgers in 1955 for a $6,000 salary and a $14,000 signing bonus. This bonus made the 19-year-old pitcher a "bonus baby," meaning the Dodgers had to keep him on the major league roster for two years before he could be sent to the minors. The young Koufax struggled mightily. Over his first six seasons (1955–1960), he had a losing record and an ERA above 4.00. He was developing into a strikeout pitcher, but his focus on throwing as hard and fast as possible led to control problems. Frustrated, he was on the verge of walking away from the sport.

Before the 1961 season, veteran catcher Norm Sherry suggested to Koufax that he not try to throw so hard all the time. The benefits were apparent right away. Focusing more on control than pure speed, Koufax won 18 games in 1961 and struck out an NL-record 269 batters. The following year, he threw his first career no-hitter, on June 30 against the Mets, at newly opened Dodger Stadium. Two weeks later he suffered an injury to his pitching hand that brought his season to a premature end. Still, he had been effective enough to win the first of what would be five straight ERA titles.

Koufax then kicked off an unmatched period of success on the mound. Between 1963 and 1966, he won three Triple Crowns and three Cy Young Awards. He won the ERA title in each of those four seasons and won 25 or more games three times. The one year during that stretch in which he didn't win 20 games or the Cy Young Award was 1964, when his season was cut short by injury. He had to settle for a 19–5 record and a third-place finish in the Cy Young vote. Koufax also pitched no-hitter number three of his career. The only Philadelphia Phillies base runner he allowed on June 4, 1964, came on a fourth-inning walk to Dick Allen, who was promptly thrown out trying to steal, allowing Koufax to face the minimum of 27 batters in the game.

In both 1965 and 1966, he again won the major league Cy Young Award by unanimous vote. Koufax set a modern (post-1893) record with 382 strikeouts in '65, and in 1966 he posted career bests of 27 wins and 1.73 ERA. On September 9, 1965, he became the eighth pitcher in major league history to pitch a perfect game, defeating the Cubs 1–0. (Chicago pitcher Bob Hendley allowed only one hit and one walk in the contest.) It was the record fourth no-no of Koufax's career.

The Dodgers won the NL pennant in both '65 and '66. Koufax caused a minor stir before the 1965 series when he refused to pitch in the opening game, since it fell on the Jewish holiday of Yom Kippur. Righty Don Drysdale, himself a former Cy Young winner (1962), took the start on short rest and was rocked for the loss. Koufax got the start, and the loss, in Game 2, but he more than made up for it by delivering two complete-game victories later in the series. He wrapped up the World Series triumph against the Minnesota Twins by going the distance in the clinching seventh game, pitching on just two days' rest. He struck out 10 batters and allowed only three hits.

More controversy arose before the 1966 season. Koufax and Drysdale joined forces and demanded to be paid $1 million, split evenly between them over three years, or $167,000 per player per year. They were negotiating with Dodgers owner Walter O'Malley and general manager Buzzie Bavasi. Prior to that, Bavasi had been playing the two off each other in separate negotiations. Working together, Koufax and Drysdale, two of the best pitchers in baseball, refused to report to training camp until their demands were met. They finally signed in the final week of spring training—to one-year contracts worth $125,000 for Koufax and $110,000 for Drysdale—and went on to lead the Dodgers back to the World Series.

Koufax's loss on the mound in Game 2 of the '66 series (which ended in a sweep at the hands of the Baltimore Orioles) proved to be his final major league appearance. Throughout the last few years of his career, Koufax had been battling injuries and pain related to an arthritic elbow. He could barely straighten the elbox on his left arm. Although he continued to put up huge numbers of innings and victories, he ultimately decided that, rather than risk permanently damaging his arm by continuing to pitch, he would walk away from the game at the age of 30. Beyond the injuries and the pain, the array of painkillers he was taking between and even during starts provided an additional wake-up call that maybe it wasn't worth it.

In 1972, Sandy Koufax became the youngest player inducted into the Baseball Hall of Fame, at age 36. Despite his relatively short career, Koufax retired with a long list of records, awards, and accolades to his credit, and for a five-year period in the mid-1960s, he was virtually unhittable. In the words of Hall of Fame slugger Willie Stargell, "Trying to hit [Koufax] was like trying to drink coffee with a fork."

SANDY KOUFAX PITCHING
DURING HIS NO-HITTER
ON MAY 11, 1963.

ASTROTURF. 1966.

64

AstroTurf, 1966

ARTIFICIAL GRASS AND
INDOOR BASEBALL

There is perhaps no development in the history of Major League Baseball more offensive to purists than the idea of playing the national pastime on anything but natural grass. Going indoors to watch a live baseball game was troubling enough, but the bright-green, nylon surface that spread like a plastic weed across baseball in the 1960s and '70s truly changed how the game looked, sounded, and even smelled. Beyond the aesthetic issues, ground balls traveled faster on the turf, and the surface was less forgiving than grass and so was harder on the body. By 1979, 10 of 26 major league teams played on artificial grass. It all started in Houston.

When the Houston Colt .45s were established in the National League's 1962 expansion, it was done with the understanding that the owners would build an indoor stadium for the club. The oppressive heat and humidity of Houston summers were not considered a conducive environment for baseball. During their first three seasons, the Colt .45s played at the open-air Colt Stadium while the domed facility was being built across the street. The temporary park was unaffectionately known as "mosquito heaven."

The enclosed Harris County Domed Stadium—better known as the Astrodome—received mixed reviews when it was unveiled for the 1965 baseball season. Lauded by the team as the "Eighth Wonder of the World," the Astrodome had a futuristic, outer-space feel to it. Mickey Mantle, who got an early look at the stadium when the Yankees played a preseason exhibition game there in April, commented that being inside the Astrodome felt like being inside a flying saucer—and that wasn't meant as a compliment. Looking to capitalize on that futuristic, out-of-this-world sensation, the team had groundskeepers and ushers dress in spacesuit-like uniforms. And the team changed its name to the Houston Astros.

Planning for an indoor baseball facility in Houston began in the early 1950s, well before the city was granted a major league franchise. Roy Hofheinz, a former mayor who spearheaded the efforts, said he got the inspiration for the idea of a roofed baseball park when he learned that the Colosseum in Rome was sometimes covered by a giant tarp to protect spectators from the hot sun.

The engineers and architects encountered several challenges during construction of the $31.6 million Houston project, not least of all figuring out how to support a 350,000-square-foot steel roof frame more than 200 feet above the playing field. They solved that engineering challenge well enough to keep the roof intact for decades. The designers also decided to incorporate 4,500 skylights in the dome to permit sunlight to penetrate and allow natural grass to grow on the field. This led to the unanticipated problem of fly balls being very difficult to pick up in the glare from the skylights during day games. Fielders struggled with fly balls during preseason workout sessions. Houston pitcher Ken Johnson commented, "Any outfielder who catches a ball should get a Distinguished Service Cross and a $50 raise."

So, the translucent skylight panels were painted over, which in turn led to the grass dying from lack of sunlight. For much of the 1965 season, the Astrodome field consisted of a mixture of dead grass and green-painted dirt. A more sustainable solution was needed.

The team turned to a synthetic surface, known as ChemGrass, which had just been patented in 1965. It was installed in phases during the 1966 season, beginning

ROLLING OUT THE ASTROTURF, 1966.

with the infield. Houston's home opener against the Dodgers was the first game played on an artificial-turf infield. On July 19, 1966, the Astros hosted the Phillies in the first baseball game played on a completely artificial grass surface.

Renamed AstroTurf, the surface soon made its way to more and more sports arenas. The cheaper costs involved in maintaining fake grass, as well as its greater durability, were advantages for facilities that functioned as more than just baseball stadiums. The multipurpose stadium was becoming all the rage in ballpark construction. Busch Memorial Stadium in St. Louis, Cincinnati's Riverfront Stadium, Three Rivers Stadium in Pittsburgh, and Philadelphia's Veterans Stadium—all built between 1966 and 1971—all served as the home field for both baseball and football teams. All but Busch Stadium were constructed with an artificial-grass playing surface; the Cardinals installed AstroTurf to replace Busch's natural grass surface in 1970. San Francisco's Candlestick Park, which opened in 1960 with natural grass, went artificial in 1971 when the NFL's 49ers moved in. Royals (later Kauffman) Stadium in Kansas City was built in 1973 as a single-purpose baseball stadium, but it too employed an AstroTurf surface; it switched to natural grass in 1994.

In addition to the increasing use of artificial turf, the trend toward multipurpose facilities produced a boring sameness in the look and feel of baseball stadiums built in the late 1960s and early '70s. The "concrete doughnuts" in Pittsburgh, Philadelphia, and Cincinnati were virtually indistinguishable from one another. Whereas the generation of ballparks built in the early twentieth century each had unique and in some cases quirky outfield dimensions in order to fit within the tight confines of their particular urban setting, the facilities of the '60s and '70s had generally symmetrical outfield dimensions. These cookie-cutter stadiums (they were no longer "parks") were often built in more open suburban locations, or simply took over the surrounding blocks, to allow for ample parking lots, greater seating capacity, and a clean if predictable footprint.

The innovation of indoor baseball, ushered in by the Astrodome in 1965, did not have as strong a pull. The Kingdome in Seattle was completed in 1976 and served as the home of the Mariners expansion team, as well as the city's pro football, basketball, and soccer teams at various points. Montreal's Olympic Stadium, built in 1976, was intended to have a retractable roof for baseball, but due to construction difficulties, it remained an open-air field until the late 1980s. When the roof was finally added, the retraction capabilities were spotty at best. The Metrodome in

10-INCH PITCHER'S MOUND, 1969.

BOB GIBSON PITCHING FROM
A 15-INCH MOUND, 1968.

since 1909. Only six players in
the majors batted over .300. The
.301 average by Boston's Carl
Yastrzemski was the lowest ever
to lead a league.

Spearheading the dominating moundsmen of 1968 was the hard-throwing Bob
Gibson. Having already established himself as one of baseball's most intimidating
and effective pitchers in seven seasons as a regular in the St. Louis Cardinals rotation,
Gibson produced numbers in 1968 that evoked the Dead-Ball Era. Gibby's 1.12 ERA
was the lowest seen in the majors for more than 60 years, and it remains the best post-
1920 ERA. His 13 shutouts were the most by a pitcher since 1916. The unanimous
Cy Young Award winner also led the National League in strikeouts. Perhaps the most
amazing thing about Gibson's year is that he lost nine games!

Gibson wasn't alone. Seven pitchers had ERAs under 2.00, the most in one
season since 1919. (In the entire decade of the 1950s, only one pitcher dipped below 2.00 in a season.) The Cleveland Indians' Luis Tiant (1.60) and "Sudden Sam"
McDowell (1.81) were the first pair of teammates to have sub-2.00 ERAs in the same
season in nearly 50 years.

Detroit's Denny McLain not only maintained an ERA below 2.00 in 1968, but
he also became the first major leaguer in 34 years—and, to date, the last—to win
more than 30 games in a season. His 31 wins, 1.96 ERA, and 280 strikeouts made
him the obvious and unanimous choice as the American League's Cy Young winner. Both Gibson and McLain also won their leagues' Most Valuable Player Awards.

McLain's Tigers bested Gibson's Cardinals in the 1968 World Series. Detroit's
Mickey Lolich was the pitching hero in October, however, winning a record-tying
three games in the seven-game series. Gibson did his part, establishing a new World
Series record with 17 strikeouts in his opening-game shutout victory.

Masterful pitching was everywhere in 1968. Drysdale threw 58 2/3 consecutive
scoreless innings for the Dodgers. Five different pitchers had no-hitters, including

NATIONAL LEAGUE CHAMPIONSHIP SERIES GAME 1 TICKET, 1969.

East Division, despite being farther west than the West Division's Braves and Reds.) In the opening game of the inaugural National League Championship Series, on October 4, 1969, the Braves hosted the New York Mets, winners of the East Division. With more than 50,000 fans on hand at Atlanta–Fulton County Stadium, the Mets won the first game of the NLCS, 9–5, in a battle of future Hall of Fame pitchers, Tom Seaver versus Phil Niekro. New York—which had an NL-high 100 wins in the regular season and won the NL East by 8 games following a monumental September collapse by the Chicago Cubs—swept the best-of-five NLCS in three games and was headed to the World Series.

Similarly, the East Division champion Baltimore Orioles dispatched the West Division champion Minnesota Twins in the American League Championship Series after winning the most regular-season games (109). Although they too swept the LCS, the Orioles didn't have as easy a time of it, needing 12 innings to topple Minnesota in Game 1 and 11 innings in Game 2 before Hall of Famer Jim Palmer led them to an 11–2 victory in the clinching third game. The powerful Orioles team then lost to the "Miracle Mets" in one of the greatest World Series upsets of all time.

After Baltimore again led the AL in wins (108) in 1970, they again played the West-champion Twins in the ALCS, with the same result. The first time that the American League team holding the best regular-season record did not get to play in the World Series was 1973, when the 97-win Orioles lost in five games to the 94-win Oakland A's. There was no shame in that, however, as the A's were on the way to their second of three straight world championships.

The story in the National League was not so tidy in 1973. The Cincinnati Reds won 99 games to secure their third West Division title since division play began. The Mets, meanwhile, were back atop the NL East for the second time in five years,

With more than 50,000 fans on hand at Atlanta–Fulton County Stadium, the Mets won the first game of the NLCS, 9–5, in a battle of future Hall of Fame pitchers, Tom Seaver versus Phil Niekro.

but this time they squeaked in with an 82–79 record, a game and a half ahead of the Cardinals. New York's .509 winning percentage would have put them in fourth place in the NL West, as San Francisco and Los Angeles both finished with better records. But the quirks of divisions meant that the Giants and Dodgers were staying home while the Mets were heading to a postseason showdown with the "Big Red Machine." In another shocking upset, the "Ya Gotta Believe" Mets beat the Reds to earn a World Series berth. They are, to this day, the team with the worst regular-season record ever to play in a World Series. They lost to Oakland in the Fall Classic in five games.

The postseason structure of two division winners from each league competing in a best-of-five series for a chance to play in the World Series remained in play until 1985, when the League Championship Series were expanded to best of seven. (In 1981, the split season caused by a players' strike led to the awarding of first- and second-half winners in each division, who then competed in a Division Series to determine who would play in the LCS.) The next full-scale realignment of divisions and playoff structure came in 1995, after MLB had expanded again, to 14 teams in each league, and split into six divisions.

67

Curt Flood's Letter to Commissioner Bowie Kuhn, 1969

TAKING ON BASEBALL'S RESERVE CLAUSE

On October 7, 1969, the St. Louis Cardinals and the Philadelphia Phillies agreed to a seven-player trade, with St. Louis outfielder Curt Flood and Philadelphia first baseman Dick Allen as the cornerstones of the deal. The only problem? Flood didn't want to be traded to Philadelphia, a city he felt was not welcoming to African-American players, to join a team that wasn't winning a lot of games. Most important, he felt he should have a say in where he played baseball. At first, he was prepared to retire rather than accept the trade. Then he decided to fight it instead.

On December 24, Flood sent a letter to MLB Commissioner Bowie Kuhn, outlining his position. "After twelve years in the Major Leagues," Flood wrote, "I do not feel I am a piece of property to be bought and sold irrespective of my wishes. I believe that any system which produces that result violates my basic rights as a citizen and is inconsistent with the laws of the United States and of the sovereign States." He hoped to play baseball in the upcoming season, Flood continued, but wanted the right to consider offers from other clubs.

Baseball players feeling as if they were being treated like property has a long history; see **Object #19**. Echoing the sentiments of countless players over the decades, Flood believed that baseball's reserve clause, which effectively bound a player to a team in perpetuity, was a violation of a player's basic rights and denied him the opportunity to control his own career.

Kuhn's response to Flood reiterated what league commissioners and team owners had been saying for decades: By the terms of his contract, his rights were

CURT FLOOD & ASSOC., INC.

CURT FLOOD STUDIOS

8007 Clayton Road
St. Louis, Missouri 63117
PArkview 5-3550

December 24, 1969

Mr. Bowie K. Kuhn
Commissioner of Baseball
680 Fifth Avenue
New York, New York 10019

Dear Mr. Kuhn:

After twelve years in the Major Leagues, I do not feel
that I am a piece of property to be bought and sold
irrespective of my wishes. I believe that any system
which produces that result violates my basic rights as
a citizen and is inconsistent with the laws of the
United States and of the several States.

It is my desire to play baseball in 1970, and I am
capable of playing. I have received a contract offer
from the Philadelphia Club, but I believe I have the
right to consider offers from other clubs before making
any decisions. I, therefore, request that you make
known to all the Major League Clubs my feelings in this
matter, and advise them of my availability for the
1970 season.

Sincerely yours,

Curt Flood

Curt Flood

CF/j

CC - Mr. Marvin J. Miller

   - Mr. John Quinn

controlled by the team, and thus he was contractually obligated to join the Phillies.

Flood went to his attorney and then to Marvin Miller, executive director of the Major League Baseball Players Association (MLBPA), and said he wanted to sue Major League Baseball. It wouldn't be the first time baseball had been taken to court over the issue. In 1922, the U.S. Supreme Court heard a case brought by the Federal League challenging Major League Baseball's monopoly. The High Court argued that MLB was not engaged in interstate commerce and thus was exempt from the nation's antitrust laws. It could continue to enforce its reserve clause. With this precedent, and others, Miller told Flood he had no chance of winning, and pursuing the case might jeopardize his career. They went ahead anyway and filed the lawsuit in federal court in New York.

Flood's case ultimately reached the Supreme Court in March 1972. As expected, in *Curt Flood v. Bowie Kuhn, et al.*, the Court upheld the lower courts' findings and ruled in favor of the defendant by a 5-to-3 decision. (Justice Lewis Powell recused himself due to his connections to the ownership of the St. Louis Cardinals.)

Although MLBPA representatives had voted unanimously to support Flood and cover his legal expenses, no active players testified on his behalf, fearing a backlash from owners. Former players Jackie Robinson and Hank Greenberg did testify for Flood. The league attorneys defended the reserve clause as bringing essential benefits and stability to the sport, and a majority of Supreme Court justices agreed. While acknowledging that baseball was, indeed, interstate commerce and its antitrust exemption was "an anomaly," the High Court felt no need to revoke the exemption or overturn the reserve clause.

Despite the defeat, the case helped to energize the players and the MLBPA to fight the reserve clause by other means. Rather than lawsuits, they turned to collective bargaining to

Flood believed that baseball's reserve clause, which effectively bound a player to a team in perpetuity, was a violation of a player's basic rights and denied him the opportunity to control his own career.

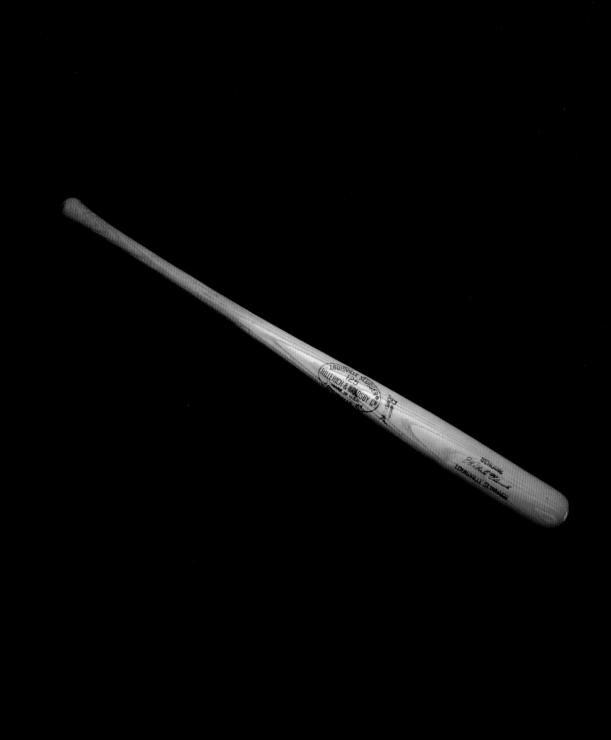

ROBERTO CLEMENTE'S 3,000TH-HIT BAT, 1972.

He struck out in his first at-bat against Jon Matlack of the New York Mets on September 30, 1972. His next time up, leading off the bottom of the fourth inning, he drove a 1–0 pitch into the gap in deep left-center field. He raced to second with a stand-up double and received a huge ovation from the modest crowd of just over 13,000 at Pittsburgh's Three Rivers Stadium. Clemente stood on second base and tipped his hat to the fans.

Clemente was pinch hit for his next time up, and with the Pirates having sewn up the East Division title, their veteran right fielder sat out the final three games of the regular season to rest up for the National League Championship Series. His last hit of the season had been a monumental one. Little did anyone know, hit number 3,000 would be the final one of his career.

On December 31, 1972, while taking relief supplies to earthquake victims in Nicaragua, Clemente's plane crashed into the sea shortly after takeoff from Puerto Rico. His body was never recovered.

The league and the nation mourned the loss of the generous and talented Clemente. Three months after his death, the Baseball Writers Association of America voted to waive the five-year waiting period for Hall of Fame eligibility and inducted Clemente into Cooperstown with 92 percent of the vote.

His on-field accomplishments were hard to dispute. A four-time batting champion, Clemente had a lifetime average of .317 to go with his 3,000 hits. He was an all-star in 12 of 13 seasons from 1960 to 1972, and he was named the National League's Most Valuable Player in 1966. That year he posted career highs in home runs (29), RBI (119), and runs (105) to go along with a .317 average, the only season from 1964 to 1967 that he did not win the batting title. Fielding was Clemente's most celebrated skill. With his rifle arm and great range, he won a record 12 consecutive Gold Glove Awards as an outfielder (he is tied with Willie Mays). He led the Pirates to World Series victories in 1960 and 1971, earning series MVP honors in '71 by batting .414 and hitting two homers in the seven games.

Clemente, who solidified his place in the national spotlight with that World Series performance, felt that he did not receive the national attention he deserved because he played in a small market. At times during his career, Clemente had a contentious relationship with the press. He could be reticent about speaking with reporters because he was not entirely comfortable speaking in English (his second language), and the quotes in the newspapers often repeated his broken or heavily

> The number
> of Latino players in
> the majors has risen
> dramatically since
> Roberto Clemente's day,
> accounting for about
> 28 percent of the
> league today.

accented speech. Many in the media insisted on calling him "Bobby" or "Bob," which displeased the proud Latino.

The Puerto Rican–born Clemente was not the first Latin American player in Major League Baseball, but he was the first Latino superstar and the first in the Hall of Fame. He was an outspoken advocate on behalf of Latino players, whom he felt were not always treated fairly or with respect.

Latinos had made tremendous strides in baseball over the 18 years of Clemente's career. In his rookie season of 1955, Latinos constituted about 5 percent of major league players. By the end of his career, the number had more than doubled, to nearly 11 percent. At his first All-Star Game in 1960, Clemente was one of five Latino players in that game, along with fellow Puerto Rican Orlando Cepeda, Cuban-born Minnie Miñoso, Venezuelan Luis Aparicio, and Cuban pitcher Camilo Pascual. Cepeda, Clemente, and Cuban shortstop Zoilo Versalles all won league MVP Awards between 1965 and 1967. Baltimore Orioles pitcher Mike Cuellar, also from Cuba, became the first Latino Cy Young Award winner, in 1969. Dominican-born Juan Marichal was among the best pitchers in the game during the 1960s and arguably the best Latino pitcher in history.

Before the sixties, Cuba was the main source of Latino players in the major leagues. As early as 1868, Esteban "Steve" Bellán, born in Havana, played for the Union Base Ball Club and then the Troy Haymakers of the National Association of Base Ball Players. Adolfo "Dolf" Luque, also of Havana, played 20 seasons in the majors beginning in 1914. He went 27–8 with a 1.93 ERA for the Cincinnati Reds in 1923, and in 1933, as a member of the New York Giants, he became the first Latin American–born pitcher to win a World Series game. Catcher Miguel "Mike" González's major league career spanned 1912 to 1932, and he became a coach with the St. Louis Cardinals after his playing days. He took over as interim manager when

Frankie Frisch was fired with 17 games left to play in 1938, making González the majors' first Latino manager. Minnie Miñoso and Venezuelan Chico Carrasquel were the first Latinos to play in an All-Star Game, in 1951. Miñoso would return for eight more Midsummer Classics.

Cuba's relationship with Major League Baseball dramatically changed following Fidel Castro's rise to power in 1959. Still, between 1960 and 1965, such Cuban talents as Hall of Famer Tony Pérez, Tony Oliva, Leo Cárdenas, Luis Tiant, Bert Campaneris, and Cookie Rojas made their major league debuts. The numbers have increased in recent years, particularly following the defection of star pitcher Livan Hernández in 1995. Cuban defectors José Abreu, Yasiel Puig, and Yoenis Céspedes were all all-stars in 2014.

Ozzie Virgil Sr., who debuted with the New York Giants in 1956, was the first Dominican-born player in the majors. Since then, more than 600 players from the Dominican Republic have played for major league teams. Guys like Pedro Guerrero, Tony Fernández, Pedro Martinez, Manny Ramirez, Vladimir Guerrero, David Ortiz, Bartolo Colón, Adrián Beltré, Sammy Sosa, Alfonso Soriano, Albert Pujols, José Bautista, Robinson Canó, Nelson Cruz, and countless others have elevated Dominican players among the elites of the game. Five of the starting position players in the 2014 All-Star Game hailed from the Dominican Republic.

Venezuela has also been a prime source of major league talent, beginning in 1939 with Alejandro "Alex" Carrasquel, Chico Carrasquel's uncle. Luis Aparicio was the first Venezuelan-born player in the Hall of Fame. Fellow shortstops Dave Concepción and Omar Vizquel had lengthy and successful careers, as did first baseman Andrés Galarraga. Johan Santana and Félix Hernández each won two Cy Young Awards (as of 2014). Miguel Cabrera, a two-time MVP, is one of the best hitters in baseball. José Altuve joined Cabrera and Hernández on the 2014 All-Star squad on his way to winning the American League batting title.

Hall of Famer Rod Carew and future Hall of Famer Mariano Rivera are just two of more than 50 Panamanians to make a baseball career in the United States. More than 100 Mexican-born players have reached the majors, most notably Fernando Valenzuela of the Dodgers, who captured the attention of the baseball world in 1981 when he won both the Rookie of the Year and Cy Young Awards. Nicaraguan Dennis Martínez holds the record for most wins by a Latino hurler. And the list of Latin American and Caribbean countries that have been represented in MLB does not end there. Players born in Aruba, the Bahamas, Belize, Brazil, Colombia, Curaçao, Honduras, and Jamaica have all made their way to the major leagues.

And Roberto Clemente's home island, Puerto Rico, is represented by three players in the Baseball Hall of Fame: Clemente, Orlando Cepeda, and Roberto Alomar. A total of nearly 250 Puerto Rican–born players have spent time in the majors. Hi Bithorn was the first, in 1942. First baseman Vic Power preceded Clemente by one year and played 12 seasons, earning seven Gold Glove Awards and six All-Star selections along the way. Willie Hernández won both the Cy Young and MVP Awards for the world champion Detroit Tigers in 1984. As of 2015, Iván "Pudge" Rodríguez has played more major league games than any Puerto Rican, and he accomplished that by being one of baseball's best catchers for more than 20 years. Puerto Rico's tradition of producing great catchers is further evident in the careers of such backstops as Benito Santiago, Sandy Alomar, Javy López, Jorge Posada, and Molina brothers Bengie, José, and Yadier. Sluggers Carlos Delgado and Juan González both hit more than 400 home runs in their careers. Carlos Beltrán has been an all-star with four different teams since winning the 1999 AL Rookie of the Year Award.

The number of Latino players in the majors has risen dramatically since Roberto Clemente's day, accounting for about 28 percent of the league today. Although it wouldn't be accurate to give credit to Clemente for all the hundreds and hundreds of players who have come from Latin American and Caribbean counties to play baseball in the United States, he was a true groundbreaker in his day and is still revered worldwide for both his playing and his humanitarianism. In 1971, Major League Baseball initiated an award to be given to the player who "best exemplifies the game of baseball, sportsmanship, community involvement and the individual's contribution to his team." In 1973, it was renamed the Roberto Clemente Award, in recognition of his contributions in those areas.

69

Ron Blomberg's Bat, 1973

THE DESIGNATED HITTER

Ron Blomberg played part of eight seasons in the major leagues between 1969 and 1978, all but one with the New York Yankees. He was a decent hitter—.293 lifetime average, .832 career OPS—but that's not what earned his bat a place in the Baseball Hall of Fame (or in this book). Rather, Blomberg secured his spot in history when, on April 6, 1973, he became the first designated hitter to come to bat in an official major league game. He walked to drive in a run his first time up and later singled, to go 1 for 3 with an RBI on the day.

The role of designated hitter has been a subject of debate among fans for the four decades since it officially entered the rule books, but the idea of allowing a more competent hitter to take at-bats for the typically poor-hitting pitcher is a concept that goes back well before Blomberg. Pittsburgh Pirates owner William Temple suggested the idea in 1891, and Philadelphia Athletics owner/manager Connie Mack took up the case in 1906, going so far as to bring the proposal before the rules committee. National League president John Heydler put it on the agenda again in the 1920s, but as with the previous attempts, the concept did not find wide support among the owners.

As pitching dominated the game in the 1960s, support for the designated hitter, or "designated pinch hitter" as it was then called, began to gain traction. Several teams experimented with it during spring training in 1969, and a few minor leagues officially instituted a designated hitter rule that year. But MLB continued to resist taking the experiment beyond a handful of preseason exhibitions.

During the "hot stove" meetings before the 1973 season, American League owners approved, by an 8-to-4 vote, adopting the designated hitter as a three-year trial. In addition to Blomberg, who hit a career-best .329 in 1973, other prominent

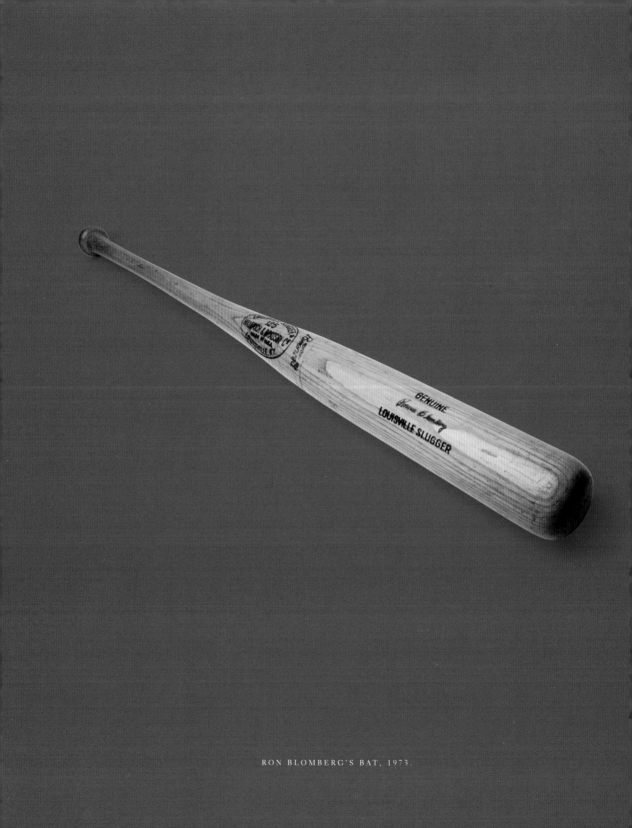

RON BLOMBERG'S BAT, 1973.

players who assumed the DH role during the '73 season were Hall of Famer Frank Robinson, who hit 30 home runs for the California Angels; Hall of Famer Orlando Cepeda, who won the inaugural "Outstanding Designated Hitter Award" during his one season with the Boston Red Sox; three-time batting champ Tony Oliva of the Minnesota Twins; former all-star outfielder Tommy Davis, who batted .306 for the first-place Baltimore Orioles; and Carlos May, who led the White Sox with 20 homers. Hal McRae was one of four Kansas City Royals to start at least 20 games at DH in 1973; he would go on to play more than 1,300 games at the position in 15 seasons with KC.

American League scoring increased from 3.47 runs per game in 1972 to 4.28 in 1973, and the leaguewide batting average jumped by 20 points. Whereas National League attendance remained more or less flat from 1972 to 1973, attendance in the AL enjoyed a 12 percent increase. In December 1975, American League owners voted to adopt the designated hitter permanently.

By the end of the decade, as scoring in the AL continued to outpace that in the NL, American League attendance had increased by more than 60 percent compared to 1972, while NL attendance was up just 30 percent. National League owners held a vote on whether to adopt the DH during the 1980 season, but the measure failed again.

Purists argue that the designated hitter sullies the game by not having players participate on both offense and defense and by giving roster spots to one-dimensional players. Supporters contend that nobody wants to watch pitchers feebly attempt to bat and that more offense makes for more exciting baseball. Some bemoan that the DH reduces the need for managerial strategy by taking much of the gamesmanship out of employing pinch hitters and double switches; others insist that the DH adds a dimension of strategy in the setting up of lineups and allows a manager to make better use of his players' talents.

To be sure, the advent of the designated hitter has allowed many great players to continue their careers after their usefulness on the field began to decline. In addition to Frank Robinson, who spent the majority of his final four seasons as a DH, Hank Aaron closed out his career as a designated hitter for the Milwaukee Brewers. Harmon Killebrew and Billy Williams both were in the lineup predominantly as DHs in the last two years of their Hall of Fame careers. Tony Oliva, who suffered from ailing knees, played exclusively as a DH from 1973 until he retired in 1976. Carl Yastrzemski was named an all-star in his final two seasons DH'ing for the Red Sox at age 42 and 43. Paul Molitor was a star infielder for more than a decade before making the switch to designated hitter, after which he led the league in hits three times and batted .316 over eight years. Jim Thome is one of only eight players in baseball history to collect at least 600 career home runs, and more than 200 of those came from the DH spot. He played there almost exclusively in his final seven seasons before retiring in 2012 at age 42.

More than just extending the careers of aging stars, the DH position has fostered some of the best hitters of the past 40 years. In addition to McRae, Don Baylor was one of the first to establish himself as a star while playing primarily DH. He got his start as an outfielder with the Orioles in the early '70s, and by the end of the decade he was taking a majority of his at-bats as a DH, amassing more than 300 career homers along the way. Harold Baines enjoyed a 22-year major league career, most of it as a DH. He held the record for most hits as a designated hitter until David Ortiz passed him.

In 2014, Frank Thomas became the first player ever inducted into the Hall of Fame after spending a majority of his career as a designated hitter. He was the Chicago White Sox's primary first baseman for most of his first eight seasons, during which time he won back-to-back AL MVP Awards (1993–1994), but after switching to DH in 1998, the "Big Hurt" continued to inflict pain on opposing pitchers. His 269 homers at the position has been surpassed only by Ortiz.

Nearly 1,400 of Edgar Martinez's 1,956 major league starts came as a DH. During his 18-year career with the Seattle Mariners he won two batting titles (the first while a third baseman), hit more than 300 home runs, and had a lifetime .933 OPS. He was honored as baseball's "Outstanding Designated Hitter" five times between 1995 and 2001—inspiring Major League Baseball to change the name of the award to the Edgar Martinez Outstanding Designated Hitter Award following his retirement in 2004.

The only man to win that award more often than the man

More than just extending the careers of aging stars, the DH position has fostered some of the best hitters of the past 40 years.

for whom it was named is David Ortiz, who has taken it seven times through 2013. Like many players with exceptional hitting skills but dubious talent in the field, Ortiz started out at first base before making the switch to full-time DH, first with the Twins and then with the Red Sox. He truly blossomed after going to Boston in 2003, where, as of 2014, he has accumulated more than 400 homers and 1,300 RBI in 12 seasons as a DH. He hasn't hit fewer than 20 homers in a season since 2001, and he has batted over .300 six times. His 54 homers in 2006 made him the first DH to lead the AL in home runs since fellow Red Sox Jim Rice did it in 1977.

When he retires, Ortiz will likely join Frank Thomas as a designated hitter with his own Hall of Fame plaque. Ron Blomberg got to Cooperstown more than 40 years earlier—or at least his bat did.

HANK AARON'S 714TH HOME RUN BALL, 1974.

Yankee, it was nothing compared to the scrutiny and hatred to which Aaron—a black man—was subjected more than a decade later.

From the final months of the 1973 season through the start of 1974, Aaron received death threats, nasty letters full of racist insults, and threats against his family. He had to be escorted to and from stadiums by security guards. He had to stay in motels under assumed names. Aaron echoed the same sentiments that Maris had in 1961: He wasn't trying to make people forget about Babe Ruth's accomplishments, he was only trying to establish his own.

Not all the mail or fan reaction was negative, however. Aaron received tens of thousands of encouraging letters of support, and he was cheered at ballparks around the country. When he went 3 for 4 without a home run in the final game of '73, leaving him stuck at 713 heading into the offseason, the home crowd at Atlanta–Fulton County Stadium gave him a standing ovation when he came out to take his position in left field for the last inning. It was a powerful moment for Aaron, who had had a tenuous relationship with the Atlanta community since the Braves moved there in 1966.

Another bit of minor controversy emerged as the 1974 campaign was about to get underway. The Braves were scheduled to open the season on the road, in Cincinnati. Hoping to see Aaron break the record in front of a home crowd in Atlanta, Braves management considered benching him for the opening three-game series. Commissioner Bowie Kuhn, however, stepped in and said that Aaron had to play in at least two of the games against the Reds.

In the 1974 opener, on April 4 at Riverfront Stadium, Aaron homered on the very first swing of his very first at-bat, a three-run shot to left-center field off Jack Billingham in the top of the first. The crowd of 52,000-plus cheered the record-tying blast. The ball now resides in the Baseball Hall of Fame in Cooperstown.

Aaron sat out the second game of the season and then went hitless in the final game of the Cincinnati series. The team then headed back to Atlanta to host the Los Angeles Dodgers for the home opener on April 8.

Facing Dodgers lefty Al Downing, Aaron walked on five pitches in his first at-bat, much to the chagrin of 53,775 booing fans. (Aaron did score that inning to become the all-time NL leader in runs, but nobody seemed to care very much about that.) He next came up in the fourth, with nobody out and a runner on. After watching the first pitch go by for a ball, Aaron made contact on Downing's next offering. The ball

72

Tommy John's Elbow, circa 1974

GROUNDBREAKING SURGERY
REVIVES CAREERS

One unfortunate constant through 150 years of organized baseball has been the risk, and reality, of a sudden injury derailing a promising career. Even as players have become more dedicated to strength training and fitness, as protective equipment like helmets and pads have gotten better, and as trainers and team doctors have become more adept at treating injuries, players are just as vulnerable to being sidelined by a fluke occurrence or the normal wear and tear of a long season.

One medical advancement that revolutionized the ability of players to come back from potentially career-threatening injuries is the development of ulnar collateral ligament reconstructive surgery, better known as Tommy John surgery.

In the late 1960s and early '70s, lefty Tommy John was emerging as a top pitcher. After averaging 12 wins in seven seasons as a starter with the Chicago White Sox, John was traded to a perennial playoff contender in Los Angeles prior to the 1972 season. He had a combined 27–12 record in his first two years as a Dodger and then got off to a torrid start in 1974, going 13–3 with a 2.59 ERA. Then, during an insignificant midsummer game, it all came to a screeching halt.

Pitching against the Montreal Expos on July 17, John felt his arm "pop" as he delivered a pitch to the plate. His left arm felt like it had gone dead. It didn't hurt so much as felt, in his words, "as if I had left my arm someplace else." He tried another pitch, and the same thing happened. He left the game and was examined by the team surgeon, Dr. Frank Jobe. Jobe couldn't identify exactly what was wrong,

TOMMY JOHN, CIRCA 1974.

341

so he prescribed rest and ice. The arm didn't improve, and x-rays did not reveal the extensiveness of damage to John's ligament.

After a month of rest and no improvement, John asked Jobe to cut him open. In those days, surgery on a pitcher's arm was rarely done, and when it was, it usually meant the end of a career. But it seemed to be the only hope for John, still just 31 years old.

On September 25, 1974, Dr. Jobe operated on John's left elbow. He found the damage to the collateral ligament was too severe to repair it, so he replaced it with a ligament transplanted from John's right wrist. It was a radical procedure to perform on a major league pitcher's throwing arm, but it was a fairly common technique in other ligament-replacement surgeries at the time.

Recovery was difficult, especially when it was discovered that a nerve had been damaged during surgery, and Jobe had to go in again. The cast was finally removed from John's arm in January 1975, and he began an extensive period of physical therapy. By late September he was pitching in the Dodgers' instructional league in Arizona.

On April 16, 1976, Tommy John made his first major league start in 21 months. He earned a loss in the game, but lasted five innings. He pitched seven shutout innings in his next outing, a no-decision. His first post-surgery victory came on April 26, against the Pittsburgh Pirates, when John allowed just one run in seven innings. He went on to finish the year 10–10 with a 3.09 ERA in 31 starts. He was named the National League Comeback Player of the Year by *The Sporting News*.

The next season, the 34-year-old John won 20 games with a 2.78 ERA for the pennant-winning Dodgers. He finished second in Cy Young voting for 1977. He won 17 in 1978, and then tested the free-agent market. John signed with the New York Yankees for a contract worth $1.725 million over three years. He earned it, posting back-to-back 20-plus-win seasons and finishing second and fourth in Cy Young voting in 1979 and 1980, respectively.

John continued pitching in the majors until 1989, when he was 46 years old. Of his 288 lifetime wins, 164 came after his groundbreaking surgery. In three World Series, two with Los Angeles (against New York) and one with New York (against Los Angeles)—all post-surgery—he had a 2–1 record and a 2.67 ERA. He struck out more than 2,200 batters in his career.

Although those numbers were not quite enough to earn John a plaque in Cooperstown (despite having more wins and a better ERA than many pitchers currently enshrined in the Hall of Fame), his impact on baseball continues to be felt.

By showing that it was possible not only to come back following major surgery but to regain pre-surgery effectiveness, John led the way for a rash of pitchers who have extended their careers despite significant injuries to their throwing arms. Since 1974, hundreds of players have undergone "Tommy John surgery." Several have inspiring comeback stories.

John Smoltz was one of the game's best starting pitchers with the Atlanta Braves in the 1990s, including a Cy Young performance in 1996. He missed the entire 2000 season recovering from Tommy John surgery. He then re-emerged as one of the game's best relief pitchers. In 2002, as the Braves' closer, he set the National League single-season record for saves, with 55. He returned to the starting rotation in 2005 and led the NL with 16 wins in 2006. Smoltz retired in 2009 with 213 career victories and 154 career saves, the only pitcher ever to have 200 wins and 150 saves.

Eric Gagne had the surgery when he was 22 and still in the minor leagues, and he went on to become one of the best relievers during the 2000s with the Dodgers. He tied Smoltz's NL record when he saved 55 games in 2003 and won the Cy Young Award. Gagne underwent a second Tommy John procedure in 2005, and although he was not as effective as he had been, he did pitch for three more seasons.

Kerry Wood was the 1998 National League Rookie of the Year but had to miss the entire 1999 season after surgery. He came back to strike out more than 200 batters in every season from 2001 to 2003. Although he never quite lived up to the phenom hype he garnered as a rookie, Wood's career lasted 14 seasons, finishing with a six-year stint in the bullpen.

The 2011 world champion St. Louis Cardinals featured four pitchers whose careers were briefly sidetracked by injury and then revived by Tommy John surgery. Jake Westbrook was an all-star pitcher with the Cleveland Indians before sitting out nearly two full seasons. He returned in 2010, was traded to St. Louis, and won 25 games over the next two years. Lefty Jaime

John led the way for a rash of pitchers who have extended their careers despite significant injuries to their throwing arms.

García spent the entire 2009 season recovering from the surgery and came back to win 13 games in each of the next two seasons. Kyle McClellan went under the knife before his rookie season in 2008 and later won 12 games as a reliever and a spot starter for the 2011 world champions.

After suffering through a variety of arm troubles earlier in his career with Toronto, Chris Carpenter came back to win 21 games and the Cy Young Award for the 2005 Cardinals. He helped St. Louis to a World Series victory in 2006 and then missed nearly all of 2007 and 2008 following both bone spur surgery and Tommy John surgery. He went 17–4 and won an ERA title in 2009. He won 11 games and led the staff with 191 strikeouts during the 2011 championship season. The 36-year-old Carpenter also pitched a league-high 237 innings, just four years after undergoing the surgery.

Not on the 2011 Cardinals staff was Adam Wainwright, who was coming off 19- and 20-win seasons for St. Louis in 2009 and 2010 before spending the entire championship year recovering from Tommy John surgery. He won 19 games again in 2013 and 20 in '14.

Young Washington Nationals pitchers Stephen Strasburg and Jordan Zimmermann both had the procedure early in their promising careers, and both bounced back to regain their stuff. Strasburg injured his ligament less than three months after making his major league debut and was sidelined for more than a year after surgery. In his first full season back, 2012, he won 15 games. Zimmermann led the NL with 19 wins in 2013, just three years after coming back from Tommy John surgery, and then pitched a no-hitter on the final day of the 2014 season.

There are other stories of pitchers who made surprising and inspiring comebacks after undergoing major surgery, and there are also countless examples of pitchers who never quite regained their stuff. Still, Tommy John surgery has become a popular—some call it "epidemic"—approach to repairing ligament damage in pitching arms. The trend has spread to minor league, college, and even younger pitchers. Some people are under the grossly mistaken impression that Tommy John surgery will help a pitcher become better even if he doesn't need it.

Still, when previous generations of players would have lost their careers to such injuries, Tommy John, Dr. Frank Jobe, and dozens of players since have shown that, through the miracle of medicine, there is always hope.

PART VII

THE
FREE-AGENT
ERA

◆ ◆ ◆ ◆

CATFISH HUNTER'S CONTRACT-SIGNING PEN, 1974.

73

Catfish Hunter's Contract-Signing Pen, 1974

BASEBALL'S FIRST BIG
FREE-AGENT SIGNING

In 1974, Jim "Catfish" Hunter won the American League Cy Young Award by leading the league in wins (25) and ERA (2.49). It was Hunter's fourth straight 20-win season, and the third consecutive world championship season for his Oakland A's. In the three World Series triumphs, Hunter went 4–0 in five starts, earned a win and a save in two relief appearances, and had a cumulative ERA of 2.08. In short, the A's couldn't have done it without him.

After the season, however, Hunter claimed that Oakland owner Charlie Finley had not paid the second half of his $100,000 salary, which according to the contract was to be a deferred payment into an annuity fund. The pitcher took the matter to arbitration, not only to get his money but to assert that Finley's failure to pay was a breach of contract that voided the agreement.

The official arbitrator ruled in Hunter's favor. The contract was voided, and the 28-year-old pitcher was declared a free agent. He was free to negotiate with any team for a new contract. Multiple appeals by Finley were all denied in the courts.

Nearly every major league team extended an offer to the new free agent, but only a handful could meet the going rate for an ace pitcher in his prime. Although the Kansas City Royals and the San Diego Padres reportedly made bigger offers, the New York Yankees, who had been purchased by George Steinbrenner two years earlier, emerged as the leading contender to acquire Hunter's services.

Sure enough, on December 31, 1974, Hunter used this 39-cent ballpoint pen to sign a five-year contract with the Yankees worth $3.35 million, or $670,000 per year. The highest-paid player the previous season had been first baseman Dick Allen of the Chicago White Sox, who earned $250,000 in 1974.

The millionaire pitcher lost his first three starts as a Yankee, but he soon got on track. Hunter finished the year with 23 wins, again tops in the AL, and he finished second in Cy Young Award voting. Hunter's wins dropped to 17 in 1976, but he helped the Yankees to their first World Series in more than a decade. He struggled with injuries the next two years as New York won back-to-back championships. By 1979, arm trouble combined with diabetes to greatly limit Hunter's abilities. After a 2–9 season in 1979, Hunter retired at the age of 33. His 224 career victories, 3.26 lifetime ERA, and nine postseason wins earned him a plaque in Cooperstown. He chose to have his likeness depicted wearing a Yankees cap, even though more than two-thirds of his games and wins were in an A's uniform.

Although Hunter is considered baseball's first free agent, the decision that led to his record-breaking deal did not directly impact the ongoing debate over baseball's reserve clause. Hunter's free agency resulted from a breach of contract by Finley. Taking down the reserve clause once and for all would follow a different path.

According to the reserve clause in contracts at the time, if a player and team did not agree on terms for an upcoming season, the team had the right to renew the previous contract "for a period of one year." MLBPA chief Marvin Miller saw this as a vital loophole. If a player did not re-sign after that one-year period, Miller argued, the player was then free to sign with whatever team he wanted. To exploit this, a player would have to first play a full season without signing a contract.

Andy Messersmith of the Los Angeles Dodgers and Dave McNally of the Montreal Expos were willing to put this to the test. After fulfilling their 1974 contracts, the two pitchers played the 1975 season without new contracts. Upon completion of the season, Messersmith and McNally announced that they were no

CATFISH HUNTER WITH THE
YANKEES, CIRCA 1976.

longer under contract with their current teams and were free to seek employment with other clubs. The owners, of course, didn't share this view and insisted that the players were still bound to their teams under the terms of the reserve clause. The case went to arbitration.

The three-man arbitration committee included Marvin Miller, who clearly sided with the players, and John Gaherin, who was representing Major League Baseball. The third, impartial member of the committee was longtime arbitrator John Seitz, who had previously ruled on the Hunter arbitration case. On December 23, 1975, Seitz delivered his decision: He ruled in favor of the players and declared that Messersmith and McNally were now free agents.

Baseball's owners immediately fired Seitz from the committee, and they took the case to court. When the U.S. Court of Appeals upheld the arbitrator's decision, Major League Baseball was out of options. The league proceeded to negotiate a new Basic Agreement with the MLBPA wherein players could declare free agency after six years in the majors. The reserve clause was finally dead.

With this freedom and the precedent of Hunter's monumental contract, seven-figure deals became almost commonplace. Messersmith's first free agent contract with the Atlanta Braves was for $1 million over three years. (McNally chose to retire.) In the first big free-agent class following the 1976 season, Hunter's former Oakland teammate Reggie Jackson signed a five-year deal with the Yankees worth in the neighborhood of $3 million. Mike Schmidt re-signed with the Philadelphia Phillies for a contract worth $560,000 per year (including deferred payments), making him the highest-paid player in annual salary. At the end of the decade, another milestone was reached when pitcher Nolan Ryan became the first player to sign a contract worth more than $1 million *per year* when he inked a four-year deal with the Houston Astros in November 1979. A year after that, Yankees owner George Steinbrenner again broke the bank when he signed Dave Winfield to a 10-year contract that, with cost-of-living increases, was worth about $23 million, or more than $2 million per year. That contract would lead to a long and ugly dispute between the owner and his all-star outfielder.

Not all the free-agent signings of the late 1970s involved such high-profile players or such high-dollar amounts, but the cumulative effect of the demise of the reserve clause and the advent of free agency was the average annual salary increasing from about $51,000 in 1975 to nearly $144,000 in 1980; by 1985, it surpassed $370,000. And it would keep growing from there.

CINCINNATI REDS WORLD SERIES TROPHY, 1975.

74

Cincinnati Reds World Series Trophy, 1975

THE "BIG RED MACHINE" CHURNS OUT BACK-TO-BACK TITLES

In the decade following the 1969 expansion and creation of division play, the Cincinnati Reds won the National League West Division six times. The pinnacle of this dynasty came in 1975–1976, when the "Big Red Machine," as it was known, won back-to-back World Series titles. The 1975 World Series trophy was the first for the franchise since 1940, gained after an all-time classic, seven-game series matchup with the Boston Red Sox.

During the regular season, the Reds won a franchise-record 108 games. Hall of Fame second baseman Joe Morgan won the first of his two consecutive NL Most Valuable Player Awards, posting a .327 average, 67 stolen bases, and a league-high 132 walks to go along with his Gold Glove fielding. Morgan's second MVP season was arguably even better, with career highs in homers (27), RBI (111), and slugging (.576), with yet another Gold Glove, his fourth in a row (and one more to come).

Finishing fourth and fifth in the MVP voting in 1975 were Reds catcher Johnny Bench and third baseman Pete Rose. Bench led the team in homers and RBI, and he took home a Gold Glove Award for the eighth year in a row. A two-time NL MVP (1970 and '72) and former Rookie of the Year (1968), Bench spent his entire 17-year Hall of Fame career with Cincinnati. He was the heart and soul of the Cincinnati teams of the '70s and retired in 1983 as the all-time franchise leader in home runs (389).

Rose does not have a plaque alongside Morgan and Bench in Cooperstown (that's another story; see **Object #78**), but his performances in 1975 and '76 were Hall of Fame caliber: combined .320 average, 200-plus hits both years, league-leading totals

"REGGIE!" CANDY BAR, 1978.

75

"Reggie!" Candy Bar, 1978

MR. OCTOBER, THE BOSS,
AND THE BRONX ZOO

"If I played in New York, they'd name a candy bar after me." So proclaimed the never-bashful Reggie Jackson in 1976, when he was playing for the Baltimore Orioles.

Sure enough, two years later, as Jackson entered his second season with the New York Yankees, the Standard Brands company released a circular-shaped candy bar of "chocolaty covered caramel and peanuts" called "Reggie!" It was handed out at Yankee Stadium and was a fixture in the candy aisle for several years.

Although it was the first snack item named for him, Jackson had already established himself as a megastar by the time he arrived in New York. As a member of the Oakland A's for 10 seasons, Jackson played in six All-Star Games, was named the 1973 American League Most Valuable Player, won two home run crowns, and helped the club to three straight championships. Like most of his teammates, he clashed with owner Charlie Finley, and it was clear that he was not going to stick around in Oakland once free agency came his way. It was also clear that Jackson was going to earn a huge payday on the open market. Finley traded him to Baltimore before the 1976 season, rather than lose him for nothing a year later.

When Jackson became a free agent in November 1976, he quickly inked baseball's biggest deal: $3 million over five years. He joined a Yankees team that was coming off its first World Series appearance in 12 years, ending the longest drought for the franchise since 1921. They lost the '76 series, however, and the team's owner was far from satisfied.

The pieces of a Yankee powerhouse had steadily been coming together since George Steinbrenner became majority owner in January 1973. The Yankees acquired Lou Piniella in a late-1973 trade with the Kansas City Royals; Piniella went on to play

LOS ANGELES DODGERS WORLD SERIES TROPHY, 1981.

76

Los Angeles Dodgers World Series Trophy, 1981

FERNANDO-MANIA IN A
STRIKE-SPLIT SEASON

When the Los Angeles Dodgers received this trophy after winning the 1981 World Series, it came at the end of a tumultuous year in baseball. A labor dispute led to nearly two months' worth of canceled games.

Prior to 1981, Major League Baseball had experienced four work stoppages since team owners and the Major League Baseball Players Association signed the first collective bargaining agreement (CBA) in 1968. A players' strike in 1972 was sparked over demands for an increase in owner contributions to the players' pension fund. The season was delayed by two weeks, but the strike ended when the owners agreed to increase payments to the pension fund and to allow salary arbitration. The very next year, the owners locked out the players during spring training over disagreement on the arbitration issue. The sides agreed to new terms by the end of February and no regular-season games were missed. When the three-year CBA signed in 1973 expired, the owners again locked out the players during spring training in 1976, largely in response to the arbitrator's ruling a few months earlier regarding free agency. That lockout lasted 17 days but again was resolved before Opening Day with a new CBA. The players struck for eight days during spring training in 1980, and although a preliminary labor agreement was reached, the issue of free agency was to be reopened the following year.

The main issue in contention was compensation to teams for the loss of free agents. The owners felt they should be compensated by receiving a player of equal value from the team to whom they lost their free agent. Players saw that as a clear undermining of the freedom they had obtained with free agency. With negotiations at an impasse, the players voted to go on strike.

When the final pre-strike games were played on June 11, the Dodgers held the major leagues' best record at 36–21. Leading the way for Los Angeles was rookie sensation Fernando Valenzuela. The 20-year-old lefty won his first eight starts that season—all complete-game performances, five of them shutouts. His distinctive delivery and affable nature made him a fan and media darling, sparking "Fernando-mania" in LA.

The owners and players finally reached an agreement on July 31. On the issue of free-agent compensation, the new contract allowed owners who lost a top-tier free agent to draft a replacement from a pool of unprotected players from all teams, not just the one that signed the free agent. This system, which proved ineffective in providing comparable replacement players, remained in force until 1985.

But baseball was back in business. Major League Baseball decided on a split-season format for 1981, wherein the first-half winner from each division would play the second-half winner in a best-of-five-game Division Series to determine the participants in the League Championship Series. The post-strike portion of the season kicked off with the All-Star Game, on August 9. Valenzuela got the start for the NL and pitched one inning of shutout ball.

The Dodgers played barely above .500 (27–26) after the strike. The Houston Astros, meanwhile, got hot, posting baseball's best second-half record, 33–20. Valenzuela cooled off a bit, going 4–3 in the second half, but still finished with 13 victories in 1981, second most in the NL; his 11 complete games, 8 shutouts, and 180 strikeouts were all tops in the league. Valenzuela barely beat out Cincinnati's Tom Seaver (who had a 14–2 record) in the voting for the National League Cy Young Award, and he edged out Montreal's Tim Raines for Rookie of the Year honors—making him the first player ever to win both awards in the same season.

The Dodgers and Astros kicked off the West Division Series on October 6 at the Astrodome. (The Cincinnati Reds had notched baseball's best *overall* record in 1981, but since they failed to win either half, they were left out of the postseason.) In the NLDS opener, Valenzuela battled Houston starter Nolan Ryan in a 1–1 match through eight innings. After Fernando was pulled for a pinch hitter in the top of the ninth, reliever Dave Stewart gave up a two-run homer for the loss. The Dodgers lost Game 2 as well, but they stormed back to win the next three at home and claim the series title.

Los Angeles then defeated the Montreal Expos in the NLCS in five games. Fernando earned the win in the final contest while allowing only three hits. Rick Monday's two-out homer in the ninth broke a 1–1 tie to clinch it for the Dodgers.

The Dodgers faced a familiar foe in the World Series, taking on the New York Yankees for the third time in five years. In a reversal of the 1978 outcome, the Dodgers lost the first two games of the series before sweeping the next four. It was the first title for Los Angeles since 1965.

Fernando-mania continued, to some degree, in the next few seasons. Valenzuela made the All-Star team from 1982 through 1986, and he struck out a record-tying five consecutive batters in the '86 contest. During that regular season, he won a league- and career-high 21 games and struck out a career-best 242 batters. The Dodgers won division titles in 1983 and '85 but lost the League Championship Series both years. They made it to the World Series in 1988, and notched a surprising victory over a powerful Oakland A's team. Valenzuela missed most the season to injury, however, and didn't appear in the postseason.

Valenzuela went 13–13 in 1990 and pitched the only no-hitter of his career. He was released during spring training of 1991. Still just 30 years old, Fernando signed with the Angels but made only two starts (losing both). After a year playing in his home country of Mexico in 1992, Valenzuela returned for five more major league seasons with four different teams. He retired in 1997 with 173 career victories.

The championship run in 1981, combined with Fernando-mania, helped the Dodgers draw a league-high 2.3 million fans. The World Series trophy shown here was given to broadcaster Rodolfo "Rudy" Hoyos, who did color commentary for the Dodgers' Spanish-language broadcasts from 1973 to 1981. He, like Valenzuela, was born in Mexico.

FERNANDO VALENZUELA PITCHES
DURING THE 1981 WORLD SERIES.

RICKEY HENDERSON'S SHOES, 1982.

77

Rickey Henderson's Shoes, 1982

THE "MAN OF STEAL" PASSES BROCK

For a quarter of a century, Rickey Henderson was one of the most entertaining baseball players to watch and to listen to. The eccentric Henderson was always good for a quote, and nobody had more confidence in Rickey's abilities than Rickey himself. He earned that confidence, however, by establishing himself as the greatest base-stealing threat the game has ever seen.

In 1982, his fourth year as a major leaguer, Henderson entered the record books as the single-season stolen base king (post-1900). Wearing these shoes on August 27, he swiped his 119th base of the season to surpass the record held by St. Louis Cardinals speedster Lou Brock. Henderson added 11 more to finish with 130—more than nine American League *teams* that year.

Two years earlier, in his first full campaign with the Oakland A's, the 21-year-old Henderson became just the third player in the twentieth century—along with Brock and Los Angeles Dodger Maury Wills—to steal 100 bases in a season, and he passed Ty Cobb as the American League single-season leader. That year he also batted over .300, scored more than 100 runs, and walked more than 100 times to earn the first of ten All-Star team selections.

Henderson would lead his league in thefts in 11 of 12 seasons from 1980 to 1991; he stole at least 40 in 14 consecutive seasons. In 1991, he became the all-time stolen base king when he stole career base number 939 on May 1, again replacing Brock at the top of the list. In his speech after breaking the record, Henderson said, "Lou Brock was the symbol of great base stealing. But today, I'm the greatest of all time."

The following year, Henderson stole the 1,000th base of his career. His 12th and final stolen base title came in 1998, when he was 39. He retired five years later with a lifetime total of 1,406, nearly 500 more than any other player.

Stealing bases was Henderson's greatest legacy, but he was also one of the best leadoff hitters. A career .279 hitter, he was a master at drawing bases on balls. Utilizing an exaggerated crouch in his stance, Henderson's 2,190 career walks constituted an all-time record when he retired (his record was later surpassed by Barry Bonds). His ability to get on base, combined with his out-of-this-world speed and confidence, allowed Henderson to score more runs than any player in history (2,295). He could also go deep when he wanted to. Finishing just three homers shy of 300 for his career, Rickey hit more than 20 in a season four times. Eighty-one times in his career, he led off a game with a home run—another major league record on his résumé.

Henderson's path through the majors was long and somewhat circuitous. He spent his first six years in Oakland, three of them with Billy Martin as his manager. Henderson's aggressive base running was a centerpiece of Martin's "Billyball" strategy, which helped Oakland reach the American League Championship Series in 1981. Henderson finished second in the league MVP voting and won the only Gold Glove of his career.

RICKEY HENDERSON ON THE BASE PATHS, CIRCA 1982.

Following the 1984 season, Henderson was traded to the New York Yankees, where he was reunited (briefly) with Martin. Rickey stepped up his power stroke in New York, belting 24 and 28 homers in his first two seasons there, while also stealing at least 80 bases both years. In 1985 he scored 146 runs in 143 games. Playing in the final year of his contract in 1989, Henderson was traded back to Oakland that June. He joined an A's team on its way to a second straight pennant. Henderson was named the Most Valuable Player of the ALCS and then batted .474 in the World Series sweep of the San Francisco Giants. He stole 11 bases in 9 postseason games.

Henderson re-signed with Oakland prior to the 1990 season and went on to win the only regular-season MVP Award of his career. He had career highs in average (.325), slugging percentage (.577), and homers (28) to go along with league highs in runs, stolen bases, and OBP; he lost the batting title to George Brett on the final day of the season. Henderson led the A's with a .333 average in the World Series, but it wasn't enough to bring a repeat title to Oakland, as they were swept by the Cincinnati Reds.

His second stint with the A's ended with a midseason 1993 trade to the Toronto Blue Jays, with whom Henderson won another World Series ring. He struggled in Toronto, though, batting .215 in 44 regular-season games and .170 in the postseason, after starting out the year hitting .327 with the A's. He decided to return to Oakland once again as a free agent in the offseason.

Henderson played 10 more seasons, but never more than two in a row with the same team. Following his two-year stay in Oakland in 1994–1995, he signed with the San Diego Padres, who traded him to the California Angels in August 1997. Rickey then inked a one-year contract to play in Oakland, for the fourth time, where he won the final stolen base crown of his career. The Mets signed him for the 1999 season. Henderson hit .315 and stole 37 bases in the regular season, and then stole 6 bases and hit .400 in the four-game Division Series victory over Arizona. Despite that, the Mets released him barely a month into the 2000 season. Rickey finished the year with the Seattle Mariners, then bounced back to San Diego in 2001, where he collected his 3,000th career hit and moved to the top of the list as the all-time leader in both runs and walks. He wrapped up his 24-year career with the Boston Red Sox and the Los Angeles Dodgers in his last two seasons, respectively.

His final major league game in 2003 came when Henderson was 44 years old, but he wasn't ready to hang up the spikes for good. He played two more pro seasons

Henderson's longevity not only allowed him to compile record-setting career numbers, but he also holds the distinction of being one of only four players ever to hit a home run in four different decades.

in the minors and helped the San Diego Surf Dawgs win the championship in the independent Golden Baseball League. Even after being inducted into the Hall of Fame in 2009, in his first year of eligibility and with 95 percent of the vote, Henderson suggested that he could still suit up and hold his own on the diamond. He was 50 years old.

Henderson's longevity not only allowed him to compile record-setting career numbers, but he also holds the distinction of being one of only four players ever to hit a home run in four different decades. He also was at the center of a stolen base resurgence in the 1980s. Although guys like Maury Wills, Luis Aparicio, Bert Campaneris, and, of course, Lou Brock were tearing up the base paths during the 1960s, it was still largely a slugger's game. In 1959, Aparicio, who led the AL in steals nine times, became the first player to steal at least 50 bases in a season since 1943. Wills took it up a notch when he eclipsed the century mark with 104 steals in 1962. It was another dozen years before Brock established the new single-season record with 118 in 1974, by which time he was one of six players with 50 or more thefts. Two years later, Brock's 56 stolen bases were only good enough for seventh best in the majors. Oakland's Billy North, Los Angeles's Davey Lopes, Cincinnati's Joe Morgan, Pittsburgh's Omar Moreno and Frank Taveras, Detroit's Ron LeFlore, and Kansas City's Willie Wilson, among others, were all bringing the stolen base back to the forefront.

When Rickey won his first stolen base crown in 1980 with 100 SBs, LeFlore had 97 with Montreal and Moreno had 96. Not since the 1890s had three players stolen at least 90 bases in the same season, and it has not happened since. Montreal's Tim Raines won the National League stolen base title as a rookie in 1981, kicking off a record streak of six consecutive seasons with at least 70 thefts. Raines's 808 career stolen bases are fifth most of all time, but his 85 percent success rate places him first among all players with at least 300 career stolen bases.

The man who ended Raines's run as the NL's perennial leader was another St. Louis speedster. As a rookie, Vince Coleman stole 110 bases in 1985. He then stole 107 in 1986 and 109 in '87, making him the only player other than Henderson to pass 100 in three different seasons, and the only one to do it three years in a row.

Led by Coleman and Seattle's Harold Reynolds, major leaguers stole more bases in 1987 than in any season since the 1890s—and Henderson missed more than a third of the year to injury, contributing just 41 stolen bases in 95 games. Interestingly, the second highest leaguewide total, post-1900, was in 1999, when teams also set a new record for most home runs in a season. (Granted the majors had expanded to 30 teams by then, but '99 remains the season with the most stolen bases in a 30-team league.)

In the post-steroid era of the 2000s, no player has gotten within 50 stolen bases of Henderson's 1982 total. (As of 2014, José Reyes's 78 for the Mets in 2008 is as close as anyone has gotten since Henderson stole 93 in 1988.) In more ways than one, Rickey's shoes are not easy to fill.

Chicago's Wrigley Field to tie the record. He sat out the next game in Chicago and then went hitless at home against the Padres the following day.

In his first at-bat against San Diego's Eric Show at Riverfront Stadium on September 11, 1985, Rose drove a hanging slider into left-center field for a single. Pete Rose became baseball's all-time hits leader. His teammates rushed out from the dugout to congratulate him, and the hometown crowd gave a standing ovation to the teary-eyed Rose lasting more than seven minutes.

Rose played in 72 games in 1986 but batted just .219. He made his last appearance as a player on August 17, at age 45. With 3,562 games under his belt, Pete Rose retired with 4,256 career hits.

He reached that monumental total by collecting more than 200 hits in a season a record 10 times over his 24-year playing career. His personal high was 230 in 1973, when he also won a batting title—his third—and was named the National League's Most Valuable Player. Rose had kicked off his career by winning the 1963 Rookie of the Year Award, and in 1965 he was named to his first of 17 All-Star teams. That year he batted .312, beginning a run of hitting over .300 in 15 of 17 years. He finished second in MVP voting in 1968 when he won his first batting crown, a .335 average during the "Year of the Pitcher." A year later he set or tied career highs in triples (11), homers (16), RBI (82), batting (.348), slugging (.512), and on-base percentage (.428). He also won the first of two Gold Glove Awards.

"Charlie Hustle," as he was known, scored more than 100 runs in a season 10 times and ranks sixth on the all-time list in that category, one of only five players in history to score more than 2,000 runs and collect more than 3,000 hits. Rose got his start as Cincinnati's second baseman before moving to the outfield, where he won his Gold Gloves. He was the third baseman during the peak years of the Big Red Machine in the mid-1970s, but after signing with the Phillies in 1979, where future Hall of Famer Mike Schmidt was already manning the "hot corner," Rose shifted to first base, where he remained for the final years of his career. He spent at least 500 games at four different positions.

The versatile Rose was Cincinnati's player-manager for three seasons before turning to managing full time in 1987. He led the Reds to four consecutive second-place finishes (1985–1988) and won more than 400 games in his managerial career.

That career was derailed, however, amid allegations that Rose had bet on baseball while working as the Reds manager. Baseball's outgoing commissioner, Peter Ueberroth, launched an investigation into the allegations in early 1989. Ueberroth's successor,

Bart Giamatti, received a report from John M. Dowd, who led the investigation as special counsel to the commissioner, on May 9. The Dowd Report contained extensive evidence—including handwritten betting slips, signed checks, and phone records—linking Rose to wagers on baseball games dating back to 1987. Giamatti acted swiftly.

At a press conference on August 24, 1989, the commissioner announced that Pete Rose would be banned from baseball for life. "One of the game's greatest players has engaged in a variety of acts which have stained the game," Giamatti said, "and he must now live with the consequences of those acts."

Though acknowledging that he bet on other sports and had been an active gambler, Rose denied vehemently that he ever bet on baseball. It was not until 2004, in his book *My Prison without Bars*, that Rose finally came clean and admitted that he bet on baseball while with the Reds. He continued to insist that he never bet against his own team and later claimed that he bet for his own team to win virtually every night. Still, he has expressed regret and remorse for tainting and disrespecting the game of baseball with his actions.

Rose applied for reinstatement with subsequent commissioners Fay Vincent and Bud Selig, but neither has relented on the lifetime ban. To this day, the all-time major league leader in hits is ineligible for induction in the Baseball Hall of Fame in Cooperstown.

PETE ROSE BECOMES THE ALL-TIME LEADER WITH
HIS 4,192ND HIT, SEPTEMBER 11, 1985.

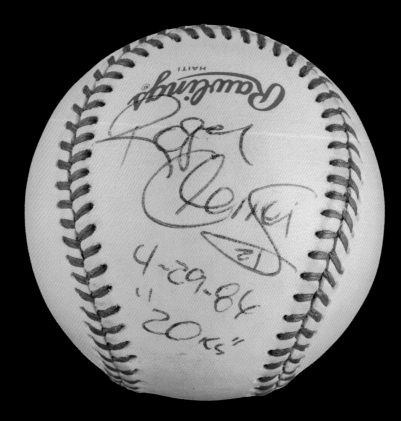

BALL FROM ROGER CLEMENS'S 20-STRIKEOUT GAME, 1986.

79

Ball from Roger Clemens's 2-Strikeout Game, 1986

THE RISE AND FALL OF "THE ROCKET"

On April 29, 1986, Boston Red Sox pitcher Roger "Rocket" Clemens struck out 20 Seattle Mariners to set the major league record for most Ks in a single game. Before that, only eight pitchers in the twentieth century had struck out as many as 18 in a game (Sandy Koufax and Nolan Ryan each did it twice). Since Clemens's feat, the only other pitchers to reach 20 in a game have been Kerry Wood of the Chicago Cubs, in 1998, and Clemens himself, against the Tigers 10 years after his first 20-strikeout game.

This ball from the 1986 game was signed by Clemens and sold at auction for over $1,000 in 2013.

Although he had shown hints of his potential as a 21-year-old rookie in 1984 when he struck out 126 batters in 133 1/3 innings, Clemens rocketed to stardom in 1986. He went 24–4 and struck out 238 batters while leading the league with a 2.48 ERA. He not only won the Cy Young Award by an overwhelming margin, but he was also named the American League Most Valuable Player. The 20-strikeout game marked his fourth straight win to start the season. He didn't record his first loss until July 2, at which point his record was 14–0. He ended the year with seven wins and no losses in his final 10 starts.

That season Clemens spearheaded a Boston team that won 95 games to claim its first division title in over a decade. After falling behind the California Angels three games to one in the ALCS, the Red Sox were one strike away from losing the series in Game 5 before a dramatic home run by Don Baylor in the top of the ninth kept them alive. They went on to win the game in 11 innings, and then Boston trounced

California in the final two games to win the pennant. Clemens earned the W in the clinching game.

In the World Series, fortunes took a 180-degree turn for Boston. The Red Sox themselves were one strike away from wrapping up the franchise's first World Series triumph since 1918, when the bottom dropped out against the New York Mets. Three consecutive two-out singles, followed by a wild pitch by reliever Bob Stanley, allowed the Mets to tie Game 6 in the bottom of the 10th. Then a Mookie Wilson ground ball that rolled between the legs of Boston first baseman Bill Buckner let the winning run score and sent the teams to a decisive Game 7. The Red Sox took an early 3–0 lead in that game before losing the game and the series.

THE FIERY ROGER CLEMENS STRUCK OUT 20 BATTERS
IN A GAME TWICE IN HIS CAREER.

Most baseball fans remember (or Red Sox fans try to forget) Stanley's wild pitch and the ground ball between Buckner's legs, but what is lost in the excitement is that Clemens had allowed just one earned run while striking out eight through seven innings before being removed for a pinch hitter. He finished the series with no decisions in two starts.

Undaunted by the heart-crushing conclusion to the 1986 season, Clemens won a second straight Cy Young Award in 1987, again leading the league in victories (20). He had 21 wins and a league-best 1.93 ERA in 1990 but lost the award to Oakland's 27-game winner, Bob Welch. Eighteen wins and league-leading totals in ERA and strikeouts brought Clemens his third Cy Young Award in 1991.

In 1996, despite posting a top-10 ERA and striking out a league-high 257 batters, Clemens finished with a losing record, 10–13. His 10th win took place on September 18 in Detroit, where he struck out 20 Tiger batters and walked none in a 4–0 shutout.

That game would prove to be Rocket's final win in a Red Sox uniform. He became a free agent after the 1996 season and signed with the Toronto Blue Jays for a deal worth $40 million over four years. In his first two seasons in Toronto, Clemens won back-to-back pitching Triple Crowns and added two more Cy Young Awards to his collection, becoming the first five-time winner of the prestigious pitching award. In 1997, he accumulated double-digit strikeout totals in 14 starts, including a season-high 16 in his first game at Fenway Park since leaving the Red Sox.

Toronto traded Clemens to the Yankees prior to the '99 season. Rocket helped New York to World Series titles in 1999 and 2000, and then he won an unprecedented sixth Cy Young Award in 2001 after posting the sixth 20-win season of his career. He played two more years in New York, winning 30 and losing 15, and announced that he was retiring after the 2003 season. On June 13, 2003, he won his 300th game and struck out the 4,000th batter of his career.

The legacy of Clemens's remarkable longevity and impressive career accomplishments took a hit when allegations about steroid use began circulating.

SKYDOME ROOF, 1989.

81

SkyDome Roof, 1989

BALLPARKS GO CONVERTIBLE

Major League Baseball first came to Canada in 1969 with the establishment of the Montreal Expos as a National League expansion team. The club initially played at the small outdoor Jarry Park until they moved into Olympic Stadium in 1977. That same year, Canada got a second team, the Toronto Blue Jays of the American League.

The Blue Jays set up shop in Exhibition Stadium, which was the home of the Argonauts of the Canadian Football League. In October 1986, construction began on a new stadium, and two-and-a-half years later, the 50,000-seat facility known as SkyDome was ready for baseball.

SkyDome exemplified a major step in stadium design by including the first fully operational retractable roof. (Olympic Stadium was intended to have a retractable roof, but technical difficulties led to the roof remaining closed for most of its life.) The $500 million SkyDome featured a four-paneled roof, with three of the steel panels sliding out in a circular motion to enclose the stadium. Sitting some 300 feet above the playing field, the 11,000-ton roof opens and closes in about 20 minutes.

SkyDome opened for business on June 5, 1989. Some 48,378 fans were on hand for the stadium's debut, and by the end of the season, the team had broken the 3 million attendance mark, despite playing the first 54 games at Exhibition Stadium. The team closed the roof at SkyDome just twice that first season; in 2011, the roof was closed 21 times, including once when it was closed during the course of the game. The first open-roofed game did not take place until May 24 during the 2014 season.

In their first full season at SkyDome, the Blue Jays set a new major league attendance record in 1990, as 3,885,284 fans came through the turnstiles. The following year, Toronto became the first team to break 4 million, and then the Jays surpassed their '91 total in each of the next two seasons. Helping to encourage those record-breaking attendance numbers were back-to-back World Series titles in 1992 and '93. To date, the Blue Jays are one of four major league teams to top the 4 million mark in a season and one of two (along with the Yankees) to do it more than once.

Beyond its high-tech roof, SkyDome introduced other innovative luxuries and amenities. A 350-room hotel is located within the stadium, with 70 rooms looking out onto the field. A large restaurant and bar also overlooked the field when the stadium opened. The massive electronic video board was the largest of its kind at the time of the SkyDome's debut, and the pitching mound can be raised or lowered by hydraulic power to allow the field to be used for other non-baseball events, of which the stadium hosts many.

Renamed the Rogers Centre in 2005, Toronto's retractable-roof stadium eventually paved the way for a wave of "convertible" facilities during the ballpark renaissance of the 1990s and 2000s. Rather than the spring and fall chill that Toronto fans would have to contend with in an open-air park, Arizona's Bank One Ballpark (now Chase Field) needed a retractable roof to address the intense heat of Phoenix summers. The air-conditioned park opened in 1998 as baseball's second convertible stadium. Safeco Field opened in Seattle a year later. A 2012 study found that the Mariners played under a closed roof fewer than the other five retractable-roofed teams. The Astros left the permanently domed Astrodome for Minute Maid Park in 2000 (when it was known as Enron Field), but they played under a closed roof in 67 of 81 home games in 2013, usually due to heat and humidity but also rain. The fourth retractable-roof stadium to open in a four-year period, Miller Park in Milwaukee has to deal with cool temperatures early and late in the season, as well as Midwestern midsummer rains. The most recent addition is Marlins Park in Miami, where heat, humidity, and heavy rain conspire to keep the Marlins playing under roof cover frequently.

To date, the Blue Jays are one of four major league teams to top the 4 million mark in season and one of two (along with the Yankees) to do it more than once.

82

Nolan Ryan's
Seventh No-hitter Ball, 1991

THE "RYAN EXPRESS" CHARGES
INTO THE RECORD BOOKS

Nolan Ryan once said that, to be an effective pitcher, "it helps if the hitter thinks you're a little crazy." The Toronto Blue Jays must have thought he was downright insane on May 1, 1991, when the 44-year-old pitcher refused to allow a single base hit. He struck out 16 in what was no-hitter number seven of his career. *Seven.*

Since George Bradley of the St. Louis Brown Stockings pitched the first major league no-hitter in July 1876, more than 280 no-hitters have been thrown in the NL, AL, and American Association. Twenty-six pitchers have thrown two no-hitters in their careers (not counting combined no-no's). Cy Young and Bob Feller threw three apiece, as did nineteenth-century hurler Larry Corcoran in the 1880s. Sandy Koufax was the first to do it four times, one per year between 1962 and 1965.

Nolan Ryan's first no-hitter came against the Royals on May 15, 1973. He struck out 12 and walked three. Two months later, on July 15, he blanked the Tigers, mowing down 17 on strikeouts—a record for a no-hitter. It took a little over a year for Ryan to join the elite group of three-time no-hit men. Although he walked eight in the game, no Minnesota Twin hit safely against the "Ryan Express" on September 28, 1974. Then, on June 1, 1975, just two years and two weeks after tossing his first no-hitter, Ryan joined Koufax with no-hitter number four.

All four of those no-hitters were with the California Angels. Ryan first broke in at the major-league level with the New York Mets. After a very brief stint in 1966, he returned in '68 as a regular starter and struck out 133 batters in 134 innings. During the Mets' championship season of '69, most of Ryan's appearances were out of

NOLAN RYAN'S 7TH NO-HITTER BALL, 1991.

the bullpen, but he worked his way back into the rotation in 1970 and '71. During his four seasons in New York, Ryan had a record of 29–38 and a 3.58 ERA—hardly Hall of Fame numbers.

After the 1971 season, he was traded to California for shortstop Jim Fregosi, in what history has proven to be one of the most lopsided baseball trades ever. The rejuvenated Ryan had 19 wins and a 2.28 ERA in his first season as an Angel in 1972. He also struck out 329 batters to become just the ninth pitcher since 1900 to top 300 in a season. He then broke the modern single-season strikeout record in 1973, surpassing Koufax's previous mark of 382 by one. Ryan also won 21 games, including the two no-hitters. He achieved his career-high output for wins in '74 with 22, despite the team's lowly 68–94 record. He again had more than 300 Ks, but injuries in 1975 limited him to 132 strikeouts and 28 starts. Over the next four seasons, Ryan had a combined record of 62–61 yet led the league in strikeouts every year.

In addition to the four no-hitters, Ryan's eight seasons in California featured seven strikeout titles and five All-Star team selections. The closest he got to bringing home the Cy Young Award was when he got 52 percent of the vote in 1973; he lost to Baltimore's Jim Palmer (who won three in four years).

In late 1979, Ryan signed with the Houston Astros in his native Texas for $1.1 million per year for four years. In his first season, his record was just 11–10, even though Houston won 93 games and its first West Division crown. He captured the ERA title (1.69) in the strike-shortened '81 season, but perhaps more significantly he broke new ground by throwing the fifth no-hitter of his career. It came in his second-to-last start of the season against the Dodgers at the Astrodome. Ten days later, against those same Dodgers at home, Ryan led the Astros to victory in the opening game of the National League Division Series, allowing just two hits and a walk in a win over Dodger phenom Fernando Valenzuela. He then took the loss in the

In addition to the four no-hitters, Ryan's eight seasons in California featured seven strikeout titles and five All-Star team selections.

NOLAN RYAN THREW A
RECORD SEVEN NO-HITTERS,
THE LAST TWO WITH THE
TEXAS RANGERS.

decisive fifth game, and the Astros' hope for a first World Series berth were dashed for the second year in a row.

Ryan averaged 15 wins over the next five seasons, but the only categories that he led the league in during that time were walks, hit batters, and wild pitches. He did become the all-time strikeout king, however, by passing Walter Johnson's career total of 3,508 on April 7, 1983.

Houston returned to the NLCS in 1986, and Ryan again failed to get a W. In Game 5, he battled New York's Dwight Gooden in a 1–1 tie through nine innings. Ryan struck out 12, walked one, and allowed only two hits, but Houston's bullpen lost it in the bottom of the 12th in a thrilling postseason contest. Four of the six games in the series were decided by one run, including the 7–6, sixteen-inning conclusion, won by the Mets.

The worst won-loss record of Ryan's career (8–16) came in 1987, despite leading the NL in both ERA and strikeouts and striking out more than three times as many batters as he walked. Following another middling won-loss record in '88, the 42-year-old took his talents north on Interstate 45 and signed a multimillion-dollar free agent contract with the Texas Rangers.

He appeared to regain his form. In 1989, at 42 years of age, Ryan became the oldest pitcher to top 300 strikeouts in a season, reaching that mark for the first time in 12 years and leading the league. He also earned the first All-Star W of his career, in his eighth and final appearance in the Midsummer Classic. In late August, Ryan notched career strikeout number 5,000, the first and to date only pitcher in history to do so. Yet another highlight came in 1990, when on June 11, Ryan pitched yet another no-hitter; he struck the Oakland A's out 14 times in the game. Career win number 300 came against Milwaukee on July 31. He was the oldest player in the major leagues that year.

The 1991 season was the 20th in which Ryan posted double-digit victories. At age 44, he pitched the second-most innings on the Texas staff. In his fifth start of the season, he simply dominated the Blue Jays in the seventh no-hitter of his career. He fell one short of matching the 17 strikeouts he got in his second no-hitter in 1973.

The Ryan Express kept chugging along. Although the stats were not what they had once been, and all his no-hitters were behind him, Ryan continued to overpower the opposition and show the fire that had allowed him to endure for 27 major league seasons. His most famous performance in the 1993 season, which he had announced would be his last, came against the first-place White Sox in early August. In the second inning, with Texas trailing 2–0, Ryan hit Chicago third baseman Robin Ventura with a pitch. The 26-year-old Ventura charged the mound to take on the pitcher 20 years his senior. Ryan got Ventura in a headlock and punched him repeatedly on the top of the head. After the combatants were separated, Ventura was ejected, and Ryan went on to hold Chicago hitless for the next 4 1/3 innings before being removed for a reliever.

The right-handed Ryan was an intimidating power pitcher in four different decades and with four different teams. His longevity not only brought prestigious career milestones, but it also left him with more losses than any pitcher since the end of the Dead-Ball Era, as well as the most wild pitches and walks in history. He is also the only player ever to have his number retired by three different franchises (the Angels, the Astros, and the Rangers).

But the milestone that will live on for years to come is the seven times that he didn't allow the opposing team to get a base hit. Nobody else has ever done that.

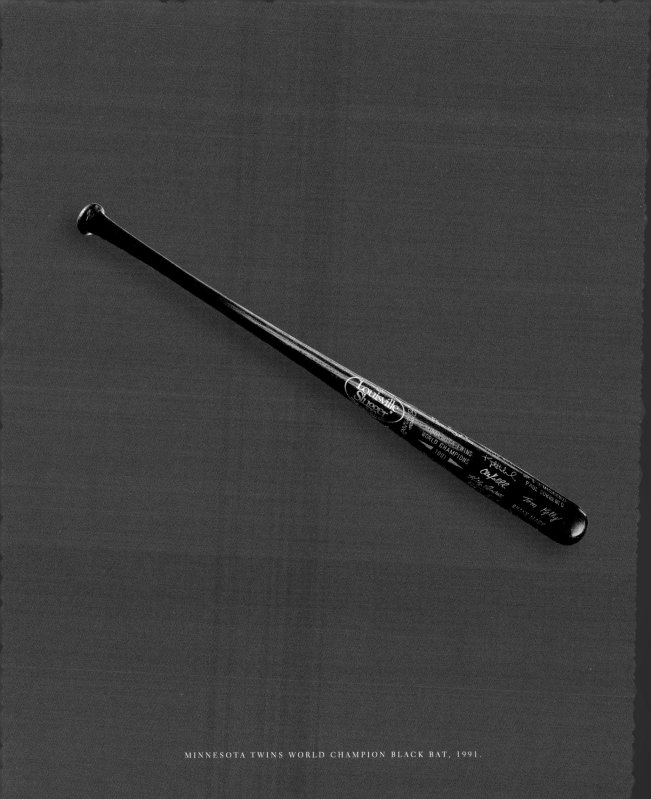

MINNESOTA TWINS WORLD CHAMPION BLACK BAT, 1991.

83

Minnesota Twins World Champion Black Bat, 1991

THE GREATEST WORLD SERIES

The 1991 World Series was a true Fall Classic. After seven intense games, culminating in a legendary Game 7, the Minnesota Twins won their second world championship in five years. This black bat from Louisville Slugger commemorates the memorable victory with facsimile signatures of players, coaches, and team staff.

The Twins and their National League foes, the Atlanta Braves, arrived at the series having clinched their divisions with more than 90 victories in the regular season. Both the Twins and the Braves were coming off last-place finishes in 1990. Both made significant roster changes that improved their outlook for '91, although neither was expected to go from worst to first quite so quickly.

The first key offseason moves for the Twins were signing veteran free agents Chili Davis and Mike Pagliarulo. "Pags" played stellar third base for Minnesota in 1991 and delivered a pinch-hit, game-winning home run against the Toronto Blue Jays in the ALCS. Davis led the Twins in homers and RBI in the regular season and belted two dingers in the World Series. Drafted by Minnesota in 1989, second baseman Chuck Knoblauch joined the big league club in '91 and went on to win the American League Rookie of the Year Award.

These newcomers joined a core of regulars that included Hall of Fame center fielder Kirby Puckett, first baseman Kent Hrbek, shortstop Greg Gagne, and left fielder Dan Gladden, all of whom had played for the 1987 champions in Minnesota. Six of the nine lineup regulars were in the prime of their careers, between the ages of 29 and 31. Gladden was the old man at 33.

ORIOLE PARK AT CAMDEN YARDS, BALTIMORE.

84

Oriole Park at Camden Yards, 1992

BALLPARK RENAISSANCE

When the Baltimore Orioles unveiled their new home before the 1992 season, it proved to be a transformative moment in baseball parks. Just as Shibe Park and Forbes Field ushered in the classic urban "jewel boxes" of the 1910s (see **Object #28**), Oriole Park at Camden Yards sparked a revival of classically styled, baseball-only facilities—a welcome change from the multipurpose, "concrete doughnuts" that had sprouted up in the 1960s and '70s.

What made Camden Yards so special was that it was unique. The quirky outfield dimensions distinguished it from the symmetrical cookie cutters of the previous generation of stadiums. The brick exterior blended with the surrounding architecture of its neighborhood, into which the ballpark nestled as an integral part of the urban landscape. Open views beyond the outfield brought the city skyline into the baseball environment.

About the stadiums of his day, 1970s ballplayer Richie Hebner commented that, when at the plate, "I don't honestly know whether I'm in Pittsburgh, Cincinnati, St. Louis, or Philly. They all look alike." There was no such trouble at Camden Yards. In addition to the views of downtown Baltimore, the historic B&O Warehouse building beyond right field, with pedestrian Eutaw Street running between it and the ballpark, could not be seen or experienced anywhere else. The arched windows and red brick façade evoked the Shibe Parks and Ebbets Fields of eight decades earlier. All the seats were oriented for optimum viewing of the baseball diamond, something that was not the case with multipurpose stadiums built to accommodate both football and baseball. And there was no artificial grass anywhere to be seen.

The architecture firm that created the designs for Camden Yards, HOK Sport (now known as Populous), went on to work with Cleveland, Colorado, Detroit, Houston, San Francisco, and Pittsburgh over the next 10 years to create similarly

Every one of the new facilities constructed between 1992 and 2012 were built for baseball use only.

retro-styled, yet distinctive ballparks. Each one was designed with features that were tied to its particular setting or team. They also tended to be smaller and more intimate than the stadiums they replaced. And it didn't stop there. Populous was behind nine other new baseball parks built between 2003 and 2012, most recently Miami's Marlins Park. Several of the more recent installations moved away from the brick-and-steel inspiration of early twentieth-century ballparks and instead invoked more modern or even futuristic design elements. The Twins' Target Field in Minneapolis combines locally quarried limestone with steel and glass to create a unique blending of classic and modern. It too offers an intimate seating bowl within a cozy urban setting that opens to the downtown skyline and connects with its surroundings—a dramatic and welcome change from its predecessor, the Metrodome. The city's light-rail transit system also pulls up directly in front of the entrance gates, similar to the trolley lines of a century ago. Bars and restaurants in the neighborhood flourish with the pre- and post-game crowds.

The ballpark renaissance of the 1990s was not all accomplished by HOK/Populous. The Texas Rangers collaborated with David M. Schwarz Architects of Washington, D.C., to build their Ballpark in Arlington (now Globe Life Park in Arlington) in 1994. The first new ballpark to open after Camden Yards, it incorporated some of the same "retro" themes and even borrowed specific design elements from old ballparks like Ebbets Field or Tiger Stadium, all within a pronounced Texas identity.

The new ballparks in Arizona, Seattle, and Milwaukee, along with Houston, brought together retro and modern with the incorporation of retractable roofs above classically styled structures.

In all, 20 of the 30 major league teams had new ballparks built within 20 years of the opening of Camden Yards. Other teams, like the Angels and the Royals, renovated their 1960s- and '70s-era stadiums with a retro aesthetic. And every one of the new facilities constructed between 1992 and 2012 were built for baseball use only.

PART VIII

STRIKES
AND
STEROIDS

◆ ◆ ◆

THE EMPTINESS OF THE MAJOR LEAGUE BASEBALL POSTSEASON, 1994.

85

The Baseball Postseason, 1994

ANOTHER WORK STOPPAGE DERAILS THE WORLD SERIES

The formation of the Major League Baseball Players Association in 1953 and the subsequent signing of the first Basic Agreement, or collective bargaining agreement, in 1968 were landmark moments in both labor and baseball history. Unfortunately, the expiration of every CBA since then had been met with either a players' strike or an owners' lockout, as the two sides battled over new contract negotiations. Beginning with the 12-day players' walkout in 1972, there had been four strikes and three lockouts in less than 20 years. Five had been resolved without the loss of any regular-season games. The 1981 strike went on for 50 days in June and July, canceling more than 700 games, but an agreement was reached in time to finish out the season (see **Object #76**). This was not the case in 1994.

Weary of escalating player salaries and declining revenues, team owners sought to institute a salary cap as part of a new CBA, following the expiration of the existing agreement on December 31, 1993. They tied the cap to a revenue-sharing plan intended to help teams from smaller markets stay competitive with big-budget clubs. They also wanted to rewrite the free-agency rules and greatly weaken players' access to salary arbitration. As far as the players were concerned, inclusion of a salary cap was a nonstarter, and had been since the very first Basic Agreement.

By this time the owners had circled their wagons by forcing out the independent-minded commissioner, Fay Vincent, in late 1992 and replacing him with fellow owner Bud Selig of the Milwaukee Brewers as acting commissioner. They were also still bitter over the court's determination that, in 1985, they had illegally colluded to keep salaries down by agreeing not to make lucrative contract offers for other teams' free agents.

The owners presented their proposal for a new CBA in June 1994. It was quickly rejected by MLBPA executive director Donald Fehr. The baseball season progressed, but as it became increasingly clear that there would be no acceptable proposal for a new CBA, the players moved toward the most powerful tool in their arsenal: a strike.

On August 12, the players officially walked out.

When the season halted, after about 115 games played, several interesting on-field story lines came to a premature end. San Diego Padres hitter Tony Gwynn was flirting with becoming the first .400 hitter in more than 50 years; after going 3 for 5 on August 11, his average was .394. With 47 games still on the schedule, Matt Williams of the San Francisco Giants had 43 homers, on pace to reach Roger Maris's single-season record of 61. Seattle Mariner Ken Griffey Jr. wasn't far behind, with 40. The American League's Most Valuable Player of 1993, Frank Thomas of the Chicago White Sox, was in the midst of another career year, with a .353 average and on pace to slam more than 50 homers and collect nearly 150 RBI. (Awards were still given for the aborted season, and Thomas won his second straight MVP.)

The Montreal Expos had the best record in the majors when the strike was called and seemed to have all the pieces in place for a run at the franchise's first pennant. The New York Yankees were atop the AL and on pace for a 100-win season and their first postseason berth since 1981. Brand-new ballparks had been unveiled in Texas and Cleveland.

Despite the lost opportunities for many individuals and teams, the players remained united in support of the strike. Gwynn said, "Never in my wildest dreams did I think I'd get this close to .400, but getting an agreement is more important than hitting .400." Various attempts at negotiations and counteroffers in August and September failed to bring agreement between the owners and the union.

On September 14, Selig announced the cancellation of the remainder of the season and the World Series.

Although most fans had no sympathy when it came to the hundreds of millions of dollars that owners and players would be losing as a result of the canceled season, the elimination of the World Series was a tough blow. The World Series had been a rite of autumn for 90 years, and in the minds of most fans, they were being denied that experience over a spat between millionaires and billionaires.

Throughout the fall and winter, every attempt to bring a resolution died. Even President Bill Clinton's order that the two sides sit down at the negotiating table and reach an agreement was unsuccessful. The acrimony continued to build.

FANS LET THEIR FEEL-
INGS KNOWN ABOUT THE
1994 PLAYERS' STRIKE.

Early in 1995, the owners announced that they were unilaterally implementing a new CBA, with a salary cap. They began enlisting minor leaguers, collegians, and former major leaguers as replacement players, or "scabs," for the upcoming season.

The threat of a season with replacement players was avoided at the 11th hour, however, after the National Labor Relations Board brought the issue to federal court on the MLBPA's behalf. Mere days before the baseball season was scheduled to start, Judge Sonia Sotomayor of the U.S. District Court in New York, later named to the U.S. Supreme Court, supported the NLRB's request for an injunction, ruling that the owners' actions were in violation of federal labor law. She ordered that the players and owners adhere to the previous CBA that had expired at the end of 1993. (A new CBA, featuring a revenue-sharing plan and a luxury tax on teams that exceeded a certain salary level, was signed in March 1997. There have been no baseball work stoppages since.)

After 232 days, the 1994–1995 baseball strike was over. The start of the 1995 season was delayed so players could have training camp, and an abbreviated 144-game schedule was announced.

Even when the players returned and the first pitches were thrown, many fans stayed away. Opening Day attendance was far below average, and the season-long attendance was down 20 percent from the previous year. Fans who did show up were not shy about showing their displeasure, directed mostly at the players, who were the more visible participants in the ugliness of the labor stoppage. Boos, and occasionally debris, rained down on the field. Fans brought signs chastising both sides for their greed.

The strike brought a serious black eye to the national pastime. It would be years before baseball regained the trust and loyalty of the American fan.

Baltimore Orioles

LINE UP CARD Date: 9-5-95

BALTIMORE ORIOLES	VISITING CLUB
8-ANDERSON-L-	5-PHILLIPS-S- ●
	PEREZ-R-
4-ALEXANDER-R- ●●	8-EDMONDS-L- ●
6-RIPKEN-R- ●	9-SALMON-R- ●●
9-BONILLA-S-	⑪-DAVIS-S-
J.BROWN	GONZALES-R-
3-PALMEIRO-L- ●	3-SNOW-S- ●
	PALMEIRO-L- ⑨
2-HOILES-R- ⑥	7-ALDRETE-L- ●
⑩-BAINES-L- ●	4-OWEN-S- ●
5-MANTO-R- ●●	2-MYERS-L- ●
HUSON-L- ●	
7-SMITH-R-	6-EASLEY-R-
1-ERICKSON	1-ANDERSON-MONTELEONE
	HARKEY-HOLZEMER
	HAYNAN-BUTCHER

LH	EXTRA	RH	LH	EXTRA	RH
HUSON	HAMMONDS		G. ANDERSON		CORREIA
GOODWIN	J.BROWN		FABREGAS		GONZALES
			PALMEIRO		ALLANSON
	ZAUN				PEREZ
	BASS				HUDLER
	BARBERIE				

LH	EXTRA	RH	LH	EXTRA	RH
LEE	BENITEZ		HOLZEMER	BUTCHER	
OROSCO	CLARK		PATTERSON	HAYNAN	
	JONES			HARKEY	
	DEDRICK			BIELECKI	
	HARTLEY			MONTELEONE	
	BOROWSKI			JAMES	
				PERCIVAL	
				SMITH	

86

Lineup Card from Cal Ripken's 2,130th Game, 1995

BASEBALL GETS A NEW "IRON MAN" AND A POST-STRIKE BOOST

As a cloud of bitterness hung over the 1995 baseball season in the wake of the eight-month-long players' strike that came to an end that April, Major League Baseball needed something to restore fans' faith in and passion for the game. Cal Ripken Jr. provided just such a restorative moment.

On September 5, 1995, Ripken was written onto the Baltimore Orioles' lineup card, playing shortstop and batting third. It was the 2,130th consecutive lineup card to feature Ripken's name on it. With it, the future Hall of Famer matched the record consecutive-game streak set by Lou "Iron Man" Gehrig 56 years earlier. A huge banner on the brick wall of the B&O Warehouse building beyond Camden Yards' right field revealed the numbers 2-1-3-0 as soon as the game became official upon completion of four-and-a-half innings.

Ripken's pursuit of Gehrig's record, one that many had considered "unbreakable," had been gradually gaining attention. Ripken eclipsed one milestone after another and surpassed other "iron men" who fell far short of Gehrig. In 1988, his seventh full season, Ripken reached 1,000 games, only the seventh player to attain that number. (Miguel Tejada subsequently joined the 1,000-consecutive-game club in 2007.) To make up the remaining 1,130 needed to catch Gehrig would require seven more seasons without missing a game.

Ripken, whose major league debut came in the first game following the conclusion of the 1981 players' strike, had played in his 2,009th consecutive game when the players walked off the job on August 12, 1994. There was no doubt that the

GREG MADDUX'S WORLD SERIES GLOVE, 1995.

In the first year of an expanded postseason featuring wild-card teams, the Braves defeated the Colorado Rockies in the National League Division Series and swept the Cincinnati Reds in the NLCS. Atlanta was headed to its third World Series in five seasons.

Maddux got the Braves on track in the series opener by allowing only two hits and no walks to the Cleveland Indians in a 3–2 triumph; both of Cleveland's runs were unearned. Maddux lost his Game 5 start, but Atlanta wrapped up the World Series in the next game behind Glavine's one-hitter. It was the Braves' first world championship since the Milwaukee team had accomplished the feat in 1957.

Teammate John Smoltz ended Maddux's streak by winning the Cy Young Award in 1996, but the Braves won another division title. They swept the Dodgers in the NLDS and then clobbered the St. Louis Cardinals 15–0 in Game 7 of the NLCS for yet another trip to the Fall Classic. Smoltz won the World Series opener against the New York Yankees, and Maddux gave Atlanta a 2–0 head start with a shutout win in Game 2. But the Yankees stormed back to win the next four and take the series. Maddux earned the loss in the Game 6 finale.

Maddux was back to his old form in 1997. He had a 19–4 record, a 2.20 ERA, and allowed only 20 walks in 232 2/3 innings. He finished second to Montreal's Pedro Martinez in the Cy Young voting, and the Braves, coming off 101 regular-season wins, lost to the Florida Marlins in the NLCS.

A 106–56 (.654) record in 1998 was the franchise's best in exactly a century, since the Boston Beaneaters went 102–47 (.700) in 1898. "Mad Dog" Maddux won the fourth ERA title of his career (2.22) and won 18 games. But once again, the team faced disappointment in October. They swept the Cubs in the LDS—Maddux won the clinching third game against his former team—but fell to the San Diego Padres in the LCS.

Known as "The Professor" for his studious approach to the game, Maddux lacked the overpowering speed of hurlers like Nolan Ryan, Roger Clemens, and Randy Johnson, but his mastery of multiple pitches and his ability to hit his spots made him a dominant pitcher for two decades.

GREG MADDUX PITCHING, CIRCA 1995.

The 1999 Braves had a chance to exact revenge on behalf of the '96 squad when they earned a rematch with the Yankees in the Fall Classic. Atlanta had won 103 games during the regular season but were no match for New York in October, losing in four straight.

That would prove to be Maddux's last chance to win a World Series with Atlanta. The Braves continued to win the NL East again and again—every year, in fact, from 1995 to 2005, plus the three pre-strike seasons of 1991–1993—but they failed to advance out of the first round in five of six postseasons from 2000 to 2005. They swept Houston in the 2001 Division Series but couldn't get past Arizona in the League Championship Series.

Maddux was not on hand for all those postseason defeats. Following the 2003 season, he re-signed as a free agent with his original team, the Cubs. In his 11 seasons with Atlanta, Maddux never won fewer than 15 games, and his cumulative ERA was 2.63, a staggering number in an era when the average ERA among NL pitchers was 4.29.

Wearing a Cubs uniform, Maddux won his 300th game in 2004. A year later he struck out his 3,000th batter to become one of only 10 members of the 300/3,000 club. His 16 wins in 2004 also marked a record 17th consecutive season with at least 15 victories. After a losing season in 2005, he was shipped to the Dodgers at the trade deadline in July 2006 and completed another 15-win year. He played out his final two seasons with San Diego and Los Angeles. He retired in November 2008 at the age of 42.

Known as "The Professor" for his studious approach to the game, Maddux lacked the overpowering speed of hurlers like Nolan Ryan, Roger Clemens, and Randy Johnson, but his mastery of multiple pitches and his ability to hit his spots made him a dominant pitcher for two decades. While he struck out 3,371 batters in his career, Maddux was very effective at getting hitters to ground out on pitches low and outside. His superior accuracy and control also allowed him to keep his pitch counts down, aiding his durability. He led the NL in starts a record seven times and compiled more than 5,000 innings pitched over his career. Maddux was inducted into the Hall of Fame in 2014 with 97.2 percent of the vote.

Maddux's records and accomplishments on the mound could fill a book, but he beat the opposition with more than just his pitches. He used his Wilson-brand glove to claim 18 Gold Glove Awards—more than any player at any position—including 13 in a row from 1990 to 2002.

DEREK JETER AT THE PLATE,
CIRCA 1996.

the opening game of the ALCS against the Baltimore Orioles. The blast, which tied the game 4–4 in the eighth, was highly controversial. A 12-year-old fan named Jeffrey Maier reached over the outfield wall with his glove in an attempt to nab a Yankee Stadium souvenir. The Orioles insisted that Maier interfered with a ball in play and Jeter should be called out, but the umpires ruled (incorrectly, as replays showed) that the fan made contact only after the ball had cleared the wall. The Yanks went on to win the game in 11 innings and the series in five games. The '96 title capped a Rookie of the Year season for Jeter in which he batted .314 and kicked off a 15-year run of double-digit-homer seasons.

Jeter and the Yankees reached the postseason again in '97, this time as the wild card, but lost to the Cleveland Indians in the American League Division Series. The 1998 season was a magical one for New York. They won a franchise-record 114 regular-season games, swept through the LDS, toppled Cleveland in the ALCS, and then swept the San Diego Padres for a second World Series title in three years. Jeter came through with his first 200-hit regular season while batting .324 and scoring a league-best 127 runs.

The Bronx Bombers kept rolling in '99, culminating in another World Series sweep, this one against the Braves. During the season, Jeter posted what would be his personal bests in batting average (.349), hits (219), triples (9), home runs (24), runs (134), RBI (102), on-base percentage (.438), and slugging percentage (.552). In the opening game of the ALCS against the hated Boston Red Sox, Jeter delivered a clutch, game-tying RBI single in the seventh; the Yanks went on to win the game on a 10th-inning, walk-off homer by Bernie Williams.

In 2000, the Jeter-era Yankees became the first team since the Oakland A's of 1972–1974 to win three World Series in a row. In a "Subway Series" against the Mets, Jeter was named the series Most Valuable Player. In Game 4, he was moved up to the leadoff spot in the batting order, and on the very first pitch of the ball game, he drilled a home run into the left-field seats at Shea Stadium. The next night, back in his familiar number two spot in the lineup, Jeter homered again, a game-tying solo shot in the sixth. The Yanks won the game 4–2 to wrap up the series. He batted .409 in the five games.

The Yankees won a fourth straight AL East crown in 2001. They had been in first place continuously since July 3 and had the division all but locked up with a 13-game lead following a win over Boston at home on September 9. Two days later, the terrorist attacks of September 11 shook the nation, and put baseball on hold for a week.

The American League Division Series with the A's opened at Yankee Stadium on October 10, and New York lost the first two games of the best-of-five series. In a do-or-die Game 3, Jeter made perhaps the most famous play of his career. With the Yankees clinging to a 1–0 lead in the bottom of the seventh, Oakland's Terrence Long drove a hit down the right-field line. Yankees right fielder Shane Spencer retrieved the ball and fired it toward the infield. He badly overthrew the cutoff men, however, and Oakland base runner Jason Giambi lumbered toward home. Jeter, who was standing near the mound, chased down Spencer's errant throw, snagged it between first and home, and in one continuous motion, made a backhanded toss to catcher Jorge Posada, who tagged out Giambi to end the inning. The remarkable play preserved the lead and sparked the Yanks to a comeback win in the series.

After advancing past Seattle—which won a record 116 games in the regular season—in the ALCS, the Yankees took on the Arizona Diamondbacks in the World Series. Although they won all three games at home in an emotional World Series return to New York, the Yankees lost a thrilling seven-game Fall Classic. Still, "The Captain" earned a new nickname. In Game 4 of the series, which began on October 31 at Yankee Stadium, a two-run homer by Tino Martinez tied the score in the bottom of the ninth. As Jeter stepped to the plate with two outs in the 10th, the clock ticked past midnight and the calendar turned to November. Facing Arizona's submarine-throwing reliever Byung-Hyun Kim, Jeter worked the count full and then knocked the ninth pitch of the at-bat over the right-field wall to win the game and tie the series. It was the first time that the World Series had extended into the month of November (as a result of the weeklong layoff following September 11), and Jeter gained the nickname "Mr. November."

The Yankees took the next five division titles and made one more appearance in the World Series under manager Joe Torre. They won the 2003 ALCS against Boston on a dramatic 11th-inning homer by Aaron Boone in Game 7, but New York lost to the Florida Marlins in the World Series. A year later the Yanks lost a devastating LCS to the Red Sox, dropping the series in seven games after winning the first three. First-round losses followed in each year from 2005 to 2007, and New York missed the playoffs altogether in 2008—for the first time in Jeter's career.

They came back with a 103-win campaign in 2009 under manager Joe Girardi. Jeter completed his fourth straight season batting over .300 and collected 100 runs and 200 hits for the fourth time in five years. On September 11 of that year, Jeter became the all-time Yankees hit leader when he passed Gehrig with number 2,722. New York marched through the American League playoffs and then defeated the Phillies for the fifth World Series victory of Jeter's career. He went 3 for 5 and scored twice in the final contest, capping a .407 performance in the six games.

Jeter slumped in 2010 with what was then the lowest batting average of his career, although he did claim his fifth Gold Glove Award. In 2011, he got his 3,000th career hit on a solo homer off Tampa Bay's David Price, making Jeter the second player (along with Wade Boggs) to reach 3,000 with a home run. Jeter went 5 for 5 in the game. It was another sub-.300 season for Jeter, however, and another first-round playoff exit for New York.

The Captain bounced back in 2012 with 216 hits and a .316 average while helping lead the Yanks back to the ALCS. In the 12th inning of the ALCS opener against Detroit, Jeter fractured his ankle making a diving play in the field. He would miss the rest of the series. The Yankees were swept in four games.

Year after year, Jeter was a leader on a winning team that made the playoffs in all but three of his 18 full seasons.

Injuries struck again in 2013. Jeter appeared in only 17 games and New York missed the playoffs for only the second time in 19 seasons. On February 12, 2014, Derek Jeter announced that the upcoming baseball season would be his last. Throughout the year, the 40-year-old Jeter was honored at ballparks around the league. He had one of the worst seasons of his career, but the fans voted him in as the AL's starting shortstop in the All-Star Game, hoping to see the Captain one last time in the Midsummer Classic. It was his ninth appearance as a starter and his 13th overall. The crowd at Minnesota's Target Field greeted him with a rousing ovation. He led off the first inning with a line-drive double down the right-field line and then scored the game's first run.

Jeter closed out his final game at Yankee Stadium with a game-winning, walk-off single against the division-champion Orioles. It was a storybook ending to a Hall of Fame career. As Jeter himself said, "I wouldn't have believed it myself."

Derek Jeter never played on a team with a losing record. He is a sure thing for induction into the Baseball Hall of Fame, but Jeter's place as an icon of baseball and of the Yankees organization had almost as much to do with his charm and his class as his statistics. He never won a league MVP Award. In 20 seasons, he never led the AL in batting average or on-base percentage or doubles or home runs. He once led in runs and twice in hits. People cite his five World Series rings, four of which were achieved in his first five years in the majors. The first championship coincided with his rookie season, but it also coincided with Joe Torre's first year as manager and Mariano Rivera's first season as the team's closer.

As a group, Jeter, Rivera, Jorge Posada, Bernie Williams, and Andy Pettitte — all products of the Yankee farm system — formed the core of a wining club under Torre that was perpetually acquiring new stars and complementary players. Paul O'Neill, Tino Martinez, Wade Boggs, Scott Brosius, Darryl Strawberry, and others brought savvy veteran experience to bolster the talented young core. But however you slice it, Jeter was the Captain and, by most accounts, the club's heart and soul for two decades.

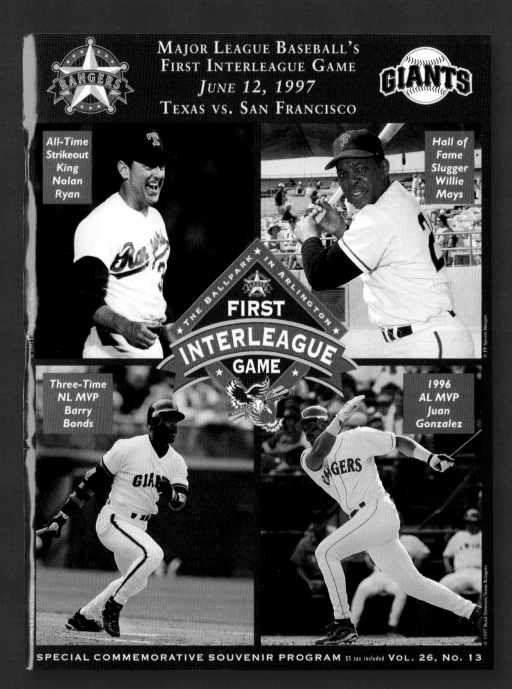

MAJOR LEAGUE BASEBALL'S
FIRST INTERLEAGUE GAME
JUNE 12, 1997
TEXAS VS. SAN FRANCISCO

RANGERS

GIANTS

All-Time Strikeout King Nolan Ryan

Hall of Fame Slugger Willie Mays

THE BALLPARK IN ARLINGTON
FIRST INTERLEAGUE GAME

Three-Time NL MVP Barry Bonds

1996 AL MVP Juan Gonzalez

SPECIAL COMMEMORATIVE SOUVENIR PROGRAM $5 tax included VOL. 26, No. 13

PROGRAM FROM FIRST INTERLEAGUE GAME, 1997.

89

Program from the First Interleague Game, 1997

A NEW TRADITION IN MAJOR LEAGUE BASEBALL

Ever since the American League declared itself a *major* league in 1900, and the National League's acknowledgment of that status with the National Agreement of 1903, the only time teams from the two leagues played each other in games that mattered was in the World Series. That all changed in 1997, when interleague play was introduced to the Major League Baseball schedule.

The first official interleague game took place on June 12 at the Ballpark in Arlington between the Texas Rangers and the San Francisco Giants. Appealing to the sense of tradition of each league, the cover of the commemorative souvenir program for the game featured all-time legends Nolan Ryan and Willie Mays to represent the two teams. Further hyping the potential excitement of this innovation, the program cover enticed fans with the prospect of watching both reigning AL Most Valuable Player Juan Gonzalez and three-time NL MVP Barry Bonds. Bonds would score the game-winning run in the seventh inning in a 4–3 Giants victory.

Three other interleague games were played later that night on the West Coast, and the American League went 3–0 in those contests. The NL won the overall head-to-head matchups for the season, winning 117 games to the AL's 97. The Montreal Expos and the Florida Marlins had the best interleague records in 1997, each going 12–3. Since 1997, the NL has won the overall interleague competition in just three other seasons (through 2014).

As Major League Baseball's announcement regarding the institution of interleague play said, "Breaking tradition always brings about controversy," and there was

**The introduction
of interleague games
was a revolutionary
move in the late
'90s, but it wasn't
the first time such
an arrangement had
been considered.**

plenty of objection from both fans and players who appreciated the separate-but-equal relationship between the two leagues that had stood for more than 90 years. But interleague play was here to stay, and it has since been expanded to more games and more varied matchups.

The initial arrangement had teams playing their counterparts in the other league's division, so the AL East played the NL East, Central Division teams played each other, and the AL West clubs matched up with the NL West clubs. A team would play one series against each interleague opponent per season, with the home team in the series alternating every year. MLB altered this in 2002 so that the matchup of divisions would vary year to year, although games between regional rivals would remain annual events—Chicago versus Chicago, New York versus New York, San Francisco versus Oakland, Washington versus Baltimore, etc. By the 15th season of interleague competition, every team had played against and defeated every other team at least once.

For many years, interleague play was held exclusively in the months prior to the All-Star break, and all interleague games took place at the same time. When the Houston Astros were shifted from the NL to the AL in 2013, interleague games became part of the everyday schedule, since each league now had an odd number of teams. That season saw the first Opening Day interleague game—Cincinnati Reds versus Los Angeles Angels of Anaheim—as well as the first on the final day of the season—Florida Marlins pitcher Henderson Alvarez threw a no-hitter against the Detroit Tigers. All teams now play 20 interleague games each season.

Designated hitters are used in interleague games when the American League is the host team, meaning that AL pitchers need to step to the plate when they play in an NL park. All stats achieved during interleague play count toward team and league records, no different from intraleague games.

The introduction of interleague games was a revolutionary move in the late '90s, but it wasn't the first time such an arrangement had been considered. William Veeck (father of innovative baseball executive Bill Veeck) proposed it when he owned the Chicago Cubs in the early 1930s but wasn't able to garner enough support from other owners. His son took up the cause 20 years later, but Bill Jr. did not have many friends among baseball's owners. Indians executive and former Hall of Fame player Hank Greenberg also proposed it, without success, in the mid-1950s. During the negotiations around possible expansion in 1959–1960, the American League actually approved interleague play, to allow for the expansion of each league to nine teams. The NL owners were not onboard, however, and instead two teams were added to each league to maintain even numbers. The AL again endorsed interleague play at the same time that the league adopted the designated hitter rule in 1973, but again the NL voted it down. The proposal finally received unanimous support by league owners on January 18, 1996.

FLORIDA MARLINS WORLD SERIES TROPHY, 1997.

90

Florida Marlins World Series Trophy, 1997

WILD-CARD WINNERS

Major League Baseball arguably experienced as many fundamental changes in the 1990s as it had in any decade since the beginning of the twentieth century. In addition to having teams from the National and American Leagues play each other during the regular season for the first time, the introduction of a "wild-card" team to the postseason meant that, for the first time, a team didn't even have to win its division in order to vie for the baseball championship. (Other than those sanctioned rule changes, the strike of 1994–1995 and the steroid epidemic taking place below the surface made the decade particularly eventful.)

The expansion of the National League to 14 teams in 1993 with the addition of the Colorado Rockies and the Florida Marlins brought the total number of franchises to 28. That offseason, as owners and players bickered over a new collective bargaining agreement, Major League Baseball did agree to realign the leagues into three divisions. Each league's East and Central Divisions contained five teams, while the AL West and the NL West each housed four clubs. The postseason competition in each league would involve the three division winners plus the non-division-winning club with the best regular-season record—the wild card. Just a quarter of a century earlier, only two teams in the major leagues were eligible for postseason play: the winner of the American League regular season and the winner of the National League regular season. Beginning in 1994, the number of postseason entrants would be eight.

What was supposed to be the first postseason involving this new arrangement did not take place, since the players' strike led to the cancellation of the entire 1994 postseason. Regrouping in 1995, the season ended with the New York Yankees seven

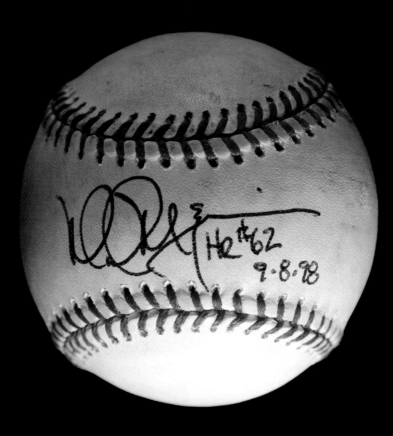

MARK McGWIRE'S 62ND HOME RUN BALL, 1998.

of June. Sosa had made some noise with a 40-homer season in 1996 and three other years with more than 30 between 1993 and 1997. But when he reached half of his personal season high in the course of a single month, suddenly there was a new presence in the Maris chase.

By the time Major League Baseball broke for the All-Star Game, McGwire had 37 homers, Griffey had 35, and Sosa had 33. Griffey won the Home Run Derby during All-Star weekend in Denver, but the 19 balls he sent over the fence in that exhibition didn't factor into the pursuit of the record.

McGwire had two multi-homer games in one week in mid-July. Sosa out-homered him by one (9–8) in the month. Griffey began to fade by August, and it became increasingly clear that the spotlight would be focused on "Slammin' Sammy" and "Big Mac." The media coverage surrounding both of them exploded. The players seemed to relish the attention, and for the most part, it was positive attention—a stark contrast to what Maris and Hank Aaron had gone through previously.

Around this time, though, a reporter noticed a bottle of pills labeled androstenedione in McGwire's locker. "Andro," as it was commonly known, increased testosterone levels in the body and often was used in conjunction with other steroids. It was, however, legal as a dietary supplement and could be purchased over the counter in any drugstore. (It had already been banned in the NFL and the Olympics, it should be noted, but not by Major League Baseball.) McGwire didn't try to hide the fact that he was using andro; he even said that "everybody" in baseball uses it.

With those assertions—it was legal; everybody was doing it—most in the media returned to putting McGwire and Sosa on a pedestal and treating fans to nonstop coverage of the great home run race. The public, too, was far less concerned with what the sluggers were pumping into their bodies than with how far they were driving the ball.

> **The public was far less concerned with what the sluggers were pumping into their bodies than with how far they were driving the ball.**

Sosa had another big month in August, going deep 13 times. McGwire's 10 long balls in August put the two in a dead tie when the calendar turned to September. With 55 homers under their belts and 25 games still to play there seemed to be little doubt that Maris's record would fall. The only question was by whom and by how many.

McGwire homered four times in his first two games in September to reach 59. On September 5, he tied the Babe with number 60. Sosa added three to his total in the first five days of the month. On September 7, Sosa and the Cubs arrived in St. Louis for a two-game series. That night, in St. Louis's 145th game of the year, McGwire tied Maris with his 61st homer. Sosa and the sellout crowd at Busch Stadium applauded Big Mac as he rounded the bases.

SAMMY SOSA CONGRATULATES MARK MCGWIRE FOLLOWING
McGWIRE'S 62ND HOME RUN, SEPTEMBER 8, 1998.

The next night, with Roger Maris's children in attendance, McGwire stepped to the plate against Chicago righty Steve Trachsel in the fourth inning and took the first offering deep, sending the ball shown here just over the wall in left field. He received hugs and slaps of congratulations from the Cubs fielders as he rounded the bases. Fireworks burst overhead and the crowd treated him to a deafening ovation while his teammates mobbed him at home plate. Even Sosa came running in from his position in the outfield to offer his congratulations. McGwire hugged his friendly rival and hoisted him in the air. Baseball had a new single-season home run king.

But that wasn't the end of the story. Sosa then hit four homers in three days and caught McGwire at 62 on September 13. They went back and forth over the next week. Going deep twice against Milwaukee, Sosa took the lead with number 66, to McGwire's 65, on September 25. Less than an hour later, however, McGwire's 66th sailed over the fence in St. Louis. Sosa went homerless the rest of the way, but Big Mac kept going, homering twice in each of the season's final two games. The new benchmark was set at a magical 70.

With a .308 batting average and a league-high 158 RBI, Sosa took home the NL Most Valuable Player Award in 1998, and his team was headed to the postseason. Over in the American League, Griffey ended up with 56 dingers for the second year in a row.

McGwire and Sosa were back at it in 1999. Big Mac won a second straight home run crown with another mind-blowing season of 65 homers and 147 RBI. Sosa belted 63 in '99, and after falling to "only" 50 in 2000, he passed 60 for a record third time with 64 in 2001.

After standing as the top record for 37 years, Maris's single-season mark had dropped to sixth best in history in a matter of four years. It moved to seventh place when Barry Bonds became the new home run king in 2001, crushing a phenomenal 73.

The steroid allegations and admissions subsequently tainted—to put it mildly—the accomplishments of McGwire and Sosa, as well as Bonds. But for anybody who was following baseball in the summer of 1998, the home run chase gave fans something to cheer for, and attendance climbed back up to pre-strike levels. The sport returned to the forefront of the American sports consciousness in a positive way—at least temporarily.

steroid-free players, the cloud that the scandals cast over the game has, in many ways, overshadowed their accomplishments.

The draw of PEDs wasn't limited to players who were driving baseballs 500 feet and crushing home run records. Since Major League Baseball instituted a formal drug policy outlining testing and suspension procedures in 2004, more than two dozen position players—ranging from backup utility infielders to all-star sluggers—have received suspensions (as of 2014), lasting anywhere from 10 games to full seasons. In addition, as many as 16 major league pitchers have been suspended, and many others have been implicated in outside investigations and in claims by fellow players.

The rumors and suspicions that players were "juicing" first got traction during McGwire and Sosa's home run frenzy in 1998. Although many fans and the media were willing to proverbially stick their heads in the sand so that they could fully enjoy the thrilling season, it soon became too big an issue to ignore. In his 2005 book *Juiced*, Jose Canseco wrote openly about his own steroid use and the widespread practice of "juicing" in baseball, including by prominent players he cited by name.

In addition to Canseco's book, the 2003 investigation into the Bay Area Laboratory Co-Operative (BALCO) for its distribution of PEDs to major league players further elevated the story to the front pages. Producer of an undetectable substance known as "the Clear," BALCO had among its listed clients Barry Bonds, Gary Sheffield, and Jason Giambi. The book *Game of Shadows* by Mark Fainaru-Wada and Lance Williams extensively explored BALCO and Bonds's PED use. Bonds was later indicted for perjury and obstruction of justice as a result of his testimony during grand jury trials. He was found guilty of the latter charge in 2011.

As the spotlight on PEDs grew brighter and drug testing began creeping in, some players turned to new, undetectable substances, such as human growth hormones (HGH), or those

---

Since Major League Baseball instituted a formal drug policy outlining testing and suspension procedures in 2004, more than two dozen position players—ranging from backup utility infielders to all-star sluggers— have received suspensions (as of 2014).

MARK McGWIRE (CENTER) TESTIFYING BEFORE CONGRESS
ABOUT STEROIDS IN BASEBALL, MARCH 2005.

not yet included on the list of banned drugs. The office of Major League Baseball struggled to keep pace with the snowballing use of steroids in its game.

Soon, the federal government got involved. In March 2005, several high-profile players, including McGwire, Sosa, Palmeiro, and Canseco, were brought before a congressional committee to testify about PED use in baseball. Commissioner Bud Selig and union head Donald Fehr were also called to testify. Although the players were evasive about their own steroid use or denied using steroids outright, the committee chastised both the league office and the players' association for not acting quickly or forcefully enough to address the issue and for the weak policy then in place.

In 2006, Selig appointed former U.S. senator and federal prosecutor George Mitchell to oversee an investigation into steroid use in the majors. Few players agreed to offer testimony, and the players' union was, as Mitchell wrote in his report, "largely uncooperative." Still, the 409-page report released in December 2007 found that the illegal use of steroids and other performance-enhancing substances had been widespread "for more than a decade" and that the response by baseball was "slow to develop." It went on to cite 89 former and current players alleged to have used steroids or HGH, including such big-name stars as Roger Clemens, Andy Pettitte, Mo Vaughn, Todd Hundley, and David Justice. Although it called out many individuals, the report held all of baseball accountable for the epidemic. Mitchell urged MLB to take all necessary steps to eliminate performance-enhancing drugs from the game, through both rigorous testing and education.

Even after federal investigations and public pressure seemed to fully expose the steroid crisis in baseball, more scandals followed. The Florida-based clinic Biogenesis of America was revealed, in 2013, to have provided HGH to numerous major leaguers during 2012. As a result of the Biogenesis investigation, three-time MVP Alex Rodriguez received a season-long suspension (it was originally to have included the final 49 games of the 2013 season but an appeal pushed the start date to Opening Day 2014); 2011 NL MVP Ryan Braun was suspended for 65 games; and three-time all-star Nelson Cruz and 11 others received 50-game suspensions.

After years of criticism, Major League Baseball gradually implemented anti-steroid policies. Following an anonymous sample-testing program in 2003 to determine the extent of PED use in the league, MLB instituted a regular program of random testing in 2004. The minimum penalties were stiffened twice during 2005 in response to criticism, from both the media and Congress, that the league was too lenient. In the ensuing years, more substances were added to the list of those being tested for, including stimulants and HGH. Regular testing during spring training and the offseason was increased, as was the amount of random testing conducted during the season. In 2014, Major League Baseball announced a further broadening of its drug policy to inject (no pun intended) more rigorous testing measures as well as still stricter penalties for players found with performance-enhancing drugs in their system. A three-strikes-and-you're-out policy is in effect, as of 2015, whereby anyone who tests positive three times for banned substances will receive a lifetime suspension from baseball.

For many fans and experts, the damage was done, and a full decade of baseball had been sullied. The stricter penalties and testing policies, however, have served to restore faith in the purity of the national pastime. Even if there aren't as many home runs flying over the fences, at least we know that they are doing so untainted.

93

Ichiro Suzuki's
Seattle Mariners Jersey, 2001

A PHENOM FROM JAPAN

In his first season in the American major leagues, Ichiro Suzuki became the second player in history, after Fred Lynn in 1975, to be named his league's Rookie of the Year and Most Valuable Player in the same year. Like Lynn, Ichiro also won a Gold Glove Award and was selected to the All-Star team—Ichiro received the highest number of fan votes, thanks to MLB opening the balloting to Japan. He won a batting title with a .350 average and led the league in stolen bases, the first player to lead those two categories in the same season since Jackie Robinson did it in 1949. Ichiro's 242 base hits set a rookie record and were the most by any player since 1930. His Seattle Mariners won a record-tying 116 games during the season.

Ichiro arrived in the major leagues at the age of 27 and was an immediate sensation. He had gotten his start in professional baseball in Japan when he was 18 years old. A superstar in Japan's Pacific League for nearly a decade, he was a three-time MVP and led his Orix Blue Wave to a championship. After participating in an exhibition series between American and Japanese all-stars, Ichiro decided to set his sights on playing in the United States. The Mariners won the bid to negotiate with him, and they subsequently signed him to a three-year, $14 million contract in late November 2000.

Before Ichiro, several pitchers had come from Japan to play in the majors, but he was the first position player to make the leap. He followed his impressive debut with nine more seasons hitting over .300, including a second batting crown in 2004 with a career-best .372. He also won nine more Gold Gloves, consecutively. The speedy Ichiro stole at least 30 bases in 10 of his first 11 major league seasons; in 2006

ICHIRO SUZUKI'S SEATTLE MARINERS JERSEY, 2001.

he stole 45 bases while getting caught only twice. He is the only player in history to collect more than 200 hits for 10 consecutive years. During his 2004 batting title season, Ichiro set a new major league record with 262 hits, topping George Sisler's 64-year-old record of 257. Sisler's daughter was in attendance at Safeco Field when Ichiro broke the record.

After dropping below .300 for the first time in his U.S. career in 2011, and with Seattle entering a rebuilding phase, Ichiro asked to be traded. He was sent to the New York Yankees in exchange for two minor leaguers and cash. He completed his 14th major league season at the age of 40 in 2014 with a .317 lifetime average and more than 2,800 hits. Combined with his career in Japan, Ichiro has accumulated 4,121 hits in professional baseball (through 2014), trailing only Pete Rose and Ty Cobb.

Emerging in the majors at a time when the McGwires, Sosas, Bondses, and Griffeys were garnering most of the headlines with tape-measure home runs, Ichiro became a star using slap hitting, bunts, speed, and placement to get on base. A fan favorite on two continents, he was voted as an All-Star starter in 9 of his first 10 seasons and selected as a reserve once.

ICHIRO RACES TO FIRST ON A BUNT, AUGUST 2001.

Emerging in the majors at a time when the McGwires, Sosas, Bondses, and Griffeys were garnering most of the headlines with tape-measure home runs, Ichiro became a star using slap hitting, bunts, speed, and placement to get on base.

As popular as he was in Seattle and throughout the United States, Ichiro's first few years in the States were a media phenomenon in his native Japan as well. Members of the Japanese media followed his every move. He further built his hero stature at home by leading Japan to victory in the first World Baseball Classic in 2006.

Baseball was introduced to Japan in the 1870s, and organized leagues began forming by the turn of the twentieth century. Numerous exhibitions between American and Japanese stars helped to bolster interest in the sport and in the American major leagues.

The first Japanese-born ballplayer to play for Major League Baseball was Masanori Murakami, a reliable relief pitcher with the San Francisco Giants in 1964 and '65. He returned to Japan after just two seasons to pursue a career there. Thirty years later, pitcher Hideo Nomo jumped from the Kintetsu Buffaloes in the Japanese Pacific League and signed a contract with the Los Angeles Dodgers in 1995. Nomo's deceptive corkscrew delivery earned him the nickname "The Tornado" and helped him to lead the league in strikeouts in his first major league season. He won the NL Rookie of the Year Award and threw two no-hitters in his career, first with the Dodgers in 1996 and later with the Red Sox in 2001.

Nomo's success led more Japanese players to seek opportunities in the United States. Mac Suzuki, also a pitcher, signed with the Mariners in 1996 but appeared in just one game before heading to the minors. He returned to the big league club to play five more years, without much success. A highly coveted Japanese star, Hideki Irabu was sold to the San Diego Padres by his Japanese club, but he refused to sign with the Padres, saying he would only play for the New York Yankees. He was sent to the Yankees in a sign-and-trade arrangement and then inked a $12.8 million deal with the Bronx Bombers for four years. Irabu completed his seven-year American career with a 34–35 record. Several other Japanese pitchers signed with American teams in the late '90s and early 2000s. Kaz Sasaki had a decent four-year run as the Mariners' closer from 2000 to 2003, winning the Rookie of the Year Award in 2000.

Ichiro followed Sasaki as another Japanese-born Rookie of the Year for Seattle in 2001, and more position players began making the move from the Japanese leagues. Hideki Matsui spent 10 years in the majors and was the MVP of the 2009 World Series while with the Yankees. As of 2014, 10 different position players from Japan have played at least 400 games in the American major leagues. Pitchers continue to have more success after coming from Japan, most recently exemplified by Yu Darvish of the Texas Rangers. He won 16 games in his rookie season of 2012 and finished third in Cy Young voting. He finished second in the balloting in 2013 after leading the league in strikeouts.

But none has matched the impact of Ichiro Suzuki, who has been not just one of the best Japanese-born players in the majors, but one of the best players, period. And he's reached sufficient star status that he is known simply by one name: Ichiro.

ALEX RODRIGUEZ'S TEXAS RANGERS JERSEY, 2001.

94

Alex Rodriguez's
Texas Rangers Jersey, 2001

THE $250 MILLION MAN

Escalating player salaries have been an ever-present concern for Major League Baseball since the dawn of free agency in the 1970s (and even earlier, when owners held all the power with the reserve clause). Players and agents salivate over each new salary milestone, while owners run around like Chicken Little crying that baseball is headed to bankruptcy.

When Texas Rangers owner Tom Hicks signed shortstop Alex Rodriguez to a contract worth $252 million over 10 years, it was the largest sports contract in history, more than double the value of baseball's previous record deal — inked by Mike Hampton just four days before A-Rod's contract. Hicks had purchased the entire Rangers franchise for $250 million three years earlier, and now he was offering more than that to just one player. If anybody was worth $25.2 million a year, though, A-Rod was the guy, or so it seemed.

Rodriguez made his major league debut with the Seattle Mariners in July 1994, just a few weeks shy of his 19th birthday. He joined an up-and-coming team that included Ken Griffey Jr., Edgar Martinez, and Randy Johnson. A-Rod made a fast impression. In his first full season of 1996, he won a batting title (.358) while hitting 36 homers and 54 doubles, scoring 141 runs, and driving in 123. He was not eligible for Rookie of the Year consideration since he had had too many at-bats the previous season, but he finished second in AL MVP balloting, losing to Juan González by the slimmest of margins. Rodriguez made the All-Star team in 1996 and was voted in as the starting shortstop in 1997 and '98 for a league that included Cal Ripken, Derek Jeter, and Nomar Garciaparra at the same position.

By the time his Mariners contract expired after the 2000 season, A-Rod had nearly 200 career home runs, including three straight seasons with 40 or more. He had a lifetime .309 average and nearly 1,000 hits. And he was still only 25 years old. He was the highest-profile free agent on the market, and Rodriguez and his agent, Scott Boras, played that to their advantage. As Rangers GM Bob Melvin commented after the signing, "We've walked away from a lot of players over salary demands. There are some players you don't walk away from. This is one of those players."

Rodriguez donned this Rangers jersey in 2001 to join a team that had won division titles in three of the previous five seasons, but had failed to advance out of the first round and then dropped to last place in the division in 2000. Texas boasted a stacked lineup that knocked a league-high 246 homers in 2001—and finished in last place once again, 43 games behind A-Rod's former team in Seattle. The Rangers' pitching staff delivered a 5.71 ERA, the worst in the majors.

Alex Rodriguez did his part by stroking an AL-leading 52 homers and a team-best 135 RBI and batting .318 in his first go-round with the Rangers. The following year he went 57-142-.300 and won the first Gold Glove of his career. Texas finished with an even worse record, by one game, than they did in 2001.

The 2003 season proved to be A-Rod's final one in Texas. He won a third straight home run title and his first MVP Award. That year he also became the youngest player ever to reach 300 career home runs. The Rangers again finished first in the league in homers, last in team ERA, and last in the standings.

Although he had set numerous franchise records, Texas was looking to unload A-Rod's hefty contract. In February 2004 they traded him to the New York Yankees in exchange for Alfonso Soriano and agreed to cover more than a third of the remaining amount owed on Rodriguez's contract.

Upon arriving in New York, Rodriguez agreed to move to third base in deference to Derek Jeter, the Yankees' all-star shortstop. He also switched his uniform number to 13, since his previous number 3 belonged to Babe Ruth and had long since been retired in New York.

In his first five years as a Yankee, A-Rod belted at least 35 home runs each season, including 54 in 2007 for his third 50-plus output; he drove in at least 100 runs and scored at least 100 every year; and he had a combined .303 batting average and .573 slugging percentage. He won two MVP Awards during that stretch (2005 and 2007) and was voted the starting third baseman for all five All-Star Games.

The Yankees lost the 2004 ALCS to the Boston Red Sox in historic fashion. They lost in the first round in each of the next three seasons, while Rodriguez batted .159 with one RBI in the 13 postseason games. In 2008, A-Rod's fifth year with the club, the Yankees failed to make the playoffs for the first time since 1993.

Following the 2007 season, Rodriguez invoked the opt-out clause of his original Rangers contract. Effectively a free agent, A-Rod used the opportunity to renegotiate his terms with the Yankees. They re-signed him to another 10-year contract, this one worth $275 million, that would last until he was 42 years old.

After posting his record 11th consecutive season with at least 35 homers, 100 runs, and 100 RBI in 2008, A-Rod missed the first month of the 2009 season following surgery and then produced his lowest home run total since his second season. But the Yankees won their first World Series since 2000, and Rodriguez was presented with the Babe Ruth Award as the most valuable player of the postseason.

Through his first 15 major league seasons, Rodriguez had compiled a lengthy list of accomplishments and established numerous records and milestones for three different franchises, for his position, and for his age. His numbers started to dip more dramatically beginning in 2010 as he approached his 35th birthday. He underwent surgery in 2011 and missed more than a third of the season. He was benched several times during the 2012 postseason, and then had another surgery to repair a hip injury prior to the 2013 campaign.

Rodriguez soon became the focus of an investigation into Biogenesis and performance-enhancing drugs. He had previously admitted, in a 2009 *Sports Illustrated* article, that he had taken steroids during his first few seasons in Texas, hoping to live up to the expectations of the huge contract he'd signed. The latest scandal cast his career accomplishments in even greater doubt.

A-Rod will be best remembered for his role in the steroid scandals of the 2000s, and for the $252 million contract that first put him in a Texas Rangers jersey.

MONEYBALL, 2003.

money, but it did pile up wins and brought people to the ballpark. After owner Walter Haas died in 1995, however, the new regime pushed Alderson to cut payroll. Instead of shelling out top-dollar contracts for high-profile talent, Alderson and company now had to find value, players who could be obtained cheaply but could still help them win.

Alderson had already begun to shift the culture in the organization to focus on new measures for player evaluation. He emphasized quantifying, through statistics, a player's ability to get on base, not whether or not he demonstrates the traditional "tools" that scouts typically and subjectively look for. The more you get on base, the logic went, the greater your chance of producing runs. The long-lionized but imperfect statistic of batting average told only part of the story. Alderson looked to the more thorough on-base percentage, which takes into account not only base hits but also reaching base by walking or being hit by a pitch. He particularly valued a hitter's patience and ability to draw bases on balls. Slugging percentage, which is essentially a weighted batting average that gives "extra credit" for each base reached on extra-base hits, was also embraced by Alderson and Beane as a crucial indicator of success at the plate.

The true guru of baseball stats was Bill James, whose annual *Baseball Abstract* had been the Bible for stat geeks since the late 1970s. He employed scientific statistical data, or "sabermetrics"—a reference to SABR, the Society for American Baseball Research—to analyze players and the likelihood of team wins and losses. James created, or inspired the creation of, a whole spectrum of new stats, and he also recognized the role of outside factors and even luck in statistics. Bill James's work greatly influenced Beane's view of the game from the front office.

Alderson stepped down as Oakland's general manager in October 1997. He had succeeded in cutting the payroll to under $25 million for the '97 season, when five other AL teams had payrolls in excess of $50 million, led by the Yankees at $62 million. But the A's had also just completed their fifth straight losing season.

Beane was chosen to take over Alderson's role as GM. Stepping up his predecessor's focus on nontraditional stats like on-base and slugging percentage, Beane pushed his scouts to locate undervalued players using these statistical methods. Many of the old-school scouts resisted, insisting that they could better tell whether a player had potential just by looking at him. That attitude did not fly in Beane's organization, however.

REMNANTS OF THE "BARTMAN BALL," 2003.

bobbled it. Everyone was safe. With the bases loaded and one out, Derrek Lee, batting .120 to that point in the series, hammered a double down the left-field line, scoring Castillo and Rodríguez and tying the game, 3–3. At that point, Kyle Farnsworth came in to relieve Prior. Following an intentional walk to load the bases, Jeff Conine hit a deep fly to right that advanced all the runners. Florida had its first lead of the night. Another intentional walk loaded the bases again. Then 35-year-old Mike Mordecai, who had led off the inning, doubled off the ivy-covered wall in left-center to clear the bases: 7–3 Marlins. That was all for Farnsworth. Reliever Mike Remlinger yielded a first-pitch, run-scoring single to Pierre before finally getting out of the inning.

Chicago's final six batters of the game went down in order. Florida had tied the series, setting up a decisive Game 7 at Wrigley Field.

The Cubs initially built a 5–3 lead in the following night's game, but the Marlins scored six more runs en route to a 9–6 clinching victory. Once again Chicago would be on the outside looking in as the World Series got underway.

Even though the usually sure-handed Alex Gonzalez bobbled a routine ground ball, and even though the Cubs pitchers yielded five base hits in the fateful eighth inning of Game 6, and even though they allowed Florida to score nine runs in the series finale, all the frustration and anger among the Cubs

LEFT FIELDER MOISÉS ALOU AND FAN STEVE BARTMAN GO AFTER THE FOUL BALL IN GAME 6 OF THE 2003 NLCS.

The Bartman incident was the latest in a line of bugaboos afflicting Cubs fans.

nation was directed at the fan who deflected the foul ball—his name, it was soon revealed, was Steve Bartman. A devoted longtime Cubs fan, Bartman was subjected to verbal abuse in the immediate aftermath of the play, and some fans threw beverages and debris at him as he attempted to watch the game from his front-row seat. He and his companions finally had to be escorted to safety by security.

Bartman's identity was revealed publicly soon after the game. Since then, he has had to live in a kind of self-imposed exile in order to avoid harassment, and potentially worse, from Chicago's rabid fans. Other than an apology written shortly after the incident, he has never addressed the incident publicly and no longer attends Cubs games.

The Bartman incident was the latest in a line of bugaboos afflicting Cubs fans. The "Curse of the Billy Goat" in Cubs lore stems from the time Billy Sianis, owner of Chicago's Billy Goat Tavern, was told that he couldn't bring his pet goat into Wrigley Field during the 1945 World Series. The offended Sianis allegedly put a curse on the team, saying they would never win another World Series. (The Cubs held a two-games-to-one lead at that point in the series but lost in seven games.) Fans have staged various ceremonies in an attempt to reverse the curse, but without success.

In 1969, the Cubs had a nine-game lead in the NL East standings as late as August 12 but went on to lose the division by eight games, following a horrendous final month of the season. During a crucial game against the New York Mets at Shea Stadium on September 9, with the Cubs clinging to a slim half-game lead, a black cat ran onto the field and walked past Ron Santo in the on-deck circle before disappearing under the stands. They lost that game and then 12 of the next 20 to end the season.

Fifteen years later, the Cubs blew a 3–0 lead in the decisive fifth game of the 1984 NLCS against the Padres. A ground ball that went through the legs of Chicago first baseman Leon Durham opened the floodgates to a 6–3 defeat.

With this legacy of bad luck, Cubs fans hoped to exorcise the demons of the "Bartman incident" the following February. The Harry Caray Restaurant Group purchased at auction, for nearly $114,000, the infamous ball that was deflected by Bartman. In a public ceremony at the downtown Harry Caray's, the ball was rigged with explosives and blown to smithereens. Bartman was invited to the event but did not attend.

Since losing Game 6 of the 2003 NLCS, the Cubs have lost seven consecutive postseason games.

BOSTON RED SOX WORLD SERIES RING, 2004.

97

Boston Red Sox
World Series Ring, 2004

A CURSE REVERSED, IN HISTORIC FASHION

When the Boston Red Sox finally won a World Series in 2004 after an 86-year championship drought for the franchise, it was a moment of pure joy for the Red Sox Nation. The four-game sweep of the St. Louis Cardinals in the Fall Classic, a series in which they never trailed in any inning, provided some measure of revenge and satisfaction in defeating a team that had beaten Boston in two previous World Series (1946 and 1967), but that was ancient history.

The phrase "Greatest Comeback in History" that adorns one side of the Red Sox's 2004 World Series ring is not a reference to the comeback of a franchise that had waited so long for a return to glory. Rather, it refers to the phenomenal comeback the Red Sox mounted in the American League Championship Series that put them in position for the World Series showdown with St. Louis.

During the course of the 86 years of Red Sox disappointment, the team most often at the source of the frustration was the New York Yankees. The franchise that had obtained Babe Ruth from the Red Sox in 1919—and, in some people's eyes, sparked the curse that led to the long drought—repeatedly came out ahead of Boston in the standings. In the 18 seasons in which the Red Sox ended the year in second place from 1919 up to and including 2004, the Yankees were the team that finished ahead of them 14 times, occasionally in particularly painful fashion.

The 1949 Boston team featuring Ted Williams had mounted an incredible late-season run in pursuit of the first-place Yanks and took a one-game lead in the standings with two games left on the schedule. Both of the games were against New

No team had ever come back from a 3–0 deficit in a best-of-seven postseason series.

York at Yankee Stadium. In the penultimate game, an eighth-inning home run by Johnny Lindell won it for the Yankees and put the teams even in the standings. The next day, New York withstood a ninth-inning flurry by Boston and secured the pennant by a 5–3 win.

Decades later, the Red Sox had the upper hand through most of the 1978 season. They were in first place continuously from May 22 until September 9, with a peak lead of 14 1/2 games in July. But as the Yankees surged, Boston stumbled, and the two finished in a tie after 162 games. In the one-game playoff to determine the division winner, Bucky "F#@%ing" Dent (the expletive added by frustrated Red Sox fans) and Reggie Jackson hit clutch homers to lead New York to victory.

The Red Sox, making the playoffs as a wild card after finishing behind New York in the division race, were ousted by the Yanks in the ALCS in 1999 and again in 2003. In the latter series, New York scored three runs against a tiring Pedro Martinez in the eighth inning of Game 7 to even the score before Aaron "F#@%ing" Boone won the game and series with a lead-off, walk-off home run on the first pitch in the bottom of the 11th.

The sting of that Game 7 loss in 2003 was still fresh when the two teams met again in the ALCS the very next year. The Yanks had finished atop the division again, but the Red Sox's 98 wins were enough to earn Boston another wild-card berth. Most of the core from the '03 team was back in '04. Catcher Jason Varitek offered key leadership from behind the plate. DH David "Big Papi" Ortiz and left fielder Manny Ramirez brought potent bats, each providing more than 30 homers and 100 RBI in '03, which they upped to 40-plus homers and 130-plus RBI in 2004 while both batting above .300. Center fielder Johnny Damon was back as the leadoff hitter and main stolen base threat. First baseman Kevin Millar rallied the Sox with the "Cowboy up!" mantra in 2003 and proudly branded the gang of

Red Sox misfits as the "Idiots" in '04. Although ace Pedro Martinez had an off year, for him, in '04, Derek Lowe and knuckleballer Tim Wakefield continued to be solid in the starting rotation. The biggest boost to the staff, however, was the offseason acquisition of Curt Schilling from Arizona. Schilling had an AL-best 21–6 record in '04 and finished second in Cy Young balloting. Another trade that reshaped the team was a midseason deal that shipped off longtime shortstop Nomar Garciaparra in a four-team trade that netted shortstop Orlando Cabrera, who would be a clutch performer in the LCS, and backup first baseman Doug Mientkiewicz. And, also significantly, manager Grady Little was fired following the 2003 postseason collapse and was replaced by Terry Francona.

After New York won the first two games of the '04 ALCS in the Bronx, defeating Schilling and Martinez, it seemed like more of the same was in store for Boston. When the Yanks pasted the Sox for 22 hits in a 19–8 thrashing in Game 3 at Fenway Park, the series appeared all but over. No team had ever come back from a 3–0 deficit in a best-of-seven postseason series.

In Game 4, for the fourth time in the series, the Yankees scored first, and by the bottom of the ninth, they were clinging to a 4–3 lead. Millar opened the inning with a walk against New York's ace closer, Mariano Rivera. Francona sent Brian Roberts in to pinch run for Millar. After several pickoff attempts from Rivera, Roberts took off and stole second base to put himself in scoring position. Third baseman Bill Mueller then drove him home with a game-tying single. New York put runners on base in the 10th, 11th, and 12th innings, even loading the bases in the 11th, but failed to get anybody home. Facing Paul Quantrill, Ramirez started the bottom of the 12th inning with a single. Ortiz then ended it with a walk-off, two-run blast. (He had previously closed out the ALDS against the Anaheim Angels with a two-run, 10th-inning walk-off homer in Game 5.) The Red Sox were still alive, for one more day at least.

The teams regrouped less than 24 hours later, and another marathon was in store. Boston tied the game in the eighth on a solo shot by Ortiz and an RBI sacrifice fly by Varitek against Rivera. The Red Sox dodged a bullet in the ninth when, with two out and a runner on first, Yankee Dave Clark's deep drive to right bounced over the wall for a ground-rule double, forcing the runner to stop at third base. Boston got out of the inning without allowing him to score. Three passed balls by Varitek while trying to catch knuckleballer Wakefield allowed Yankee runners to advance to second and third in the top of the 13th, but again the Red Sox got out of it with no damage done. Finally, in the bottom of the 14th, after 5 hours and 49 minutes of baseball, Ortiz delivered yet another game-winning hit, a two-out RBI single, to put Boston within one game of New York.

Extra innings were not needed in Game 6, but there was no shortage of drama or controversy. Making the start for Boston, Schilling was recovering from a torn ankle tendon suffered during the League Division Series, and blood began seeping through his sock during the game. He still managed to hold the Yankees to one run in seven innings. Boston got three runs on a Mark Bellhorn homer, which had initially been ruled a ball in play after bouncing off a fan and onto the field; the umpires convened and reversed the call, declaring it a home run—much to the dismay of the Yankee Stadium crowd. In the seventh inning, Derek Jeter drove in a Yankee run with an RBI single, and then Alex Rodriguez effectively killed the rally when he slapped the

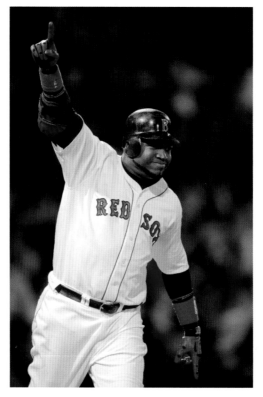

DAVID ORTIZ CELEBRATES HIS GAME-WINNING HOMER
IN THE 12TH INNING OF GAME 4 OF THE 2004 ALCS.

ball out of the glove of pitcher Bronson Arroyo as Arroyo tried to tag him on his way to first base. The ball rolled free and Jeter came around to score. Following another long umpire conference, A-Rod was called out for interference, Jeter had to return to first base, and Arroyo escaped the inning with no runs scoring. The game ended in a 4–2 Boston victory. The Red Sox had tied the series.

Boston was striving to make history with a Game 7 victory at Yankee Stadium the next night. A two-run dinger by Ortiz in the first and a grand slam by Johnny Damon in the second put them well on the way. Another Damon homer, a two-run job in the fourth, provided Boston with a commanding 8–1 lead. Pitcher Lowe retired 11 consecutive Yankees after allowing a third-inning RBI single. In a rare relief appearance, Martinez came in in the seventh and allowed two runs before extinguishing the rally. Boston added another run in each of the last two innings, and the 10–3 pounding capped what truly was a historic comeback.

As a postscript, the Boston Red Sox went on to win two more World Series championships in the next 10 years (2007 and 2013) to establish their place as one of the dominant teams of recent years.

BARRY BONDS'S 756TH HOME RUN HELMET, 2007.

98

Barry Bonds's 756th
Home Run Helmet, 2007

MORE RECORDS FALL AS MORE
STEROID ALLEGATIONS RISE

Barry Bonds's major league career is really a tale of two players. Over the course of his first 13 seasons, seven with the Pittsburgh Pirates and six with the San Francisco Giants, Bonds was a three-time MVP, an eight-time all-star (seven as a starter voted by the fans), and an eight-time Gold Glove winner. He had 411 career home runs and 445 stolen bases, making him baseball's first and to date only 400/400 man. In 1996 he became the second player in history (after Jose Canseco) to hit 40 homers and steal 40 bases in the same season. He had not won any batting titles at that point in his career, but he hit over .300 six times and had an on-base percentage of .411 while averaging more than 100 bases on balls per season. He had only one home run title (46 in 1993) but finished among the league's top five every year from 1992 to 1997, as well as in 1990.

Bonds's Pittsburgh teams won consecutive division titles in 1990–1992 but went 0 for 3 in the National League Championship Series. Bonds batted .191 and hit only one home run in those 20 postseason games. He left for San Francisco after the 1992 season when it became clear that the small-market Pirates couldn't afford the going rate for the reigning MVP.

Bonds wasn't exactly a favorite with the media, given to curt if not outright surly responses to reporters' questions, and he rubbed teammates and opposing players the wrong way with his arrogance. But few would deny that Bonds, who was 34 years old when the 1998 season came to an end, had put up Hall of Fame–caliber numbers over his first 13 years in the majors.

MIGUEL CABRERA'S TRIPLE CROWN AWARD, 2012.

For his efforts, Cabrera was voted Most Valuable Player of the American League in 2012. Some experts believed that Mike Trout of the Los Angeles Angels of Anaheim deserved the award. The 2012 Rookie of the Year, Trout certainly had an amazing season and was the number one guy in WAR as well as in stolen bases and ranked high in many other categories. But Cabrera's dominance across a range of stats, both old and new, convinced a majority of voters to cast their ballot for him.

The 2012 season was Cabrera's sixth year in a row and eighth overall with at least 30 homers; he added one more in 2013. He has topped 100 RBI in each of his first 11 full seasons and has scored more than 100 runs in eight of those seasons. Cabrera won a second MVP Award in 2013 with his third batting title (.348), another 44-homer output, and a league-best 1.078 OPS. As of the end of 2014, Cabrera's .320 lifetime batting average was the best among all active major leaguers.

When Cabrera won the 2012 Triple Crown, he was the first person in either league to earn the distinction since Boston's Carl Yastrzemski did it in 1967. That 45-year gap was the longest between Triple Crown winners in history, illustrating its increasing difficulty. Frank Robinson accomplished the feat with the Orioles the year before Yaz. The Yankees' Mickey Mantle did it in 1956, his 52 homers the most ever in a Triple Crown season. Ted Williams won two Triple Crowns with Boston in the 1940s. Joe Medwick's 1937 Triple Crown with the St. Louis Cardinals is the last by a National Leaguer (to date). Lou Gehrig became the first Yankee to lead in all three categories in 1934. The previous year, Jimmie Foxx of the Philadelphia Athletics and Chuck Klein of the Philadelphia Phillies became the first players to win their respective leagues' Triple Crowns in the same season. Rogers Hornsby was a two-time winner (1922 and '25) while batting over .400 both times. Although RBI was not an official statistic before 1920, Ty Cobb's retroactive 115 RBI in 1909 completed the trifecta for him. In the very first season of the American League, Napoleon "Nap" Lajoie of the Philadelphia Athletics led all fellow ALers in all three stats, including a .426 average. Everybody on this list (except for Cabrera, who's not yet eligible) is a member of the Baseball Hall of Fame.

Even if batting average is not the perfect measure of a hitter's efficiency at the plate, and runs batted in have a lot to do with what the hitters in front of you in the lineup do, and home run hitters don't necessarily breed championships, there's no denying that to lead a league in all three of these categories is a rare and impressive achievement.

WORLD BASEBALL CLASSIC CHAMPIONSHIP TROPHY, 2013.

100

World Baseball Classic Championship Trophy, 2013

A TRUE WORLD SERIES?

Baseball has been known as the "national pastime" of the United States since the earliest years of the sport. Its origins and precursors may be traced back to Old World games in Europe, but the specific rules and culture of the sport that we know as baseball has uniquely American origins.

It didn't take long, however, for baseball to extend its reach to other nations. American merchants, sailors, and missionaries introduced the game to distant lands during the late nineteenth century, and early baseball pioneers like Harry Wright and Albert Spalding organized tours of American teams across the world. The sport hasn't been able to rival soccer on a global scale, and even basketball, another American invention, has spawned respectable pro leagues in more foreign nations than baseball has. But in some areas, namely Far East Asia and Latin America, the passion for the game is as widespread as it is in the United States.

International competitions between all-star teams of different nations dates back to the earliest tours of the 1870s and 1880s. Baseball appeared at the Summer Olympics in the 1904 games in St. Louis and sporadically in various Olympic Games afterwards. It was included as a demonstration sport at the 1984 Los Angeles Olympics and the 1988 Games in Seoul, South Korea. Baseball became an official medal game in 1992 but would only remain so for five Olympic cycles. In those five competitions, Cuba claimed three gold medals and two silvers. South Korea won the 2008 gold, while the United States, fielding only amateur athletes, won its lone gold medal at the 2000 games in Sydney, Australia; the United States also won

Bibliography

Baseball Americana: Treasures from the Library of Congress. New York: Smithsonian Books/HarperCollins Publishers, 2009.

Block, David. *Baseball Before We Knew It: A Search for the Roots of the Game*. Lincoln: University of Nebraska Press, 2005.

Brackin, Dennis, and Patrick Reusse. *Minnesota Twins: The Complete Illustrated History*. Minneapolis: MVP Books, 2010.

Fost, Dan. *Giants Past & Present*. Rev. ed. Minneapolis: MVP Books, 2011.

Gentile, Derek. *The Complete Chicago Cubs*. New York: Black Dog & Leventhal Publishers, 2002, 2004.

Henderson, Robert W. *Ball, Bat and Bishop: The Origins of Ball Games*. Champaign: University of Illinois Press, 1974, 2001.

James, Bill. *The New Bill James Historical Baseball Abstract*. Rev. ed. New York: The Free Press, 2001.

Johnson, Steve. *Chicago Cubs Yesterday & Today*. Minneapolis: Voyageur Press, 2008.

Jones, David, ed. *Deadball Stars of the American League*. Dulles, VA: Potomac Books, 2006.

Leventhal, Josh. *Baseball Yesterday & Today*. St. Paul, MN: Voyageur Press, 2006.

Leventhal, Josh. *Take Me Out to the Ballpark*. New York: Black Dog & Leventhal Publishers, 2000–2011.

Lewis, Michael. *Moneyball: The Art of Winning an Unfair Game*. New York: W. W. Norton & Company, 2003.

Miller, Marvin. *A Whole Different Ball Game: The Sport and Business of Baseball*. New York: Birch Lane Press, 1991.

Morris, Peter. *A Game of Inches: The Story Behind the Innovations that Shaped Baseball*. Chicago: Ivan R. Dee, 2010.

Murphy, Cait. *Crazy '08*. New York: Smithsonian Books/Collins, 2008.

National Baseball Hall of Fame and Museum. *Baseball As America: Seeing Ourselves Through Our National Game*. Washington, D.C.: National Geographic Society, 2002.

National Baseball Hall of Fame and Museum. *Inside the Baseball Hall of Fame*. New York: Simon & Schuster, 2013.

Nemec, David. *The Great Encyclopedia of 19th-Century Major League Baseball.* New York: Donald I. Fine Books, 1997.

Piccione, Peter. "Pharaoh at the Bat." *College of Charleston Magazine.* Spring/Summer, 2003, p. 36.

Pietrusza, David, Matthew Silverman, and Michael Gershman. *Baseball: The Biographical Encyclopedia.* Kingston, NY: Total Sports Publishing, 2000.

Ritter, Lawrence S. *The Glory of Their Times.* New York: Vintage Books, 1966, 1985.

Seymour, Harold. *Baseball: The Early Years.* New York: Oxford University Press, 1960.

Seymour, Harold. *Baseball: The Golden Age.* New York: Oxford University Press, 1971.

Silverman, Matthew. *New York Mets: The Complete Illustrated History.* Minneapolis: MVP Books, 2011.

Simon, Tom. *Deadball Stars of the National League.* Dulles, VA: Brassey's, Inc., 2004.

Sugar, Bert Randolph. *Bert Sugar's Baseball Hall of Fame: A Living History of America's Greatest Game.* Philadelphia: Running Press, 2009.

Sullivan, Dean A., ed. *Early Innings: A Documentary History of Baseball, 1825–1908.* Lincoln: University of Nebraska Press, 1995.

Sullivan, Dean A., ed. *Middle Innings: A Documentary History of Baseball, 1900–1948.* Lincoln: University of Nebraska Press, 1998.

Sullivan, Dean A., ed. *Late Innings: A Documentary History of Baseball, 1945–1972.* Lincoln: University of Nebraska Press, 2002.

Thorn, John. *Baseball in the Garden of Eden: The Secret History of the Early Game.* New York: Simon & Schuster, 2011.

Thorn, John, "Play's the Thing," *Woodstock Times,* 12/28/2006. Accessed from http://thornpricks.blogspot.com/2006/12/bruegel-and-me_27.html

Veeck, Bill, with Ed Linn. *Veeck as in Wreck.* Chicago: University of Chicago Press, 1962, 2001.

Waggoner, Glen, Kathleeen Moloney, and Hugh Howard. *Spitters, Beanballs, and the Incredible Shrinking Strike Zone: The Stories Behind the Rules of Baseball.* Chicago: Triumph Books, 1987, 2000.

Ward, Geoffrey C., and Ken Burns. *Baseball: An Illustrated History.* New York: Alfred A. Knopf, 1994.

www.baseball-reference.com